access to history

Change and Protest 1536–88: Mid-Tudor Crises? FOURTH EDITION

access to history

Change and Protest 1536–88: Mid-Tudor Crises? FOURTH EDITION

Roger Turvey and Nigel Heard

 HODDER EDUCATION

AN HACHETTE UK COMPANY

Study Guide authors: Angela Leonard (Edexcel) and Sheila Randall (OCR)

The Publishers would like to thank the following for permission to reproduce copyright material:
Photo credits: © Bettmann/CORBIS, pages 8, 41, 102; © Corpus Christi College, Oxford, UK/The Bridgeman Art Library, page 63; Mary Evans Picture Library, pages 45, 105; Fotomas/The Bridgeman Art Library, page 126; © The Gallery Collection/Corbis, page 66; Hulton Archive/Getty Images, page 4; Lambeth Palace, London, UK/The Bridgeman Art Library, page 100; The National Archives UK, page 39; National Portrait Gallery, London, UK/The Bridgeman Art Library, pages 59, 90; Private Collection/The Bridgeman Art Library, pages 51, 145; The Stapleton Collection/The Bridgeman Art Library, page 142; Ken Welsh/The Bridgeman Art Library, pages 42, 53.
Acknowledgements: Cambridge University Press for an extract from *Tudor Monarchies 1485–1603* by John McGurk, 1999; Hodder Education for an extract from *Disorder and Rebellion in Tudor England* by N. Fellows, 2001; Hodder Education for an extract from *The Tudor Years* by Edward Towne, 1994; Hodder Murray for an extract from *The Early Tudors: England 1485–1558* by David Rogerson *et al.*, 2001; Longman for an extract from *Elizabethan Parliaments 1559–1601* by M. Graves, 1987; W.W. Norton & Company for an extract from *The Government of Elizabethan England* by A.G.R. Smith, 1967; NPI Media Group for an extract from *The Tudors* by Richard Rex, 2002.
Every effort has been made to trace all copyright holders, but if any have been inadvertently overlooked the Publishers will be pleased to make the necessary arrangements at the first opportunity.

Hachette UK's policy is to use papers that are natural, renewable and recyclable products and made from wood grown in sustainable forests. The logging and manufacturing processes are expected to conform to the environmental regulations of the country of origin.

Orders: please contact Bookpoint Ltd, 130 Milton Park, Abingdon, Oxon OX14 4SB. Telephone: (44) 01235 827720. Fax: (44) 01235 400454. Lines are open 9.00–5.00, Monday to Saturday, with a 24-hour message answering service. Visit our website at www.hoddereducation.co.uk

© Roger Turvey and Nigel Heard 1999
First published in 1999 by
Hodder Education,
An Hachette UK Company
338 Euston Road
London NW1 3BH

Second Edition published in 2000.
Third Edition published in 2006.
This Fourth Edition published in 2009.

Impression number   5   4   3   2
Year   2013   2012   2011   2010

Cover image: King Edward VI (1537–53) and the Pope, c1570 (oil on panel), English School (16th century) © National Portrait Gallery, London, UK/
The Bridgeman Art Library
Typeset in 10/12pt Baskerville and produced by Gray Publishing, Tunbridge Wells
Printed in Great Britain by the MPG Books Group

A catalogue record for this title is available from the British Library.

ISBN: 978 0340 986 776

Contents

Dedication

Keith Randell (1943–2002)

The *Access to History* series was conceived and developed by Keith, who created a series to 'cater for students as they are, not as we might wish them to be'. He leaves a living legacy of a series that for over 20 years has provided a trusted, stimulating and well-loved accompaniment to post-16 study. Our aim with these new editions is to continue to offer students the best possible support for their studies.

1

A Crisis in Mid-Tudor England?

POINTS TO CONSIDER

This chapter is designed to help you to understand what historians mean by the term mid-Tudor crisis. It explains how the views of historians about mid-sixteenth-century England have changed and how they use the ideas of crisis and the development of the State to explain events. By examining the problems created by political, social, economic and religious change you should be able to come to a firm decision about whether there was a mid-Tudor crisis. These issues are examined as four themes:

- Mid-Tudor England 1536–88
- The historiographical background
- A crisis of the State: government, politics and foreign affairs
- A crisis of the State: social, economic and religious change

Key dates

1532		Thomas Cromwell became the king's chief adviser
1534		Henry VIII became Head of the Church in England
1540	June	Fall of Thomas Cromwell
1546		Duke of Norfolk (Thomas Howard) imprisoned
1547	January	Henry VIII died
		Duke of Norfolk released from prison
		Edward VI became king
		Duke of Somerset (Edward Seymour) became Lord Protector
1549	November	Somerset replaced by the Duke of Northumberland (John Dudley) who became Lord President of the Council
1553	July	Edward VI died
	July	Lady Jane Grey crowned queen and 'reigned' for nine days
	July	Mary became queen of England
1558	November	Mary died and was succeeded by Elizabeth
1559		Elizabeth crowned queen of England

1 | Mid-Tudor England 1536–88

Key question
Who were the major political figures in mid-Tudor England?

It has been argued that the England of 1588 was very different from that of 1536. The period witnessed changes in government, politics and religion but the intensity and influence of those changes has been a subject for debate. Some historians argue that the changes were so radical and wide-ranging that they contributed to what has been termed a mid-Tudor crisis. In fact, this idea of crisis in the State has been extended to encompass the economy, society and even foreign affairs. On the other hand, there are historians who disagree, stating that the changes that did occur were natural and what one might expect from a period spanning over 50 years. However, there is no doubt that if one compares England in 1588 to that in 1536 there are some stark differences. For example,

- for the first time in English history the kingdom was governed by a female rather than a male monarch
- the State religion had been transformed into Protestant Anglican as opposed to Roman Catholic
- the monastic system that had endured for over 800 years no longer existed
- Spain had turned from an ally of England into its mortal enemy.

This period witnessed the rise of the bureaucrat, men like Thomas Cromwell and William Cecil, and the emergence of

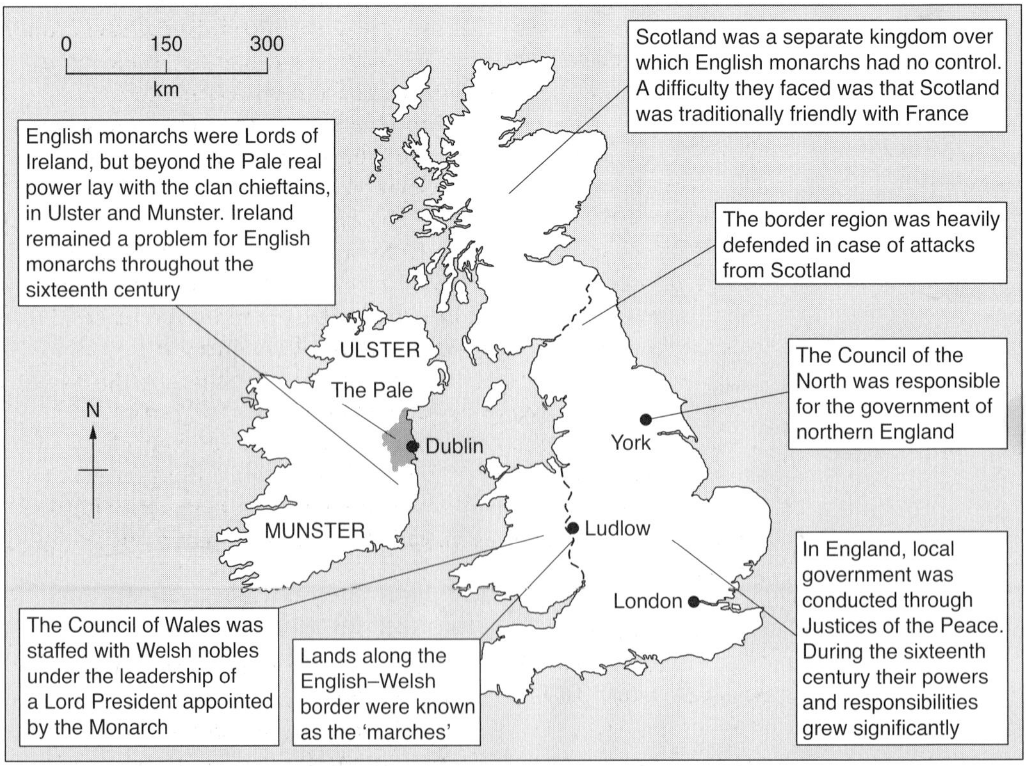

Key date

Thomas Cromwell became the king's chief adviser: 1532

Figure 1.1: The geography of mid-Tudor England.

Key dates

Henry VIII became Head of the Church in England: 1534

Fall of Thomas Cromwell: 1540

Key question

What problems did Henry VIII face in the second half of his reign?

Key terms

Factions
Rival or opposing political groups led by powerful noblemen or noble families. Factions fought for control of the monarch.

Ruling élites
The landowning class of nobles and gentry who attended parliament and the Court, and who controlled the forces of law and order, government and administration both locally and, in the case of the more powerful, centrally.

Protestant
Term used to describe those who had protested against and separated from the Roman Catholic Church.

Anglo-Catholicism
Term used to describe the English Catholic Church set up in 1534 with the king as its head rather than the Pope.

parliament as a more significant institution of government. Inflation, depression and trade dislocation heralded economic changes that affected society, and the individual within that society, as much as the State. In short, the period between 1536 and 1588 is so significant that it is worthy of in-depth analysis and investigation.

Henry VIII: faction and rivalry at Court 1536–47

Faction was a fact of life at Court but during the period of Thomas Cromwell's ascendancy (1532–40), Henry VIII's chief adviser was, with the support of the king, largely able to control it. Cromwell was a shrewd political operator being skilled at making and breaking alliances almost at will. His alliance with the Boleyn faction to see off the supporters of Catherine of Aragon proved successful. However, once the Aragonese faction had been destroyed Cromwell bided his time before turning against the Boleyns. He did so only when it became obvious that the king had tired of Anne Boleyn and fallen in love with Jane Seymour. Cromwell proved as ruthlessly successful in ridding the king of Anne Boleyn, and the leading members of her powerful faction at Court, as he had been in pushing them together. Her conviction for treasonous infidelity was achieved on the flimsiest of evidence.

Cromwell's hand in the destruction of Anne Boleyn earned for him the enmity of her uncle Thomas Howard, duke of Norfolk. Already hated by Norfolk on account of his low birth and powerful position at Court, the duke determined to destroy Cromwell once the opportunity presented itself. In the meantime, Cromwell's attempt to form an alliance with the Seymour family, by encouraging the king's marriage to Jane, seemed to be bearing fruit. However, neither side trusted the other and when Norfolk used the disaster of the king's marriage to Anne of Cleves to destroy Cromwell, Seymour, now the Earl of Hertford, did nothing to help the king's chief adviser.

The fall of Cromwell in 1540 heralded a period of increased political instability. There was a growth in the rivalry between **factions** at Court. The main issue lay between the reformists who supported reform in politics and religion, and the conservatives who were opposed to reform. The rivalry between these two factions began in 1534 when Henry had broken away from the Roman Catholic Church and made himself Supreme Head of the Church of England. Since then the **ruling élites** had been split over the issue of whether the English Church should remain essentially Catholic or become more **Protestant**.

The reformists

The reformists were led by Archbishop Cranmer and Edward Seymour, later Duke of Somerset, the uncle of Prince Edward. The reformists were unhappy with the **Anglo-Catholicism** established by Henry VIII and Cromwell in 1534. They wanted the Church of England to become more Protestant.

Profile: Thomas Cromwell 1485–1540

1485	–	Born the son of Walter Cromwell of Putney, a blacksmith and cloth-merchant
1503	–	Joined the French army and marched with them to Italy, fighting in the battle of Garigliano
1504–13	–	Entered the household of the Italian merchant-banker Francesco Frescobaldi. He later worked as a cloth merchant in the Netherlands
1514	–	Stayed in the English Hospital in Rome
1520	–	Established in London mercantile and legal circles
1523	–	Entered the House of Commons for the first time
1524	–	Appointed a subsidy commissioner in Middlesex. Entered Wolsey's service
1530	–	Became a member of the King's Council
1531	–	Took control of the supervision of the king's legal and parliamentary affairs
1532	–	Became master of the King's Jewels
1534	–	Confirmed as Henry VIII's Principal Secretary and Chief Minister
1535	–	Appointed Royal Vicegerent, or Vicar-General
1540 April	–	Granted the Earldom of Essex
June	–	Imprisoned in the Tower of London prior to his trial and execution for treason in July

Cromwell was a dedicated bureaucrat who served Henry VIII well. His greatest achievement was in planning and piloting the legislation responsible for the break with Rome. His survey, closure and eventual destruction of the monasteries represent a model of administrative speed and efficiency. Unfortunately, his skill and effectiveness in government, his promotion of the key aspects of Protestantism and his leadership of the religious reform movement at Court caused jealousy and made him powerful enemies. When he made mistakes, such as arranging the marriage between Henry VIII and Anne of Cleves, his enemies pounced and ruined his reputation with the king. Barely three months after being ennobled as Earl of Essex he was executed on trumped-up charges of treason.

The Conservatives

The conservatives were headed by Thomas Howard, Duke of Norfolk, and Stephen Gardiner, Bishop of Winchester. Some conservatives wanted the Church to return to Roman Catholicism but most were content to continue the Anglo-Catholicism established by Henry VIII. The conservatives were united in opposing a Protestant Church of England.

Duke of Norfolk (Thomas Howard) imprisoned: 1546

Duke of Norfolk released from prison: 1547

Key dates

Key terms

Reformation
The religious changes of the sixteenth century in England and continental Europe.

Privy Council
Élite body of councillors drawn from the nobility and more powerful gentry who met with the monarch on a regular basis to offer their advice, frame laws and govern the country.

Key dates

Henry VIII died: 1547

Edward VI became king: 1547

Duke of Somerset (Edward Seymour) became Lord Protector: 1547

Key question
What problems did Somerset face?

Key terms

Minority government
Government by councillors when the ruler is a child or minor.

Regency Council
A select group of noble councillors who govern the kingdom on behalf of a ruler who is a child. Between 1547 and 1549 the Council was headed by Somerset to rule on behalf of Edward VI.

Disputes between the factions

The disgrace and execution of Cromwell, the architect of the **Reformation**, had been a success for the conservatives. This was confirmed by Henry VIII's marriage to Catherine Howard, the Duke of Norfolk's niece. The conservatives hoped to influence the king and the shaping of royal policy via his new wife. However, Catherine's trial and execution for adultery in 1542 marked a victory for the reformists. In seeking out the evidence to destroy her, the reformists hoped to ruin the reputations of both Norfolk and Gardiner.

For the next five years the two factions strove for supremacy at Court. Henry VIII's final marriage, to Catherine Parr, a committed Protestant, showed that the conservatives were losing ground. In 1546 the reformists gained a decisive advantage when the Duke of Norfolk was arrested and put in the Tower of London on a charge of treason, and Stephen Gardiner was dismissed from the **Privy Council**. It was against this background that Edward VI, brought up as a Protestant, came to the throne in 1547.

Some historians see these disputes between the factions as a sign of increasing dynastic weakness. Others argue that factions were a normal part of Tudor politics, and that such rivalry was necessary for healthy government. Nevertheless, the fact remains that Henry VIII's death in 1547 marked the beginning of years of less stable government and this has prompted many historians to see it as a period of crisis.

Edward VI: the Somerset years 1547–9

Henry VIII was succeeded by the nine-year-old Prince Edward, his son by his third wife, Jane Seymour. This was a problem in itself because Edward was too young to rule, and periods of **minority government** were often times of potential political unrest. Henry VIII had tried to prevent trouble by establishing a **Regency Council** led by Edward Seymour, Edward's uncle. Edward Seymour quickly gained control of the Council, and, under his new title of Lord Proctector Somerset (he had been made Duke of Somerset by his young nephew), ruled the country until 1549. During this time the political situation deteriorated steadily. Whether this was caused by Somerset's lack of ability, or by the numerous difficulties which he had to overcome is hotly debated by historians.

Three major problems were inherited from the policies of Henry VIII.

1. Religious policy

Should the Church of England remain essentially Catholic or become more Protestant? Somerset inherited a divided Church that lacked decisive leadership and a clear direction. Somerset himself was a moderate reformer, as were most members of the Regency Council, whereas Edward VI, despite his youth, favoured more radical changes. However, powerful politicians such as the Duke of Norfolk and Bishop Gardiner were opposed to change, and such differences only increased the in-fighting among the political factions.

2. Foreign policy

Should the war with France and Scotland begun by Henry VIII in 1542 be continued or stopped? Somerset inherited a war that Henry VIII had hoped would secure the marriage of Edward VI to the young Mary, Queen of Scots. Although the government was already bankrupt, Somerset continued the war and thereby further crippled the country's finances. At the same time he strove to continue Henry VIII's policy of keeping on good terms with Charles V, ruler of Spain and the **Holy Roman Empire**, for fear of provoking him into war.

Holy Roman Empire
Collection of states of varying sizes that covered central Europe (Germany and Austria) and northern Italy that was governed by an elected ruler, the Emperor.

Key term

3. Economic policy

Should the economy, which had been neglected by Henry VIII, be reformed or left to repair itself? Somerset inherited an English economy that was in a very weak condition. Population levels had been increasing rapidly since the 1530s, causing prices to rise and making it difficult for young people to find work. The problem was made worse by a fall in demand for English textiles abroad, which caused growing unemployment among cloth workers. By 1549 there was widespread discontent among the mass of the population, leading to large-scale popular uprisings in Norfolk and the West Country.

Although the rebellions were eventually suppressed, Somerset's enemies on the Council seized the opportunity to overthrow him and take power.

Edward VI: the Northumberland years 1550–3

From the ensuing power struggle John Dudley, Earl of Warwick, emerged as the new leader. He was made Duke of Northumberland and Lord President of the Council. He ruled the country as the Lord President Northumberland for the remainder of Edward VI's reign. While Northumberland seems to have adopted more practical policies than Somerset there is some debate as to whether he was any more successful in overcoming the problems that faced the country.

Although the popular discontent had been subdued, Northumberland faced the same problems as his predecessor. These problems were three-fold:

Key question
What problems did Northumberland face and how did he deal with them?

Somerset replaced by the Duke of Northumberland (John Dudley) who became Lord President of the Council: 1549

Key date

1. Foreign policy

Somerset's fall from power caused a temporary breakdown in military leadership. This enabled the French to gain the initiative in the war and they went on the offensive. This, combined with a lack of money, forced Northumberland to make peace with both France and Scotland. This annoyed many of the ruling élites who thought that this was a humiliating climb-down.

Key term

Catholic élites
The most powerful and influential Catholic politicians and landowners in the kingdom.

Key dates
Edward VI died: 1553

Lady Jane Grey crowned queen and 'reigned' for nine days: July 1553

Key question
Why did Northumberland attempt to make Lady Jane Grey queen of England?

Key terms

Poor laws
Laws passed to deal with the poor and vagrant in society. Because they did not understand the causes of poverty and vagrancy and they feared rebellion, many of the early poor laws had been designed to punish and control the poor. However, by mid-century some attempt was made to assist the poor by promoting charity and providing work.

Constitution
The rules and regulations that determine how a country is governed.

2. Religious policy

At the same time, possibly to secure the support of Edward VI, Northumberland allowed increasingly radical reforms to be introduced into the Church of England. For example, altars were ordered to be removed and the church service was modelled on the Lutheran system of worship. Such a move not only angered the **Catholic élites** at home, but also antagonised Emperor Charles V, England's major continental ally, who was an active supporter of the Roman Catholic Church.

3. Economic policy

Northumberland had learned from Somerset's mistakes and introduced measures to try to restore stability. The Privy Council and the government were reorganised, finances were reformed, and debts created by the war began to be paid off. Although the economic situation continued to worsen, new **poor laws** were introduced to help the poorest sections of society.

Northumberland and Lady Jane Grey

Whether Northumberland would have succeeded in establishing himself firmly in power is a matter of speculation because Edward VI died in 1553. This created an immediate **constitutional** crisis. Under Henry VIII's will, Mary, the daughter of his first wife, Catherine of Aragon, was to succeed if Edward died childless. However, Mary was a devout Roman Catholic and it was feared that she would restore the authority of the Pope and so end the Royal Supremacy over the Church of England.

In an effort to prevent this, Northumberland tried to change the succession by disinheriting Mary and her younger sister Elizabeth, the daughter of Henry VIII's second wife, Anne Boleyn. Instead, the Crown was to pass to Lady Jane Grey, the Protestant granddaughter of Henry VIII's sister Mary. Moreover, to secure his own position, Northumberland arranged for Lady Jane Grey to marry his son Guildford Dudley.

The plot seemed to have succeeded and Jane was crowned queen, but the ruling élites, both Catholic and Protestant, rallied to the support of Mary. Whether they did this through dislike of Northumberland or to preserve the legitimate succession is not altogether clear. Northumberland was arrested and quickly executed. Early in 1554 Lady Jane Grey and Guildford Dudley too were executed.

Profile: Lady Jane Grey 1537–54

1537 – Born
1553 – Married Guildford Dudley, youngest son of Lord
President Northumberland
1553 – Crowned Queen of England. Reign lasted for nine days
from 6 to 15 July
1554 – Executed for treason

Lady Jane Grey was the daughter of Frances Brandon, Duchess
of Suffolk and Henry Grey, Marquis of Dorset. Through her
mother, Jane was a granddaughter of Henry VIII's sister Mary.
Because of her royal connections Jane became a victim of Tudor
politics. Edward VI named Jane as his heir because of her
attachment to the Protestant faith. The young king was
determined to prevent his half-sister, Mary, from succeeding to
the throne. In this he was helped by the Lord President
Northumberland and by Jane's mother and father.

Jane was persuaded to marry Guildford Dudley and accept the
crown after Edward VI's death. The Privy Council initially agreed
to proclaim her queen but they soon deserted her when
Northumberland's military expedition to defeat Mary failed. By
the beginning of August 1553 Jane, her husband and father-in-
law were imprisoned in the Tower. Northumberland was quickly
executed but Mary was reluctant to execute Jane because she
recognised her as an innocent political pawn. However, when
Jane's father led a rebellion against the Crown, Mary felt she had
no choice but to execute her young cousin.

Henry VII *m.* Elizabeth of York

Arthur
(1486–1502)

Margaret *m.* James IV
(1489–1541) | of Scotland

Henry VIII *m.* (i) Catherine of Aragon
(b. 1491   (divorced, d. 1536)
reigned   (ii) Anne Boleyn
1509–47)   (executed 1536)
               (iii) Jane Seymour
                    (died in childbirth 1537)
               (iv) Anne of Cleves   (ii)
                    (divorced, d. 1557)
               (v) Catherine Howard
                    executed 1542)   Henry   Frances *m.* Henry Grey
               (vi) Catherine Parr   Brandon   Duke of
                    (d. 1548)   (d. 1534)   Suffolk

Mary *m.* (i) Louis XII
of France
(d. 1515)
(ii) Charles
Brandon
Duke of
Suffolk
(d. 1545)

James V *m.* (i) Madeleine
of Scotland | of France
(d. 1542)   (d. 1537)
            (ii) Mary of Guise
                of France
                (d. 1540)

(ii)

Mary,   *m.* (i) Francis II
Queen   of France
of Scots   (d. 1560)
(1542–87) (ii) Henry Stuart,
executed)   Lord Darnley
              (d. 1567)

(i)

Mary I   *m.* Philip II
(b. 1516   of Spain
reigned   (d. 1598)
1553–8)

(ii)

Elizabeth I
(b. 1533
reigned
1558–1603)

(iii)

Edward VI
(b. 1537
reigned
1547–53)

Henry Grey
Duke of
Suffolk
(executed
1554)

Jane Grey *m.* Guildford
(executed   Dudley
1554)   (executed
                 1554)

James VI of Scotland
I of England
(reigned in England 1603–25)

STUART SUCCESSION

TUDOR SUCCESSION   GREY SUCCESSION

Figure 1.2: The Tudor/Stuart succession.

Mary Tudor 1553–8

Key question
What were the main problems facing Mary and how successfully did she deal with them?

Until quite recently historians dismissed Mary as lacking political experience and leadership qualities. In addition, she is accused of being over-zealous in her support of Roman Catholicism and Spain. Certainly, by the end of her reign her religious and overseas policies had made her widely unpopular. However, it is now suggested that her reign was not altogether disastrous, and that, but for her early death, her policies might have succeeded.

Mary was widely popular on her accession and had the full support of parliament. Her two major objectives were:

Key date
Mary became queen of England: July 1553

- to return England to Roman Catholicism
- to create closer links with the Habsburgs, her mother's family headed by the Holy Roman Emperor Charles V.

Creating closer links with the Habsburgs

Before Mary could achieve her primary objective of returning England to the Roman Catholic Church she had first to secure an alliance with the most influential ruling Catholic family in Europe, the Habsburgs. Mary believed that an alliance with the Habsburg rulers of the Holy Roman Empire, Spain and the Netherlands would strengthen her religious position both at home and abroad. To achieve this she proposed to marry Charles V's son, Philip II of Spain. Although the Council and parliament somewhat reluctantly agreed to the marriage, there was increasing opposition to the proposal. Many of the ruling élites feared that England would be dominated by Spain and drawn into the Habsburg wars against France.

Key terms

Habsburgs
Family name of the ruling family of Spain and Austria. The head of the family from 1519 until his retirement in 1555 was Charles V who, as Holy Roman Emperor, also ruled Germany, the Netherlands and parts of Italy.

Repeal
The procedure in parliament whereby laws are cancelled and removed from the book listing current laws known as the Statute Book.

Marian government
Term used to describe the government of Mary I.

Returning England to Roman Catholicism

With the **Habsburg** alliance secured, Mary began the task of restoring the Church of England to Roman Catholicism. In the first year of her reign, parliament agreed to **repeal** and thereby ignore all the Protestant legislation passed under Edward. Nevertheless, many of the ruling élites had misgivings about such a policy. Some disliked the idea of the Royal Supremacy over the Church being ended, while others feared that they might have to return the Church lands which had been sold off to the ruling élites during the reigns of Henry VIII and Edward VI. In the end Mary had to compromise, and although papal authority was restored, no attempt was made to reclaim any Church lands that had been sold. At the same time, the **Marian government** began another round of financial reform to reduce costs and increase revenues, and initiated a thorough review of the navy.

Before any benefits could be gained from these reforms the reign was overtaken by events. The persecution and execution of Protestants made Mary increasingly unpopular with all levels of society. Popular discontent was made worse by the steadily worsening economic situation and rising unemployment. Anti-Spanish feelings rose to fever pitch when Philip II, despite his promises to the contrary, involved England in his war with

France. As a result, Calais, England's last continental possession, was lost to the French. Mary's death in 1558 was greeted with just as much enthusiasm as had been her accession five years earlier.

Elizabeth I: 1558–88

Mary was succeeded as queen of England by her 25-year-old half-sister Elizabeth. Given the political, religious and economic problems she had inherited from Mary, Elizabeth was well aware that the enthusiasm and popular support that accompanied her accession could evaporate overnight. She was determined to learn from the errors made by her predecessors and, in an effort not to repeat them, she quickly identified those issues that required careful attention: religion, faction and the succession.

The settlement of religion

The question of whether the England inherited by Elizabeth was more Catholic than Protestant, or vice versa, is hotly debated. Indeed, the debate over the relative strengths of Protestantism and Catholicism is unlikely to be resolved because the issue is complex and the evidence contradictory. There were probably as many enthusiastic and committed Catholics as Protestants in England but given the years of change and confusion, the majority of the people were possibly more inclined to be religiously indifferent. If the law compelled them to go to church habit rather than conviction impelled them to attend its services.

   In such volatile circumstances the majority of the population were ripe for conversion to either faith, which is why the settlement of religion was thrashed out in Elizabeth's first parliament. Meeting within eight weeks of her accession, between January and April 1559, parliament enacted the so-called **Elizabethan Church Settlement**. The legislation reconfirmed the **Royal Supremacy**, set out the way in which the Church was to be run and established the content and conduct of services in every parish church. Although the Settlement included an Act of Uniformity that restored the Edwardian Prayer Book of 1552, the government hoped that by being deliberately vague on some aspects of doctrine the legislation would appeal to Protestants without alienating Catholics. In short, the Settlement was a compromise capable of either a Catholic or Protestant interpretation.

Faction

According to one contemporary observer, Sir Robert Naunton, the queen was said to 'rule by faction'. In other words, aware of the rivalry that existed between her courtiers and her ministers, Elizabeth used her advantageous position to play off one against the other. By careful manipulation Elizabeth was able to control those who sought royal patronage. Her choice of first minister, Sir William Cecil, later Lord Burghley (after 1571), did much to cause envy among those who sought a more influential position in government.

Key question
What were the main problems facing Elizabeth and how successfully did she deal with them?

Key dates

Mary died and was succeeded by Elizabeth: November 1558

Elizabeth crowned queen of England: 1559

Key terms

Elizabethan Church Settlement
Term use to describe the organisation, ritual and teaching of the Church of England as enforced by Acts of Parliament.

Royal Supremacy
Act of Parliament restoring the Crown as Head of the Church of England. Elizabeth was proclaimed Supreme Governor of the Church.

Elizabeth's firm support of Cecil did not deter the queen from employing and favouring others such as Robert Dudley, Earl of Leicester, Sir Francis Walsingham and Sir Christopher Hatton. Few of the significantly powerful nobility were deliberately alienated so that rebellion like that of the Northern Earls (see pages 146–50) was rare. The only high-profile casualty of Elizabethan faction politics was the duke of Norfolk, who was executed in 1572.

The succession

The question of the succession preoccupied the queen's ministers and her members of parliament for almost the whole of her reign. As early as 1562, when Elizabeth fell dangerously ill with smallpox, the question of the succession was top of the political agenda and there it remained, even after her recovery, as an ever-present blot on the political landscape. Fearful of her marrying a foreign prince, the political establishment was equally afraid of the consequences of taking a member of the English nobility to be her husband. Yet the alternative was also unthinkable: to remain unmarried would almost inevitably lead to the succession of her Catholic cousin, Mary, Queen of Scots. The issue was not resolved until the very end of Elizabeth's reign.

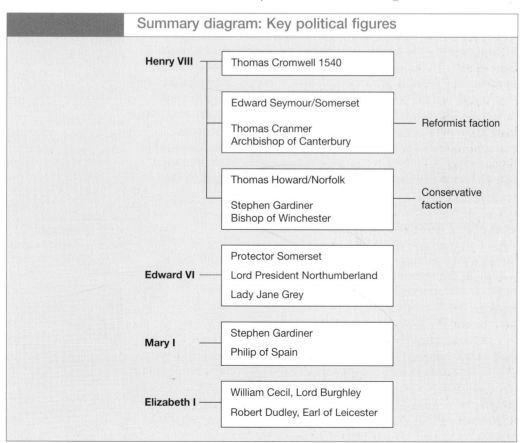

Summary diagram: Key political figures

2 | Historiographical Background

'History' commonly carries two meanings: it refers to what actually happened in the past, and also to the way in which that past has been written about by historians. Therefore, when historians study a particular event or period in history, mainly through the reading and interpretation of original sources, they naturally record their opinions in print. In this way historical information is compiled alongside historians' opinions that, together, builds into a body of work.

Over time successive generations of historians studying the same event or period in history change their opinions and in doing so they might disagree with or even criticise what previous historians have thought or written. The historians who first study and publish their opinions or interpretations on an historical event or period establish the orthodox or traditional view of that history. The historians who come after and who disagree with their predecessors are usually referred to as **revisionists** because they revise earlier interpretations. It is important to remember that whereas historians generally agree on the facts of history – these do not change unless they are proved to be incorrect – they often disagree on their interpretation of them.

Historiography is the term used to describe the study of this history-writing by taking account of changing ideas and opinions. The historiography referred to in the title to this section of the book deals with the way in which historians have changed their opinions on the mid-Tudor period. Whereas earlier historians firmly believed that there was a mid-Tudor crisis in the period between 1536 and 1558, modern historians are not so convinced. Indeed, some historians have argued that a period of crisis endured in England for some 30 years beyond 1558. That is why this period of history is a controversial one. It is likely that what historians have thought or written today will be revised in the future.

The Whig interpretation of history

Until the Second World War English historical writing was still largely dominated by the **Whig interpretation of history**. The middle of the sixteenth century was seen as a 'dead' period between the exciting changes under Henry VIII and the consolidation and expansion of the reign of Elizabeth I. This was because the Whig historians of the nineteenth century did not see any great or 'progressive' events taking place in England at this time. They therefore regarded the reigns of Edward VI and Mary as unimportant. Whig historians assumed that events were shaped by 'great' men (or women). This attitude has created the traditional view of the period, and the years between 1547 and 1558 have tended to be seen in terms of personalities rather than events.

Key question
What is meant by the term 'historiography' and how does it apply to the period 1536–88?

Key terms

Revisionists
Historians who believe that older or more traditional interpretations and ideas in history should be regularly reviewed and changed if necessary.

Whig interpretation of history
Belief that historical events are shaped by great men or women, so that the study of history should be seen in terms of personalities rather than events.

Key question
What is meant by the Whig interpretation of history?

Marxist
Historians who see historical change as a series of events caused mainly by social and economic tension leading to conflict between the poorer and richer classes.

Key question
What is meant by the revisionist/Marxist debate?

Feudalism
The political and social system of medieval England. The system was based on the relationship between lord (master) and vassal (servant): in a ceremony known as homage the vassal promised to serve his lord in war and peace in return for land.

Key question
What are the major theories concerning the rise of the State and of the idea of crisis?

The major and tragic figures have been the dying boy king and the haunted, half-Spanish Mary, driven by love for Philip II and the Catholic religion to commit atrocities against her Protestant subjects. In the background lurked the obscure and slightly sinister figures of the Lord Protector Somerset and the Lord President Northumberland, one provoking popular rebellion and the other plotting to seize the Crown. These were the people who were thought to have created history and little attention was given to the mass of the population, or to the underlying issues that shaped events.

The revisionist/Marxist debate

During the 40 years following the end of the Second World War, historians changed their views about the mid-sixteenth century. There were two broad schools of historical thought: revisionist and **Marxist**.

- Revisionist interpretation largely concentrated on the short-term changes in the constitution, politics and foreign policy brought about by the ruling élites.
- Marxist interpretation largely concentrated on the long-term changes in the economy and society.

Not only were the two groups of historians mutually opposed, but members of both schools disagreed among themselves about the causes of change. Nevertheless, both schools saw England as a part of the momentous changes taking place throughout western Europe. To explain these developments they created general theories into which they tried to fit the ever-growing range of conflicting evidence. Of these theories the two with the greatest bearing on mid-Tudor England were those concerning the rise of the State and of crisis.

General theories concerning the rise of the State and of the idea of crisis

It is particularly important to understand the basis of these theories and how they applied to England in the middle of the sixteenth century. The idea of crisis became very popular among historians in the 1970s. Most revisionist and Marxist historians used these theories to explain the various problems experienced by western European countries. For example, there was

- the crisis of **feudalism** in the fifteenth century
- the religious crisis of the sixteenth century.

However, it must be remembered that the so-called mid-sixteenth-century crisis was confined to England and did not form part of a general European crisis.

Defining crisis

A major difficulty for the student trying to understand any theory of crisis is to decide what historians mean by their use of the word. It could be said that a crisis results from an immediate short-term problem such as a foreign invasion, a rebellion or a harvest failure. Equally it could be maintained that a crisis is created by a combination of long-term problems, which together threaten the collapse of government or the State. The problems in England during the reigns of Edward VI and Mary combine all these possibilities. Yet, even so, it has to be decided whether the English State was in serious danger of collapse. Even before trying to answer this question it is necessary to establish exactly what is meant by the sixteenth-century State.

Defining the State

Revisionist and Marxist historians were generally agreed that the **feudal crisis** and chronic anarchy of the late Middle Ages enabled western European monarchs to gain power at the expense of the Church and the aristocracy. There is broad agreement that those monarchs who were able to take advantage of this situation increased their power and became the centrepiece of a new type of State. They achieved this by creating permanent central and local **bureaucracies** dependent on royal patronage, and by controlling military power. At the same time these monarchs had to maintain a balance between the various sections of their subjects by gaining their acceptance of the legitimacy of royal authority. Thus when historians of either school discussed the sixteenth-century State they were visualising it as the monarch and the permanent machinery of central and local government.

It was generally accepted that, within this broad framework, the states of western Europe were created and developed along different lines depending on their geographical, religious, social, political and economic background.

Finance

Unlike '**absolutist**' states on the continent where, theoretically, the monarch was above the law, had independent sources of taxation and controlled paid officials and mercenary armies, England was more like a **constitutional monarchy**. English monarchs were, to some extent, answerable to parliament and tended to rule through **Statute law**. At the same time they had to rely on the revenue from royal estates, and whatever money they could persuade parliament to grant them. In turn this meant that they could rarely afford to keep a standing army of mercenaries and had to rely on the goodwill of the aristocracy and gentry to raise troops from among their tenants.

Shortage of money also meant that they depended on these same landowners to act as an unpaid bureaucracy to run local government – as Justices of the Peace, for instance. While this might seem to indicate that the English State was in a weaker position than its more authoritarian counterparts on the

Key terms

Feudal crisis
The breakdown in the relationship between lord (master) and vassal (servant). The relationship changed from one based on rewards of land for service to one based on money payments.

Bureaucracy
The means by which a State is governed by officials responsible for routine administration.

Absolutist
Similar to dictatorship where the ruler has absolute power, i.e. unchallenged rule.

Constitutional monarchy
A system whereby a monarch governs the kingdom within the limits of an agreed framework of rules that includes institutions such as the Privy Council and parliament.

Statute law
Laws passed in and by parliament.

Key terms

Bourgeoisie
Term used by Marxist historians to describe the middle class of lawyers, landowners and merchants.

Plague cycle
Term used to describe the regular occurrences of plague. For example, the Black Death of 1348–51 was followed by plague outbreaks in 1361–2, 1369, 1393.

Key question
Why was the period between 1536 and 1588 seen as being in crisis?

Key terms

Husbandmen
Tenant-farmers who rented their land from the local landowners.

Cottagers
Poorer peasant farmers who were obliged to work on the landowner's land either for free or for a fixed sum of money.

Yeomen
A social class of richer peasants that may have been as wealthy as some of the gentry but were below them in social class.

continent, this was not true. One could argue that the English taxpayer was getting government on the cheap and was therefore less likely to rebel.

Order

Order was seen as the central problem for the sixteenth-century State. Monarchs had to raise money for the ever-increasing machinery of government needed to maintain peace and security, manage the economy and create social harmony. To achieve this they had to increase their revenue, but extra taxation was unpopular and likely to provoke rebellion, so leading to the collapse of government. English monarchs depended on the active support of the majority of landowners and the middle classes (described by Marxist historians as the '**bourgeoisie**'), and on the passive obedience of the great mass of the population who had no share in the running of the country. Anything that upset this delicate balance could create a crisis for the English State, if not necessarily for the English people.

The potential for mid-Tudor crises

In terms of these broad theories, the break with Rome in 1534 and the death of Henry VIII in 1547 were seen, especially by G.R. Elton, as times of crisis. Although Henry had avoided civil war and had made careful provision for the succession of his young son Edward, the prospect of a minority (see page 5) posed a serious threat to the stability of the government, particularly as the factions at Court were deeply divided over religious issues. This certainly represented a potential crisis for the State, which might have led to widespread rebellion, or invasion by a foreign power to restore the Catholic religion (see G.R. Elton, G.W. Bernard and D.M. Loades).

As well as these political difficulties, England faced a number of long-term socio-economic problems. By the beginning of the sixteenth century the English population had begun to recover from the worst effects of the Black Death of 1349 and the subsequent **plague cycle**. Rising population forced up rents and food prices and made it difficult to find work, causing distress among the urban and rural poor. These difficulties were made worse in the middle of the century by the temporary decline of the English cloth trade, which threw large numbers of people out of work (see D.C. Coleman, D.M. Pallister and Nigel Heard).

Popular unrest was increased by the rapidity of religious changes – from Roman to Anglo-Catholicism between 1534 and 1547, from Anglo-Catholicism to Protestantism between 1547 and 1550 and from Roman Catholic to Protestant between 1558 and 1570 – as many people felt that their old, traditional way of life was under threat. This was reflected in the growing tension between **husbandmen** and **cottagers** on the one side and **yeomen** and gentry on the other. The former felt that landowners and richer tenant farmers were using the commercial and religious situation to their own advantage (see P. Williams, J. Loach and D. MacCulloch).

So in 1547, 1553 and 1558–9 England seemed to be in a precarious position with possible conflict among the ruling élites, the threat of foreign invasion – the threat became reality in 1588 – a failing economy and rising popular discontent.

New approaches to the historical debate

Most historians have recently become suspicious of general theories, particularly of crisis. They have come to the view that history should be seen in terms of separate crises occurring in individual countries or regions at different times without any common linkage or cause. Although this does not necessarily rule out a mid-Tudor crisis, the concept is now no longer fashionable.

Continued research has led to a considerable revision of ideas about all aspects of the latter half of the reign of Henry VIII, the reigns of Edward, Mary and the early part of the reign of Elizabeth. Far from a danger of collapse, mid-Tudor government is now considered to show considerable strength in overcoming a series of potentially damaging difficulties. Religious change is similarly seen as having been achieved with remarkably little disruption when compared with developments on the continent. Although there was popular unrest, this is thought to have been caused by economic stresses rather than any weakness on the part of the authorities. The major crisis point is now thought to have been the economy, which suffered not only from government mishandling, but also from a whole range of long- and short-term problems.

These are the issues that will be examined in the following sections to see which, if any, of them constituted a 'mid-Tudor crisis'.

Key question
How and why did the approach to the study of the mid-Tudor period change?

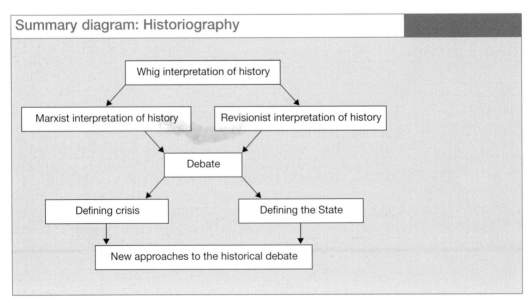

Summary diagram: Historiography

- Whig interpretation of history
  - Marxist interpretation of history
  - Revisionist interpretation of history
    - Debate
      - Defining crisis
      - Defining the State
        - New approaches to the historical debate

3 | A Crisis of the State: Government, Politics and Foreign Affairs

The State

Key question
How and why did the State change during the sixteenth century?

By the early sixteenth century the State was assuming greater responsibility for every aspect of life. In much of Europe government was becoming centralised in capital cities such as London, Paris and Madrid, and growing numbers of civil servants were being employed to administer both central and local affairs. At the same time, the State was trying to take control in areas in which it had had little or no influence during the Middle Ages. As the administration grew in size, statesmen realised that they had to take more control of the economy to ensure that the country was creating the wealth needed to pay the cost of government. Consequently, the government began to pass legislation to try to regulate the economy, and place restrictions on the way in which individual merchants and industrialists could operate.

Many European countries, including Catholic ones, were deciding that religion was such a fundamental concern that it could no longer be left under the control of the Pope in Rome. In England the Henrician Reformation of the 1530s had made the monarch Head of the Church and given parliament control of religious policy. This meant that religion had become part of the State's social policy, by which the government tried to maintain stability and cohesion. Yet, while the English State had gained great power and influence, it was becoming recognised that the government was responsible for the welfare of all the people in the country. Not only was the State expected to help the poor by taking over the charitable work previously carried out by the monasteries, but, also, to find employment for all the able-bodied.

This broad picture of the English State is widely accepted. Although it may appear very much like the creation of the twentieth-century historians using hindsight, it was precisely in these terms that the people of sixteenth-century England saw it as well. **Commonwealth**, or 'commonweal', the word used by contemporaries to describe the country, was a **nationalistic** and patriotic concept, but at the same time it contained the idea that the government was responsible for the welfare of all citizens, just as all citizens had the obligation to serve the State. This is well expressed by John Pym, a radical MP and critic of the monarchy:

Key terms

Commonwealth
A community of shared interests where everyone, in theory, worked for the common good.

Nationalistic
People who are particularly proud of their country and who might distrust or even hate foreigners.

> The form of government is that which doth encourage every member of a state to the common good; and as those parts give strength to the whole, so they receive from it again strength and protection. If this mutual relation be broken, the whole frame will quickly be dissolved, and fall to pieces.

Although this was written in the 1620s, Pym is describing what he saw as the good and well-balanced parliamentary constitution and government of the sixteenth century. Of course, this was an idealistic view of government and society, which only worked partially and for some of the time. The government found it difficult to see all the connections between different parts of the frame. Individuals at all levels of society, like modern historians, had their own biases and priorities. The sixteenth-century English State could only function with the consent of a majority of the people, and the art of government was to achieve as much as was practicable in the circumstances.

The monarchy

Crucial to the delicate structure of checks and balances was the monarch. Although the State was growing in power and becoming more stable with the development of new offices of State and permanent civil servants, it was still dependent upon the personality of the king or queen. Much of the thinking concerning the duties of the State was **paternalistic**. Just as a father was head of a family and was responsible for its well-being, so the monarch was to the nation. Equally, just as the father expected obedience from all members of the family, so the monarch expected unswerving loyalty from his subjects. The relationship between the monarch and his people and his place within the State is clearly shown in the **Treason Act** of 1547:

> Nothing being more godly, more sure, more to be wished and desired, between a Prince the Supreme Head and Ruler and the subjects whose governor and head he is, than on the Prince's part great understanding and flexibility ... and on the subject's behalf that they should obey rather for ... love of a king and prince, than for fear of his strict and severe laws; yet some times there cometh in the commonwealth problems that make it necessary for the repressing of the insolvency and unruliness of men and for the forseeing and providing of remedies against rebellion.

Here is another view of the State, which is very similar to John Pym's idealistic picture of the sixteenth-century constitution. Edward VI, although only nine years old, is seen as the father of his people. It is a relationship based on mutual co-operation and love, but the king, like a father, has to punish his children if they become fractious and unruly. In mid-sixteenth-century England the king was seen in these paternalistic terms, and was regarded as the keystone of the constitution.

The succession

Such paternalistic attitudes meant that many members of the ruling élites thought the monarch should be male. Many continental countries recognised **Salic Law**, which excluded women from succession to the throne. Although England did not do this, there was no tradition of female monarchs. Henry VIII's anxiety for a male heir suggests that he considered that a female heir would create dynastic weakness. When Edward VI died in 1553, the Lord President Northumberland tried to exclude the princesses Mary and Elizabeth from the throne on the grounds

Key question
What part did the monarch play in the State?

Key terms

Paternalistic
The idea that a monarch would govern his kingdom and rule his subjects as a father would his house and family.

Treason Act
Law passed in parliament to punish those who betray the State and its monarch. Political and religious disloyalty was punishable by death if convicted under the Treason Act.

Salic Law
A law originating in France and dating from the eleventh century, which excluded females from succeeding to the throne.

Key question
Why was the royal succession such a problem?

that they were illegitimate (their mothers' marriages to Henry VIII had been declared invalid so that their father could marry again), and, because as women, they might endanger the security of the State by marrying foreign princes (see pages 61–2). Northumberland did not oppose the idea of a female monarch which is why he attempted to strengthen his control over the Crown by replacing Mary and Elizabeth with Lady Jane Grey. However, Queen Jane would be a ruler in name only, she would be guided by him and by the advice of an all male Council. As an additional guarantee of her co-operation Jane was married to Northumberland's youngest son.

Although Northumberland was unsuccessful, it is clear that Mary, after she had overthrown him in 1553, was reminded that there was opposition to the idea of a female monarch, especially one who was unmarried. In 1554 parliament passed an Act concerning Regal Power which made it very clear that, within the English constitution, royal authority was 'invested either in male or female, and are and ought to be taken in one as in the other'. Some constitutional historians see this as a very significant piece of legislation, which, by removing doubts about the right of women to rule in England, prevented constitutional crises in the future. For other historians, however, the crucial point concerning the succession was not one of gender, but the question of age and ability.

It is widely agreed that if there was to be a constitutional crisis in mid-sixteenth-century England, it was likely to be caused by the succession of the nine-year-old prince Edward. There is little doubt that England in 1547 could have seen a return to the chaos and anarchy of the **Wars of the Roses** in the second half of the fifteenth century. That there was no real crisis in 1547, 1553 or 1558 is seen to be the result of the loyalty and support of the majority of the population for the process of legitimacy and law.

The fact that the succession of a minor in 1547 did not cause an immediate crisis does not lessen the potential gravity of the situation. Historians are in broad agreement that a central feature in the development of the State was the struggle for power among the ruling élites. In such circumstances a strong, adult monarch was needed to maintain control, and the accession of a nine-year-old minor clearly opened the way for ambitious men to attempt to gain power.

Key term

Wars of the Roses The sequence of plots, rebellions and battles that took place in England between 1455 and 1485. The idea of the warring roses of Lancaster (red) and York (white) was invented by Henry VII after he seized the throne in 1485.

The key debate

> How and why do historians disagree on the nature of the factions and power struggles of the period?

Revisionist theory

Early revisionist historians like Joel Hurstfield and G.R. Elton saw this power struggle within the ranks of the ruling élites as taking two main forms.

- At the Court, the centre of government, the courtiers formed groups, or factions, which were constantly striving to gain royal favour. This is not considered to have been particularly dangerous, because factions are seen as a normal part of Tudor government.

- A much greater threat was thought to have been the rivalry between the '**court party**' and the '**country party**'. (It must be remembered that these were not political parties in the modern sense of the term.) Members of the 'country party' were considered to have resented the growth of the central bureaucracy because they thought it was sucking power and wealth into London at the expense of the provinces.

Although this early revisionist theory is now treated with caution, particularly by Alan G.R. Smith and David Starkey, the hostility displayed towards Somerset and Northumberland by many of their fellow members of the ruling élites is thought to have been part of this struggle.

Marxist theory

Marxist historians like Christopher Hill, E.P. Thompson and Eric Hobsbawm interpreted this struggle for power as part of the class conflict between the old aristocracy and the rising commercial and professional groupings drawn from town and country. It was once fashionable to describe this in terms of 'the rise of the middle class' – a conflict between the new, commercially orientated smaller landowners, merchants and professional men, and the old military or feudal aristocracy for the control of central and local government.

Now it is agreed that these distinctions are much less clear-cut, and that it is often difficult to show the difference between merchants, rising gentry, and the old aristocracy. Most Marxist historians came to agree that the conflict was between active reformers and conservatives, who were drawn equally from the ranks of the aristocracy and the new rising groups. This was seen as the beginning of a struggle for power between Protestant commercial interests and the conservative, Catholic forces of paternalism.

Key terms

Court party
Seen as consisting of the members of the Privy Council, government officers and courtiers, all of whom held office and enjoyed royal patronage.

Country party
Made up of those among the élites who did not hold office or enjoy royal favour, and generally lived on their estates in the countryside.

Debasement of the coinage
A process whereby the government tried to preserve its gold and silver reserves by reducing the amount of precious metal that went into making coins.

Some key books in the debate
Christopher Hill, 'Marxism and history', *The Modern Quarterly* NS 3 (1948), 52–64.
Eric Hobsbawm and Terence Ranger (eds), *The Invention of Tradition* (Cambridge, 1992).
E.P. Thompson, *The Making of the English Working Class* (Harmondsworth, 1968).

Foreign policy

Most historians have considered foreign policy to be central to the political development of the State. It is generally agreed that the major problem for the early modern governments was to find fresh sources of revenue to meet their rising costs. Increased taxation was unpopular and might lead to rebellion, while borrowing, or **debasement of the coinage**, was equally dangerous

Key question
Why did foreign policy become so important?

Inflation
Price rises in goods, materials and foodstuffs.

Valois
Name of the ruling royal family of France between 1328 and 1589.

Hundred Years' War
Fought between England and France for control of France between 1338 and 1453.

New World
Term used to describe the continent of America.

and might result in bankruptcy or high **inflation**, which merely added to the cost of government. The alternative was for the State to adopt an aggressive foreign policy to acquire land, wealth and trade. Unfortunately, warfare was extremely expensive, particularly because of the rapid changes in military technology. As a result a country waging war, even a successful one, might bankrupt itself.

By the middle of the sixteenth century England was neither strong nor wealthy enough to compete with the great continental powers such as the Holy Roman Empire, or France. This meant that it was necessary for England to ally with one or other of her more powerful continental neighbours. Until 1559 western European foreign policy was dominated by the conflict between the **Valois** kings of France and the Habsburg rulers of the Empire and Spain. Several diplomatic considerations made it natural for the early Tudors to ally themselves with the Habsburgs. France had been England's national enemy throughout the Middle Ages. Henry VIII's marriage to Catherine of Aragon in 1509 linked England dynastically with Spain and the Empire. This alliance not only offered more protection against possible French aggression, but it was hoped it might also help the English kings to regain the territories lost to France during the **Hundred Years' War**.

Another important consideration was that the Habsburgs ruled the Netherlands, the major industrial centre for textiles in northern Europe. As the English economy was dependent on the export of cloth to the Netherlands, it was essential to maintain good Anglo-Habsburg relations. Although the English Reformation of the 1530s had soured relations with the Catholic lands and Spain, the Anglo-Habsburg alliance was maintained until the death of Mary in 1558.

Thereafter, the fate of the Anglo-Habsburg alliance remained in the balance as Philip of Spain and Elizabeth of England sought to maintain good relations without really trusting each other. It broke down in 1568–9 when Elizabeth imprisoned the Catholic Mary, Queen of Scots, put down the pro-Catholic Northern Rebellion and sought improved relations with France. Alliance turned to annoyance between 1569 and 1585 when relations between England and Spain deteriorated to such an extent that Philip declared war on Elizabeth culminating in the launch of his Armada in 1588. The reasons why England and Spain went to war may be summarised in four key points:

- the plundering raids by English privateers on Spanish treasure ships from the **New World**
- English support for the Protestant Dutch rebels under William of Orange who was attempting to free the Netherlands from Spanish rule
- the trial and execution of Mary, Queen of Scots, a fellow Catholic monarch
- England's improving relations with France.

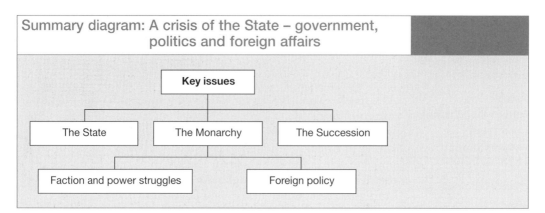

Summary diagram: A crisis of the State – government, politics and foreign affairs

4 | A Crisis of the State: Social, Economic and Religious Change

It is widely agreed that fundamental structural changes were taking place in western Europe in the sixteenth century and that these changes were the result of the breakdown of the late medieval economy. Despite differing opinions over detail, it is generally thought that the underlying structural change taking place was a movement away from a **self-sufficient rural economy** towards a **commercial market economy**.

Social change

The changes influencing the economy also had a considerable impact upon the structure of society. Medieval society has been described as a feudal pyramid. It was based upon the ownership of land, military service and peasant agriculture.

At the top of the pyramid was the king, who was the largest landowner. The military élites were made up of the aristocracy and their families, who held land from the king, and the knights and their families, who held land from the aristocracy. Below them came the great mass of the peasantry, who worked the land and provided food and labour for the élites. The only groups outside this structure were the clergy and the small number of people who lived in towns.

The élites

The economic developments of the late Middle Ages began to change this structure, but it was a very gradual process. It is widely agreed that a highly significant shift among the élites was the rise of 'the gentry', the class of landowners socially just below the aristocracy:

- Revisionists linked this development with the expansion of the State. They considered that the gentry increased in numbers and power because of the growth in royal patronage and in the opportunities to hold government office.
- Other historians, particularly Marxists, saw the gentry rising at the expense of the aristocracy because of their greater ability

Key question
What were the key changes in the economy and society?

Key question
How did society and the social structure change during this period?

Key terms

Self-sufficient rural economy
Growing enough food to feed the nation without having to rely on foreign imports.

Commercial market economy
Landlords leased out their land in larger units to commercial farmers for greater profit which resulted in smaller tenant farmers being forced off the land to work for wages in agriculture.

and willingness to take advantage of commercial opportunities available after the breakdown of the medieval economy.

It is difficult to choose between these two theories. What is certain is that there were more openings by the sixteenth century than during the Middle Ages for men of initiative to increase their power and wealth.

The gentry are regarded both by contemporaries and by historians as an expanding group ranked below the aristocracy and above the yeomen. They included younger sons from the aristocracy and the upper ranks of the yeomen, as well as wealthy merchants, lawyers and professional men from the towns.

Many Marxist historians saw the English gentry as the rising, capitalistic 'bourgeoisie', which was in conflict with the aristocracy. This is a difficult argument to sustain because many gentry families were related to the aristocracy, and the ambition of successful gentry families was to join the ranks of the aristocracy. It is certainly true that the gentry, who were becoming increasingly educated through attending university and being trained in law, competed with the aristocracy for offices in central and local government. They are seen also as supplying the capitalistic drive needed to bring about economic expansion, but there is no real evidence to show that the gentry were more commercially motivated than many of the aristocracy.

What can be said is that the ruling élites in general benefited during the sixteenth century from rising prices, and the redistribution of monastic and other Church lands. Only by the end of the century did the rising demand for land and titles begin to cause real competition among the ruling élites. However, this process was only just beginning by the middle of the century.

The non-élites

Equally significant changes were taking place among the non-élites or peasantry. By the beginning of the sixteenth century, peasant society, as it was to be found in Scotland, Ireland and continental Europe, is considered to have been rapidly disappearing in England. The spread of commerce placed considerable restraints on the traditional village framework. The generally loose peasant society was being replaced by a more rigid structure. This consisted of yeomen (holding more than 60 acres), husbandmen (farming between 15 and 40 acres), and cottagers (who had a cottage and a small plot of land).

The **enclosure** of open fields and commons in some areas meant that smallholdings were being absorbed into larger commercial farms. Loss of access to common land deprived poorer families of grazing rights for their animals and stopped them from collecting firewood or gathering wild fruit and other necessities. This meant that the way of life for the rural poor, where the centre of work for the family was the home and smallholding, was being eroded. Those people who could not find work as wage labourers on the large commercial farms run by the gentry, yeomen and husbandmen, or in local rural industry, were forced to move away

Key term

Enclosure
The enclosing of land by fences or hedges in order to divide large, open fields into smaller more manageable units.

The old élite became divided into two parts

Aristocratic society: the nobles and their immediate families ranked below the monarch

The gentry: the younger children of the aristocracy, their families and their descendants evolved into a lesser élite

There were three ranks in this new social group

At the top were the **knights**. The title had partially lost its old military significance, although it still was not hereditary. Knights could be created for a variety of reasons, yet the title increasingly came to denote a landowner with estates worth at least £100 a year

Next in rank to the knight was the **esquire**: a title given to the children of knights and their descendants

The lowest rank among the gentry was the **gentleman**: a title given to the younger children of esquires and their descendants

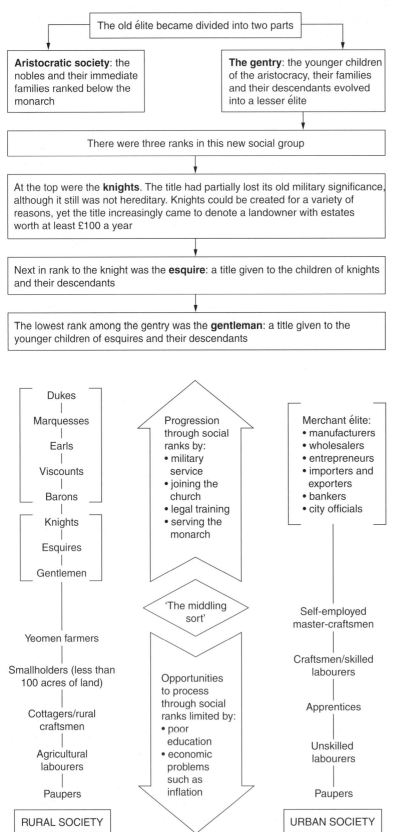

Dukes
|
Marquesses
|
Earls
|
Viscounts
|
Barons
|
Knights
|
Esquires
|
Gentlemen
|
Yeomen farmers
|
Smallholders (less than 100 acres of land)
|
Cottagers/rural craftsmen
|
Agricultural labourers
|
Paupers

RURAL SOCIETY

Progression through social ranks by:
• military service
• joining the church
• legal training
• serving the monarch

'The middling sort'

Opportunities to process through social ranks limited by:
• poor education
• economic problems such as inflation

Merchant élite:
• manufacturers
• wholesalers
• entrepreneurs
• importers and exporters
• bankers
• city officials

Self-employed master-craftsmen
|
Craftsmen/skilled labourers
|
Apprentices
|
Unskilled labourers
|
Paupers

URBAN SOCIETY

Figure 1.3: The early Tudor social hierarchy c1550.

from the village. Many migrated to the towns where they joined a growing urban population dependent on wage labour.

It must be stressed that changes were generally very slow, and varied widely across the country. A great many villages remained entirely unaltered. Only in the Midlands and around expanding towns, where commercial farming was profitable, were large numbers of people forced off the land. Even so, for a government anxious to maintain the status quo and the traditional village structure, this was not an ideal situation. In an attempt to stop people moving away from the villages the government tried to legislate against enclosure, which they thought was the main cause of depopulation. To stop people moving about the countryside, laws of increasing severity were passed against **vagrancy**. For example, vagrants were to be whipped and branded on their first conviction but executed if caught a second time.

However, what Tudor governments failed to realise was that a rising population and the shortage of job opportunities were the real underlying causes of this problem. It was this situation, worsened by increasingly frequent food shortages, that was the major cause of popular discontent in mid sixteenth-century England.

The key debate

Why was there a breakdown of the rural economy?

Marxist theory

Marxist historians saw the breakdown in terms of a 'feudal' crisis caused by a deterioration in the relationships between 'peasant' tenants and their landlords. This resulted in a change from a feudal or self-sufficient 'mode of production' to a capitalist or commercial market 'mode of production'.

These landlords, it was claimed, spent their income on luxury goods, warfare and castle-building, and as costs increased they had to raise rents, **tithes** and taxes – a process called 'extra surplus extraction'. As the landlords did not invest their money to improve the efficiency of their estates by improving the quality of their land or introducing new farming techniques, the soil became exhausted and the level of food production fell.

By the end of the Middle Ages there was growing resentment among the tenants who were faced by falling crop yields and rising rents. They began to abandon their farms, to refuse to pay rents and to stage rebellions, for example, as in the Peasants' Revolt of 1381. Such 'peasant' resistance forced the landlords to lease out their land in larger units to commercial farmers, and this resulted in more tenants being forced off the land to work for wages in agriculture and industry. This was the new and more exploitative 'mode of production', based on wages, which was spreading in England during the sixteenth century. In turn, this new form of economic relationship caused further resentment, leading to class conflict between the wage-earners and the commercial 'bourgeoisie' in both town and country.

Key terms

Vagrancy
Term used to describe the wandering poor who have no permanent work or home.

Tithes
Tax amounting to 10 per cent of a parishioner's income (usually paid in goods) levied by the Church.

Revisionist theory

While non-Marxist historians agreed that these changes took place, they accounted for them very differently and saw no evidence of class conflict. For them the late medieval economic breakdown came as a result of drastic changes in the level of the population. By the end of the thirteenth century the population growth during the Middle Ages had put great pressure on land and food supplies. This population pressure, combined with inefficient farming techniques, had led to soil exhaustion and a **Malthusian crisis**.

The Black Death solved this problem by reducing the population by about a third. Further outbreaks of bubonic plague maintained a high death rate, so that the population of England had been reduced from about six million in 1300 to about one and a half million by the middle of the fifteenth century. Such a drastic loss of population led to a deep **recession** which caused a sharp reduction in food prices and rents, but created a demand for labour. As a result, wages rose. While this was very advantageous to the husbandmen and wage labourers, it was disastrous for the great landowners, who lost income from rents and the sale of foodstuffs. Furthermore, they had great difficulty in finding tenants, especially as many of the cottage smallholders found it more profitable to leave their farms to work for wages.

The great landowners were left with no alternative but to rent out all their land cheaply on long leases of up to 99 years to ambitious members of the gentry and prosperous husbandmen, or yeomen. When the population began to recover by 1500 a new group of **commercially oriented** small landowners – the gentry and yeomen – had emerged. They benefited from the rise in food prices and rent levels, while themselves enjoying low rents because of the long leases obtained in the fifteenth century. The great landowners could not profit from the upturn in the economy until the long leases ran out in the second part of the sixteenth century, while the husbandmen suffered from rising rents, and the wage-earners from increased food prices. The apparent consequence was the rise of this new commercial group at the expense of the great landowners, husbandmen and wage-earners. The lower orders, looking back on what for them was the 'golden age' of the fifteenth century, resented these changes, and this was to be a major cause of popular unrest during the sixteenth century.

Key terms

Malthusian crisis
Socio-economic theory of T.R. Malthus (d. 1834), an English clergyman and economist who argued that when a country's population outstrips food production the result is famine.

Recession
A fall in the demand for goods which leads to a drop in prices and unemployment.

Commercially oriented
A system whereby landowners and merchants became more businesslike in order to make a profit.

Some key books in the debate

Eric Hobsbawm, *The Age of Capital* (Weidenfeld & Nicholson, 1975).
D.M. Pallister, *The Age of Elizabeth, 1547–1603* (Longman, 1983).
E.P. Thompson, *The Poverty of Theory and Other Essays* (Merlin Press, 1978).

Economic change
Problems of mid-Tudor agriculture

Key question
What problems affected Mid-Tudor agriculture?

These two long-term explanations of change (or some combination of them) are still widely accepted as the cause of fundamental structural shifts in England. By the middle of the sixteenth century the government was beginning to face severe economic problems. The population had risen to 2.3 million by the 1520s and had possibly increased to over three million by 1550. This necessitated feeding the extra people – a difficulty made worse because of the drift of the rural unemployed into the towns to find work. As the towns were dependent upon the countryside for food this created great problems for the urban authorities.

Many historians consider that continued rural self-sufficiency, whereby many farmers produced only enough to feed themselves and their families, made the situation even more difficult. This can be seen as the basic crisis of mid-century English farming: commercial expansion being severely limited by traditional self-sufficiency. However, there is little evidence that commercial farming was very successful in increasing the levels of food production because many of the gentry and yeomen were more interested in sheep farming in order to benefit from high wool prices.

To improve efficiency and to increase production many commercially orientated landowners fenced off their land from the old open fields. This was the cause of most of the complaints about enclosure of land and the eviction of tenants, particularly when former **arable** land was converted to **pasture**. Yet it was necessary to create compact farms and to fence off the common land to bring it under cultivation if farming was to become more specialised and productive. Such was the dilemma facing the government, and by the late 1540s the growing shortage of foodstuffs showed that population was possibly again outstripping food supply. This position was made worse by a growing number of harvest failures – posing the threat of another Malthusian crisis.

Key terms

Arable
Farming land set aside for the growing of crops.

Pasture
Farming land set aside for the rearing of animals.

Enclosure

The potential danger of widespread starvation presented the authorities with long-term social problems. The government aimed to maintain social stability and order while, at the same time, accepting increased responsibility for poor relief and welfare. The government did not wish to see smallholders evicted or forced to leave the land because they would either drift into the towns or become vagrants, creating a source of riot and unrest.

Enclosures were seen as the major cause of economic distress and social instability, and the government tried to pass laws against the practice. The difficulty was that parliament, representing the landed interests, often blocked such legislation. Even when anti-enclosure laws were passed, the local magistrates (who were landowners themselves) frequently refused to enforce

Key question
Why was enclosure seen as a major cause of economic problems?

them. Consequently, not only did the State show itself to be incapable of taking effective action, but it antagonised the landowners by trying to prevent enclosure, and the lower orders by not preventing it.

Urban problems and the cloth industry

Although in the sixteenth century most people lived on the land and depended on agriculture for a livelihood, an increasing minority of the people dwelt in towns and were employed in industry. Here again the government encountered severe difficulties. It is widely accepted that there was an urban crisis in the sixteenth century, which was heightened by a slump in cloth exports. Once again the long-term causes of this situation can be traced back to the late Middle Ages. Early medieval industry was carried out in the towns and was controlled by **craft guilds**. The largest industry was clothmaking but output was on a small scale: most of the goods manufactured were sold locally. The major international export was wool, which was sold mainly to the Netherlands and Italy.

By the thirteenth century many merchants and industrialists were beginning to leave the towns because of strict guild regulations that restricted the freedom of craftsmen to ply their trade, and the high cost of urban overheads. The result was the establishment of a commercial rural cloth industry, based on the 'putting-out system'. It produced large quantities of semi-manufactured cloth which were exported to the Netherlands for finishing and sale. The new industry, mainly based in East Anglia and the West Country, continued to expand during the recession of the fifteenth century. This encouraged landowners to convert arable land into sheep pasture to meet the ever-increasing demand for wool.

The transfer of the cloth industry to the countryside caused problems for many towns, and these were made worse by the recession during the late Middle Ages. In addition, because of the very high urban death rate, towns were dependent upon migrants from the countryside to maintain, or increase, their population level. The sharp decline in national population during most of the fifteenth century reduced the flow of migrants, and many towns began to shrink in size.

When population levels began to recover about 1500, people who could not find work in the countryside drifted into the towns. Consequently, many towns were faced with a new problem of having too many migrants and were unable to feed, house or employ them. In addition, the number of migrants increased because the country-based textile industry was facing growing competition from new types of cloth made on the continent. This meant that from the 1520s there were frequent slumps in demand, and many laid-off workers were forced to go to the nearest town to seek work.

By 1550 the Antwerp market had begun to decline, causing widespread unemployment among English cloth-workers. Other sources of work were scarce. Although many people were leaving

Key question
Why was there an urban crisis and what part did the cloth industry play?

Craft guilds
Similar to trade unions, formed to protect and promote the particular trade of their members.

Putting-out system
Manufacturing system whereby the raw material is put out for others to finish off.

Key terms

the land and were available for employment in industry, there was little investment in towns to create new jobs. Consequently, the towns faced a very real crisis. The urban authorities had to contend with the problem of housing and feeding large numbers of unskilled migrants with little prospect of finding employment for them.

By the mid-sixteenth century the government was threatened by rising discontent in both towns and countryside. The poor agricultural performance meant that the towns had great difficulty in feeding their rising populations and this created the threat of serious bread and unemployment riots. The situation was no better in the countryside. Discontent over enclosures and rising rents was increased by the loss of employment in the rural cloth industry on which many of the agricultural poor relied for subsistence. In these circumstances it is hardly surprising that the Lord Protector Somerset was confronted by widespread popular uprisings in 1549.

Overseas trade

To a large extent these economic problems were outside the control of the mid-Tudor government. To meet the increasing cost of the administration and expand the national economy the English State needed to find new markets both in and beyond Europe to raise national wealth. The exploration of west Africa, Central and South America carried out mainly by Spain and Portugal in the fifteenth century, is seen as part of this general process of State development. Yet while Spain and Portugal were gaining new markets, colonies and raw materials and France and the Holy Roman Empire were growing in strength, England was preoccupied with the Wars of the Roses. Far from gaining new territories and trade, she lost all her continental markets apart from the Netherlands.

Clearly, in order to overcome her economic problems England needed to participate in world trade to gain the raw materials and markets to stimulate demand and create new jobs. The first two Tudor monarchs, however, showed little interest in **Atlantic trade**. Henry VIII in particular was much more concerned with his continental ambitions. In any case, England at this stage could not afford to antagonise its Habsburg allies by breaking their **monopoly** of the American trade. Not until after 1550, with the decline of the Antwerp market, did the English government show any serious interest in colonial exploration and the establishment of new markets.

Protestantism and the expansion of trade

The emergence of the expansion of trade is still seen by many historians as being linked with the development of Protestantism. It has been suggested that it was significant that the countries of north-western Europe which were to dominate world trade were all strongly influenced by Protestantism, and especially **Calvinism**, while the more economically backward countries were all Catholic. Consequently the conflicts between

---

Key terms

Atlantic trade
The triangular trade route between Europe, America and Africa.

Monopoly
Total control of trade by one country to the exclusion of others.

Key question
How important was the growth in overseas trade?

Key term

Calvinism
A term used to describe the influence and religious ideas and teachings of John Calvin of Geneva, a radical Protestant religious reformer who attacked the Catholic Church's wealth and privileges.

Key question
What part did Protestantism play in the expansion of trade?

the countries of the reformation and the **Counter-Reformation** can be interpreted as economic wars just as much as wars of religion.

Although it is widely agreed that such explanations are too simple to be totally acceptable, they still play an important part in interpretations of western capitalism. In 1550 England was still a backward, off-shore European island and was not to take any significant part in world trade until the end of the sixteenth century. However, some historians accept that the economic and, to a lesser extent, religious changes taking place laid the basis for England's political and economic dominance by the eighteenth century.

Religious change

Religious change is still seen by many historians as being very important in this economic and social restructuring. Support for the English Reformation by a large cross-section of the more commercially motivated aristocracy and gentry is interpreted as showing hostility towards the Roman Catholic Church. The break from Rome can be seen as the removal of the 'dead hand' of a Church which, by its opposition to commerce and competition, was slowing the pace of economic development. At the same time the enormous wealth and great territorial possessions of the Roman Catholic Church in England were perceived as unproductive.

The ruling élites

It is suggested that support from the ruling élites for Henry VIII's religious policy was based on their desire to acquire confiscated Church property, which they could use commercially to their own profit. Certainly the seizure and, after 1540, the sale of monastic lands, was the largest redistribution of property since the Norman Conquest of 1066 and enabled an expansion in the number of the land-owning élite. However, there is little evidence to show that the Catholic élites were any less eager to acquire Church property, or were less commercially successful, than their Protestant counterparts. Consequently, while it is possible to say that the Reformation promoted commercial change, it is more difficult to maintain that it was brought about for commercial reasons.

The non-élites

The impact of religious change on the lower orders or non-élites is equally difficult to define. Many among the rural population were opposed to Protestantism, seeing it as a threat to their traditional way of life. Others, especially in the towns, welcomed the ideas of the reformers on the rights of man, equality, and the redistribution of Church wealth. These different responses to Protestantism have been cited by many Marxist historians as evidence of the loss of solidarity among the lower orders and of the beginning of the breakdown of community values and mutual support.

Key term

Counter-Reformation
Catholic reaction against the spread of Protestantism. Led by the Pope, the Catholic Church attempted to reconvert Protestants and bring them back to the Catholic faith.

Key question
How and why did religion change?

Protestantism is perceived as introducing more radical ideas into popular protest, or, at least, strengthening those ideas that already existed. Although extreme radical groups among the lower orders in England were always to be a minority, they are seen as playing an important part in increasing social tensions and pressures. For them the Reformation marked the beginning of the millennium, the thousand-year rule of Christ, when all men would be equal and there would be no more hardship, poverty and unemployment.

Obviously such ideas were very attractive in a period of sharply rising prices, food shortages and a lack of job opportunities, and increased the possibility of popular riot and rebellion in years of particular hardship. This was clearly a dangerous situation, and fear among the élites of popular rebellion added to the stresses already being felt within society. Although many of these social, economic and religious changes were only beginning in England by 1550, they can be seen as posing very serious problems to the government and represented a potential crisis for the State.

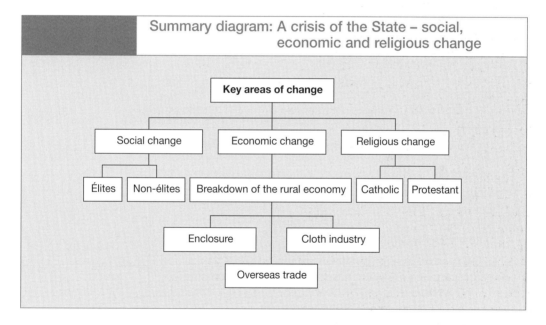

Summary diagram: A crisis of the State – social, economic and religious change

Study Guide: A2 Question

In the style of Edexcel

'Essentially a period of continuity rather than of significant change in the structure of government and the operation of its authority.' How far do you agree with this view of England in the years 1536–53?

Exam tips

This question requires you to assess the extent of change in the structure of government and the way in which authority was exercised over the period. As the question is concerned with overall structures, you do not need to consider transfers of power between key individuals unless you feel they have a direct bearing on that. You should, however, develop some criteria for assessing change and come to a conclusion about whether these changes are extensive enough to be regarded as significant.

You will be able to add to your notes in preparation for this question after you have studied Chapters 2 and 5.

You should examine the following:

- How far the nature of royal government changed in the period – setting the increased intervention in religion and the economy and changes in administration and the growth of bureaucracy against the evidence of the continued personal role of the monarch and the monarch's relationship with the aristocracy.
- The extent to which the growth of the gentry can be seen – and how far this was associated with a change in the way in which royal authority operated through the authority of the élites in rural society.
- The extent to which authority at all levels was weakened as a result of religious change and a growth in a distressed, workless and mobile section of society.

In coming to a conclusion, you should acknowledge the gradual nature of change in this period, but you should consider whether the work of Thomas Cromwell did result in significant change in the nature of government and how far the exercise of authority in Tudor society showed continuity rather than change.

2

Government, Politics and the State 1536–88

Key dates

1547	January	Death of Henry VIII and accession of Edward VI
	February	Edward Seymour created Duke of Somerset and Lord Protector
	October	Fall of Somerset
1549		Rebellion in East Anglia and the West Country
1550	February	John Dudley created Lord President of the Council
1551	October	John Dudley created Duke of Northumberland
1552	January	Execution of the Duke of Somerset
1553	July	Death of Edward VI, brief reign of Lady Jane Grey, and succession of Mary I
	August	Execution of the Duke of Northumberland
1554	January	Wyatt Rebellion
	July	Mary I married Philip of Spain
1558	November	Death of Mary I and accession of Elizabeth I

1562	Succession crisis
1570	Pope excommunicated Elizabeth
1587	Execution of Mary, Queen of Scots

1 | The Political Situation in Mid-Tudor England 1536–88

Key question
How have historians changed their views about the political situation in mid-Tudor England?

Political history is about an élite of men and women who run the day-to-day affairs of a country. In trying to interpret events, political historians have to rely upon written evidence. **State papers** make it easier to discover what happened when. It is more difficult to find out why things happened. This is particularly true for the sixteenth century because many of the documents have been lost or destroyed. However, lack of evidence is only part of the political historian's problem. Successful political leaders tend to manufacture their own history. Being in power they can create evidence which sets their actions in the best possible light. On the other hand, politicians who fail are often unjustly condemned by those who replace them. The 22 years between 1536 and 1558 saw many such shifts in political power. It is for these reasons that political historians continue to reassess their views about mid-Tudor politicians.

State papers
Documents drawn up by ministers that record the decisions made and show the decision-making process undertaken by central government.

Key term

Until the end of the revisionist/Marxist debate (see Chapter 1) historians generally accepted that the mid-sixteenth century was a time of political conflict and confrontation in England – a period of failure and lack of progress, set between the great achievements of the 1530s and the recovery of the national economy under Elizabeth I. This period of conflict and confrontation was seen to stem from weak political leadership. The result was a contest between Crown and parliament, and bitter strife between Catholics and Protestants. The five major political figures listed below have been blamed for this failure for various reasons:

- Henry VIII: in his final years Henry was seen as an increasingly weak ruler unable to control the factional disputes that came to dominate the Court.
- Duke of Somerset: traditionally referred to by some historians as the 'good Duke', Somerset was seen as a moderate reformer, who fell from power because of his tolerant and fair-minded policies.
- Duke of Northumberland: considered ruthless and greedy, creating a constitutional crisis by trying to change the succession (see page 58).
- Queen Mary: condemned for being politically inept, for her obsession with Philip II of Spain and for her devotion to Catholicism.
- Elizabeth I: has been criticised for her almost instinctive reluctance to take decisive and creative action. She has been portrayed as a 'do-nothing queen'.

General theories of crisis and the rise of the State only strengthened the opinion that the mid-Tudor period was one of failure. However, new evidence and research has caused these views to be questioned and revised.

The idea of a mid-Tudor political crisis is no longer popular. Considerable reservations are felt about the theories of the State and the **Tudor revolution in government**. Although there were disruptions in the day-to-day running of the country, the machinery of government continued to operate normally. The period 1536–88 is now seen in terms of co-operation rather than conflict – as a time of definite political and administrative development. In part this change results from revised opinions about the political leaders:

- Although Henry VIII's final years were marked by the king's failing health and power he managed to maintain the authority of the Crown and preserve the unity of the realm.
- The Duke of Somerset is now seen as a Tudor soldier and statesman who was more interested in war than social reform.
- The Duke of Northumberland is still regarded as ruthless and self-seeking, but he is becoming recognised as an able and reforming administrator.
- Although few would claim that Mary was a great queen, her reign is being seen as a time of significant political and administrative progress.
- Some historians have revised their opinion by suggesting that Elizabeth's 'do-nothing' approach was sometimes the wisest course of action: to put off until tomorrow what need not be done today.

Key term

Tudor revolution in government
Theory first put forward in the 1950s by G.R. Elton to explain the changes that took place in government under the guiding hand of Cromwell.

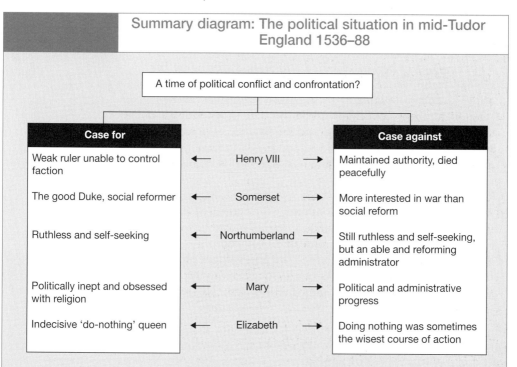

Summary diagram: The political situation in mid-Tudor England 1536–88

A time of political conflict and confrontation?

Case for		Case against
Weak ruler unable to control faction	← Henry VIII →	Maintained authority, died peacefully
The good Duke, social reformer	← Somerset →	More interested in war than social reform
Ruthless and self-seeking	← Northumberland →	Still ruthless and self-seeking, but an able and reforming administrator
Politically inept and obsessed with religion	← Mary →	Political and administrative progress
Indecisive 'do-nothing' queen	← Elizabeth →	Doing nothing was sometimes the wisest course of action

2 | Henry VIII, Thomas Cromwell and the Changes in Government 1536–40

Key question
What did Elton mean by his use of the term 'revolution in government' and how significant was Cromwell's part in it?

It is almost impossible to discuss Thomas Cromwell and the changes that took place in government during the 1530s without reference to the historian G.R. Elton. This is because Elton is responsible for identifying what he termed a Tudor revolution in government as taking place between 1532 and 1540, when Cromwell was Henry's chief minister. His main contention was that during these years a series of changes was made that in their totality marked a change from medieval to modern forms of government. Allied to this theory was the significance Elton attached to the part played by Cromwell in these 'revolutionary' changes in government.

'Revolution' in government

Elton's theory can be broken down into four parts:

- The structure and organisation of central government. The 'administrative revolution' was responsible for a radical change in the structure and organisation of central government. The major part of this recasting of central administration revolved around the reorganisation of the financial departments and the creation of the Privy Council. The result was that *government by the king* was replaced by *government under the king*.
- The role of parliament and the scope and authority of Statute law. The essential ingredient of the Tudor revolution was the concept of national sovereignty and the creation of a sovereign law-making parliament. In using parliament to enforce the Reformation the Crown was emphasising that nothing lay outside the competence of parliamentary statute. The result was that *king and parliament* had been replaced by *king-in-parliament*.
- The relationship between Church and State. By bringing the Church firmly under the control of the king the Royal Supremacy had initiated a 'jurisdictional revolution' in the relationship between Church and State. The independence of the Church had been quashed and the balance of power between Church and State had tipped firmly in favour of the latter. The result was that *Church and State* had been replaced by *Church in State*.
- Extension of royal authority in the regions. By bringing the outlying regions of the kingdom under the control of the central government Cromwell was aiming to create a nation that was a jurisdictional entity. He gave more authority and purpose to the Council of the North and reformed the government of Wales by empowering the Council of Wales and the Marches. Although short-lived, he also set up a Council of the West. The result was that a *fragmented polity* was replaced by a *unitary state*.

Elton argued that, as these developments were one of the two or three major turning-points in the history of British politics, they well deserved the title of revolution.

This then was Elton's overview statement into which all Cromwell's endeavours could be accommodated: his remodelling of the king's finances by bureaucratic procedures, his creation of the Privy Council as the body collectively responsible for executing the king's policies, his methods of containing opposition while the revolution took place, his attempts to introduce social and economic reform along the lines advocated by the commonwealth men, his establishment of the king in parliament as the highest authority in the State, and his destruction of the Church's position as a State within a State.

'Evolution' in government

Although some historians do not support Elton's 'revolution' in government theory, they do agree that changes did take place. The argument between the pro- and anti-Elton groups of historians can be simplified by focusing on the use of the term 'revolution'. Revolution suggests that far-reaching, radical and innovative changes took place, but those historians who reject the use of this term prefer to use evolution as a means of describing the changes in that they were measured, piecemeal and conservative. The argument now centres on how the changes introduced in the 1530s built upon existing systems and departments.

Changes in financial administration

Financial departments such as the Court of Exchequer and the Duchy of Lancaster were long-established departments of State that administered:

- the income that came in from sheriffs and customs duties
- the extensive lands and rights that had come to the Crown from the house of Lancaster.

The Duchy of Lancaster became the model for a number of new departments which were established to administer most of the Crown's other sources of income. The most famous of these new departments were the Court of First Fruits and Tenths and the Court of Augmentations, set up to handle the Church wealth that was newly coming to the king.

The establishment of the Privy Council

Some time in the 1530s (probably in 1536) the informal medieval system of a large council, with between 70–90 members, was replaced by a more formal Privy Council system in which an élite group of about 20 trusted permanent councillors assumed responsibility for the day-to-day running of the government. As the informality of the medieval system had normally resulted in one or two councillors gathering most power into their own hands, the change was seen as the movement of control away from a small number of influential individuals to a powerful bureaucratically organised group.

  The Privy Council's small size and the eminence and competence of its members enabled it to function effectively during periods of crisis such as the rebellion known as the

Pilgrimage of Grace (see pages 131–4) and even during the royal minority of Edward VI. The creation and importance of the Privy Council by 1540 are not in doubt but some historians have questioned Cromwell's part in its creation.

The role of parliament and the relationship between Church and State

Elton claimed that Cromwell's work radically enhanced the power of the State and the competence of parliament within the State. It is claimed, with some justification, that Cromwell not only paved the way for royal government to take control of the English Church, he masterminded the method through which this could best be achieved: by means of parliamentary statute. By making Henry VIII the Supreme Head of the Church in England Cromwell had affected a revolution in the relationship between Church and State. In using parliament to enforce the Reformation, Cromwell had established the principle that king-in-parliament constituted the highest form of authority in the kingdom.

Extension of royal authority in the regions

Cromwell intended to extend royal authority into the wilder and remoter parts of the kingdom but his success in this field was limited. He had no choice but to depend on the unpaid co-operation of local gentry acting as **Justices of the Peace** and on the willingness of powerful noble landowners or influential clerics who invariably filled the offices of president of the regional Councils of the North, West and Wales. The fact that some gentry and nobility joined the rebellion known as the Pilgrimage of Grace shows how precarious this policy was.

Key terms

Pilgrimage of Grace
Popular rebellion in northern England (1536–7) caused by distrust of Cromwell and discontent over religious changes, particularly the closure of the monasteries.

Justices of the Peace
Magistrates, largely landowners, who enforce the State's rules and regulations in local courts of law.

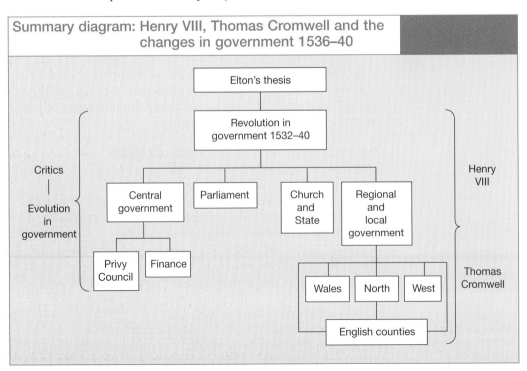

Summary diagram: Henry VIII, Thomas Cromwell and the changes in government 1536–40

Key question
Why was the succession such a problem and how was it resolved?

Key term
Succession Acts
Acts of Parliament passed to clarify and enforce the right of succession to the Crown of England.

3 | Henry VIII and the Succession 1544–7

Apart from the wars with Scotland and France, which had begun in 1542 and 1544, Henry VIII's major concern in his last years was the succession. Since 1527 he had been obsessed with the need to safeguard the dynasty by leaving a male heir to succeed him. The birth of Prince Edward in 1537 had seemed to achieve this objective. By 1546 the king's declining health made it clear that his son would come to the throne as a minor. To avoid any possible disputes Henry made a final settlement of the succession in his will of 1546. This replaced the **Succession Acts** of 1534, 1536 and 1544, although the terms of the will were similar to the Act of 1544.

In the event of Edward dying without heirs, the succession was to pass first to Mary, the daughter of Catherine of Aragon. If Mary died without heirs her sister Elizabeth, daughter of Anne

The last will and testament of Henry VIII. Why has Henry VIII's will been described as one of 'extraordinary political significance'?

Boleyn, was to succeed. The major change to the previous settlement was that if all Henry's children were to die without heirs, the throne was to pass to his niece Frances Grey.

Lady Frances was the elder daughter of Henry VIII's sister Mary, who first had married King Louis XII of France and then Charles Brandon, Duke of Suffolk. This clause meant that the other possible claimant to the English throne, the infant Mary, Queen of Scots, was excluded.

Mary was the descendant of Henry VIII's sister Margaret, who had married James IV of Scotland (see page 8). Henry was anxious to preserve the Royal Supremacy, hence the inclusion of the Protestant Grey family and the exclusion of the Catholic Stuart dynasty. Although the will had replaced the earlier succession settlements, the Acts of 1534 and 1536, which had made Mary and Elizabeth illegitimate to remove them from the line of succession, were not repealed.

Henry's major concern in his will was to secure the peaceful succession of his son and safeguard the Royal Supremacy. By 1546 it had become clear that the surest way to achieve this, and so prevent a power struggle, was to give authority to Seymour and the reform faction. The disgrace of Howard and Gardiner (see pages 41 and 63) had secured the position of Seymour and his supporters, and this was strengthened by adjustments to the terms of the will right up to the time of Henry VIII's death.

A Regency Council was nominated consisting of Seymour and 15 of his most trusted allies. Members of the Council were to have equal powers, and were to govern the country until Edward reached 18 years of age. In order to secure the loyalty and co-operation of the Council its members were to be rewarded with new titles and lands taken from the monasteries and the Howard family.

Key dates

Death of Henry VIII and accession of Edward VI: January 1547

Edward Seymour created Duke of Somerset and Lord Protector: February 1547

Summary diagram: Henry VIII and the succession 1544–7

Acts of Succession	1534 – Mary out		Elizabeth in
	1536 – Elizabeth out		Any future child in
	1544 – Elizabeth and Mary out		Edward in
Will of Henry VIII	1546 – Edward first	Mary second	Elizabeth third

Profile: Thomas Howard, Duke of Norfolk 1473–1554

1473 – Born
1513 – Fought at the battle of Flodden. Rewarded with the title Earl of Surrey
     – Appointed Lord High Admiral (1513–25)
1520 – Appointed Lord Lieutenant of Ireland (1520–2)
1522 – Appointed Lord High Treasurer (1522–47)
1523 – Appointed Warden-General of the Northern Marches
1529 – Contributed to the downfall of Cardinal Wolsey
1533 – Appointed Earl-Marshal
1536 – Presided over the trial of his niece Anne Boleyn
1537 – Put down Pilgrimage of Grace with severity
1539 – Supported passing of Act of Six Articles
1540 – Contributed to downfall of Cromwell. With Gardiner led conservative faction at Court
1542 – Disgrace and execution of his niece Catherine Howard damaged his position at Court. Recovered to take command of an army against the Scots
1544 – Appointed Lieutenant-General of the army in France
1546 – Ousted from royal favour by leader of reformist faction, Seymour. Norfolk's son executed for treason
1547 – Imprisoned in the Tower awaiting execution but spared when Henry VIII died. Remained a prisoner in the Tower throughout Edward VI's reign
1553 – Released from Tower on accession of Mary. Took part in trial and execution of Northumberland
1554 – Served against Wyatt's rebels. Died aged 80.

Norfolk was among the most powerful nobles in England. He was well connected having married as his first wife, a daughter of Edward IV, and as his second, the grand-niece of Edward IV's queen. His Yorkist background counted against him during Henry VII's reign but he gradually proved his loyalty and was rewarded for his service.

He actively encouraged his nieces Anne Boleyn and Catherine Howard to become involved with the king but their disgrace and execution damaged his position at Court. His leadership of the conservative faction there brought him into conflict with the reformists under Somerset. The death of Henry VIII saved Norfolk's life but the accession of Edward VI ensured his continued imprisonment. He resumed his career under Mary but he never regained his former high position at Court or in government.

4 | The Protector Somerset 1547–9

Somerset was the son of a Wiltshire knight, Sir John Seymour, and so came from the middle or gentry class. His father had served both Henry VII and Henry VIII in war and he was personally known to them but he did not secure a permanent place at Court. Somerset's rise to prominence began with his knighthood in 1523 for military service in France under the Duke of Suffolk. The king's chief minister, Cardinal Thomas Wolsey, thought him worthy of promotion and in 1524 he joined the king's service as a member of the **Royal Household**. He survived Wolsey's fall from power in 1529 by publicly supporting the king in the divorce issue.

His sister Jane's marriage to Henry VIII in May 1536 brought him into the royal family and he was soon showered with honours. Within a week of the marriage he was made Viscount Beauchamp and in 1537 he was created Earl of Hertford. In the same year he became a member of the king's ruling council. In 1542–3 he became Lord High Admiral and Lieutenant-General

Royal Household
Term used to describe the living arrangements of the monarch. It consisted of servants who looked after the monarch's person and his financial and political affairs.

Key term

Edward Seymour, Duke of Somerset (c1502–52).

in the north in 1544–5 when he waged a successful war against the Scots. On the king's death in January 1547 he became protector of the realm and Duke of Somerset. His younger brother, Thomas, was created Baron Seymour of Sudeley and appointed Lord High Admiral.

In the opinion of some historians Somerset was a kindly and amiable man but a contemporary who knew him thought him 'dry, sour and opinionated'. His friend and ally, Sir William Paget, described him as a quick-tempered man who was prone to taking the wrong decisions when put under pressure. He was a better soldier than he was a politician and within two years of taking power he had completely lost control of the situation.

Rise to power

Key question
Why was the Duke of Somerset able to rise to power so rapidly?

In spite of Henry's precautions, it soon became apparent that the plans for the regency were not practical. Even if there had been no tensions between the conservative and reform parties, it is doubtful whether a Regency Council made up of 16 equal members could have operated successfully. The Council system of government in England was designed to function with a chief executive, the monarch, to make final decisions. For the Regency Council to operate successfully it was necessary for one of its members to act as its chief. Somerset quickly emerged as the leader of the Council. He had been high in favour during the last part of Henry VIII's reign and this, coupled with the reputation that he had earned through his successful campaigns in the Scottish war, placed him in a very strong position.

He and his ally and fellow councillor, Sir William Paget, had custody of Henry VIII's will. They kept the king's death secret for four days. This gave them time to take advantage of the weakness of the conservative party and to rally support among the reformers and moderates for the nomination of Somerset as leader of the Council. The reason why he gained power so quickly is not altogether clear, although his being the new king's uncle certainly helped. Clearly, the reformers among the clergy hoped for the introduction of religious reform, and it is likely that many moderates regarded Seymour as the best means of preserving stability and the Royal Supremacy.

Higher clergy
The bishops and two archbishops of England and Wales.

Chancellor
Senior minister in the royal government who had control of the Great Seal used to authenticate and give legal force to laws.

Henry's death and the terms of the will were made known to an assembly of nobles and **higher clergy** at the Tower of London on 1 February 1547. At the same time Lord Wriothesley, the **Chancellor** and new head of the conservative faction, announced that Somerset had been made leader of the Council for 'the better conduct of business'. By the end of February Somerset had secured the firm support of the majority of councillors and was made Lord Protector, with the right to appoint and dismiss members of the Privy Council. These powers made Somerset the undisputed ruler of the country. He was created Duke of Somerset and was given confiscated monastic property to support his new titles. Other members of the Council were given new titles and estates, roughly along the lines laid out in Henry VIII's will.

Key terms

Somerset's character

Somerset's success in reaching supreme power is often attributed to the support of the very able Paget. Therefore, any valid judgements about Somerset's character and capability have to be based on his achievements, or lack of them, over the ensuing two years if they are to be valid. There are three main views about Somerset's character:

- In the past he has been regarded as a genuine reformer, sympathetic to the plight of the poor.
- More recently, doubts have been expressed about whether he had any interest in social reform and it has been claimed that he was an arrogant self-seeker who refused to accept advice, and who enriched himself with confiscated Church property.
- Using the same evidence, historians currently see him as a Tudor soldier and statesman, whose main interest was the war against Scotland and France.

Somerset is regarded as being no more greedy, and no more sympathetic to the poor, than his fellow aristocrats. Certainly in February 1547 the other members of the Council were just as quick to accept lands and titles as Somerset himself.

System of government
Parliament

Somerset took over a form of administration that had been developed by Henry VII and Henry VIII. Due to changes introduced by Cromwell in the 1530s (see pages 36–8), Tudor government had come to rest on the principle that the power of the monarch was based in parliament. Both Houses of Parliament had to approve proposals for taxation and confirm any new laws before they became permanent statutes. On the other hand, the monarch could call parliament to meet as often, or as infrequently, as he chose.

When parliament was not in session the Crown could make new laws through **proclamations**, or could suspend existing laws, but these actions had to be confirmed when parliament met again. Certain things such as diplomacy and the making of war or peace were part of the **royal prerogative**, over which the monarch had complete control. Religion had always been considered part of the royal prerogative until Henry VIII used parliament to carry through the English Reformation. Under Mary, and later Elizabeth I, religion was to become a matter of dispute between Crown and parliament.

Privy Council

The day-to-day administration was carried out by the Privy Council. Members of the Council were chosen by the monarch from among the nobles, higher clergy and more important gentry. They were selected for their loyalty and their administrative or military skills, and could be dismissed at will. The work of the Privy Council was supported by a staff of

Key question
What were Somerset's aims while he was in power?

Key terms

Proclamations
The Crown's official or public announcements that included the right to make new laws, especially when parliament was not in session.

Royal prerogative
Certain rights held by the monarchy enabling it to make proclamations, enforce the royal will, and suspend or repeal acts of parliament.

Profile: Sir William Paget 1505–63

1505	–	Born in Wednesbury in Staffordshire
1529	–	Entered parliament as an MP
1530	–	Employed by Henry VIII and Archbishop Cranmer to persuade the universities of northern Europe to support the king's divorce from Catherine of Aragon
1541	–	Appointed ambassador to France (1541–3)
1543	–	Appointed to the Privy Council
c1545	–	Became, with Somerset, Henry VIII's chief adviser (1545–7)
1547	–	Supported Somerset's protectorate; he and Somerset became close friends
1549	–	Created Baron Beaudesert. Supported Somerset against Northumberland. After initially being arrested was allowed to return to government office
1551	–	Arrested on a charge of conspiring against Northumberland
1552	–	Released from prison and forcibly retired from government
1553	–	Invited to return to government by Northumberland who sought his help in proclaiming Jane Grey queen. Initially supported Jane Grey but soon deserted her for Mary. Appointed to lead Mary's government along with the Earl of Arundel
1554	–	Rewarded for supporting and negotiating Mary's marriage with Philip of Spain
1554–5	–	Refused to support Gardiner's religious legislation, which angered the queen
1556	–	Given the less important office of Lord Privy Seal. Virtually ignored in government
1558	–	Served on the Privy Council of Queen Elizabeth
1560	–	Virtually retired from government
1563	–	Died

Paget was one of the most able and influential men in government. He was trusted by Henry VIII and Somerset but not by Northumberland, who distrusted his loyal support of Somerset in the **coup d'état** of 1549. Nevertheless, Northumberland initially employed him for his talent as a minister. His religion was not known to contemporaries, who thought him variously a Protestant reformer and a Catholic conservative. The truth is he kept his religious convictions very much to himself.

His support of Mary earned her trust and gratitude and his handling of the marriage negotiations won the admiration of Philip of Spain. However, his opposition to what he regarded as extreme religious legislation drawn up by his one-time friend Gardiner, with whom he quarrelled quite violently, led to his losing his leading place in Mary's government. For the last three years of her reign she all but ignored his advice.

Key term

Coup d'état
French term to describe a rebellion that removes the head of State and the government from power.

permanent civil servants chosen mainly from the gentry, lawyers and minor clergy.

The Privy Council was responsible also for the running of local government, with the support of the nobles, higher clergy and gentry. The two parts of the country that were thought most open to rebellion or invasion, Wales and the Scottish border, were administered by the Councils of Wales and of the North. These were regarded as sub-committees of the Privy Council, and were run by members of the local ruling élites chosen by the Privy Council in London.

Local government

Local government in the remainder of England was administered by the nobles and higher clergy in each county. They were expected to maintain order, administer justice, collect taxes, raise troops and carry out instructions from the Privy Council. These duties had to be organised through their own households, and frequently at their own expense. In turn they were supported by the local gentry, who, among other things, acted as Justices of the Peace and commissioners for collecting taxes and assisting the Lord Lieutenants in mustering the **county militia**.

The major problem with this system was that if the leading local families did not support the government, or did not like the legislation, they often failed to carry out instructions from London. This meant that the central administration had to be careful to maintain the confidence and support of the majority of the landed élites.

County militia
Non-professional military force raised from among the able-bodied local population that lived within the bounds of a county.

Key term

Government under Somerset

There is little evidence to suggest that the administration during the first two years of Edward VI's reign was markedly different from that of the last years of Henry VIII. The Privy Council was made up of men who had risen to power under Henry and who were using the same methods and machinery of government to cope with similar problems. The real differences were the lack of effective leadership, and the fact that existing problems had grown worse. Economic and financial expedients and a half-hearted religious reform policy created confusion and uncertainty among both the landed élites and the general public.

It has been suggested that Somerset was neither more nor less to blame for these problems than his aristocratic colleagues. But whether this was because he was unwilling or unable to change their attitudes is uncertain. While there is no evidence that he tried to corrupt the government, it is equally true that he introduced no reforms. What can also be said is that he failed to show the leadership necessary to compensate for the absence of an adult monarch. Whether this was because of his preoccupation with war, or because of his stubbornness and inability to adjust to new conditions is difficult to judge.

Somerset and the problems of government
Short-term problems

The new regime inherited three pressing short-term problems from the previous reign. Decisions had to be made about:

Key question
What problems did Somerset face in government?

- whether or not to continue the wars against Scotland and France
- the question of religious reform
- how to find ways of raising more revenue.

War

Whether or not Somerset's main interest was to bring the war against the French and the Scots to a successful conclusion, its continuation was seen as a matter of national pride by most of the aristocracy and gentry. Consequently, any move to end the war would have lost him support among the landed élites. In any case, the Council was bound by Henry VIII's last wishes to arrange a marriage between Edward VI and the infant Mary, Queen of Scots to secure the succession. This meant continuing a war based on the ill-founded belief that a military victory would force the Scots to agree to the marriage.

Religious reform

In 1539 Henry VIII had tried to prevent any further religious changes by passing the **Act of Six Articles**, which had laid down doctrines and forms of worship for the Church of England. Since then pressure had been mounting among the Protestant clergy and **laity** for the introduction of reforms along the lines of **Lutheranism** and Calvinism as practised on the continent. Although the Privy Council was made up mainly of moderates, it was anxious to keep the support of influential reformers such as Bishops Ridley and Latimer. For this reason the administration had to make some gesture towards introducing religious reform. If it did not then it would risk losing the support of the Protestant activists and encourage a Catholic revival, which might well have resulted in the administration losing power.

Revenue

Revenue was the most pressing problem. In 1547 the government was virtually bankrupt. The crippling cost of the war was the main reason for this. By 1546 Henry VIII had already spent £2,100,000 on the war, and borrowed a further £152,000 from continental bankers. To pay for this he had sold off most of the monastic lands seized between 1538 and 1540, as well as some Crown lands. By 1547 the annual revenue from Crown lands had fallen to £200,000. This was insufficient to run the country and pay off government borrowing, let alone finance the war.

There was an urgent need to reform the taxation and customs systems, and to bring the way that finances were administered up to date. Somerset and the Council did none of these things because of their preoccupation with the war and the concern that if they raised taxes this would be unpopular with the élites and other taxpayers. Instead, they fell back on the old expedients of seizing more Church property and debasing the coinage.

Key terms

Act of Six Articles
Passed in 1539, the Acts were intended to protect and promote Catholic religious ideas and prevent the further spread of Protestantism in England and Wales.

Laity
Term used to describe the non-clerical general population, the parishioners as opposed to the priests.

Lutheranism
A term used to describe the influence and religious ideas and teachings of Martin Luther of Wittenberg in Germany. His protest against the corruption and wealth of the Catholic Church and criticism of the Pope led to him being thrown out of the Church (1520s), after which he set up his own Protestant Church.

Long-term problems

As well as these immediate political and administrative difficulties, the government faced a number of serious long-term economic and social problems. Population continued to increase, and this presented a major threat to the government. Increasing population was the main cause of inflation because greater demand for goods pushed up prices. Not only did this add to the cost of administration, but it also threatened most people's living standards at a time when wages were not increasing. In addition, it meant that more people were available for employment. This, in turn, caused more poverty because it also raised the number of vagrants looking for work.

Fortunately, a run of good harvests kept the price of grain stable until 1549. Then a poor harvest made the situation worse, and the level of popular discontent rose (see page 128). The root causes of these problems were largely beyond the government's control, but continuing high levels of taxation and debasement of the coinage only made the economic situation worse.

The administration was well aware that there was rising popular discontent over the worsening economic conditions. They feared that this might lead to popular uprisings, but they were uncertain how to tackle the economic problems. Therefore, whatever action the government took it was likely to cause as many problems as it solved. In the event, it appears from its actions over the next two years that the government's main objective was to continue the wars. At the same time it cautiously introduced some religious reforms and tried to damp down popular discontent.

Laws and proclamations 1547–8

When the government had established itself in power and decided its **legislative programme**, parliament was summoned to meet in November 1547. One of its first actions was to pass a new Treason Act. This repealed the old heresy, treason and censorship laws and the Act of Six Articles, which had maintained **doctrinal orthodoxy** since 1539.

The removal of the **heresy laws** allowed people to discuss religion freely without fear of arrest, while the ending of censorship on printing and publishing enabled the circulation of books and pamphlets on religion, and the importation of Lutheran and Calvinist literature. A whole mass of unpopular legislation passed during the previous reign was thus swept away.

In the past this has been seen as clear proof of Somerset's tolerant attitude, although it could equally well be interpreted as the normal action of a new regime trying to gain popularity by abolishing the oppressive legislation of its predecessor. However, 'oser examination suggests that the government was clearing the · for religious reforms (see Chapter 3).

Key terms

Legislative programme
The key points of a government's plan to govern the country by passing laws, deciding levels of taxation and controls on trade.

Doctrinal orthodoxy
The traditional or long-held beliefs of, in this instance, the Catholic Church and religion.

Heresy laws
Laws to punish those people who reject the State religion and the teachings of the Church.

Key question
Why was it necessary to pass new laws and issue proclamations?

Key question
What was the impact
of the passing of the
new Treason Act?

The Treason Act

Whatever prompted the government to pass a new Treason Act, it immediately created problems for itself. The removal of the restrictive laws encouraged widespread debate over religion (see pages 89–91), particularly in London and other towns. Public meetings frequently ended in disorder and riots, with attacks on churches to break up statues of saints and other Catholic images. At the same time, the repeal of the old laws left the county and urban authorities with much less power to deal with such situations. Consequently the government had helped to promote the very disorder that it was trying to avoid. In the process, it had undermined the confidence of the authorities who now felt themselves powerless to enforce order.

The new Treason Act also repealed the Proclamation Act of 1539 that stated that royal proclamations should be obeyed as if they were acts of parliament, providing that they did not infringe existing laws. The Proclamation Act had been regarded with suspicion because it was feared that it would allow the monarch to rule without parliament. It has been suggested that Somerset was trying to give himself more freedom to rule by proclamation by ignoring parliament.

There is no evidence to suggest that this was his real intention, although there was a considerable increase in the use of proclamations during his period of office. Under Henry VIII proclamations were, on average, used six times a year. During Edward VI's reign they averaged 19 per year, and of these, 77 – well over half – were issued by Somerset. This increase is now seen as a strategy adopted by a government, faced with severe difficulties, which needed to react as quickly as possible to changing circumstances. Certainly contemporaries did not seem to think that Somerset was trying to corrupt the constitution. There is evidence that he lacked the backing of the Privy Council, and there was no sign of protest from parliament about their use.

Dissolution of the monasteries
The closure of the monasteries of England and Wales by Henry VIII between 1536 and 1540.

Chantries
Small religious houses endowed with lands to support one or more priests whose duty it was to sing masses for the souls of the deceased founder or members of the founding organisation.

The Chantries Act

The Chantries Act of 1547 can be regarded as another measure of religious reform. Undoubtedly it was a logical step, after the **dissolution of the monasteries**, to close the **chantries**. Yet, in reality, this Act was a device to raise money to pay for the wars. A similar plan had already been discussed by Henry VIII and his advisers. Commissioners were sent out early in 1548 to visit the chantries, confiscate their land and property, and collect all the gold and silver plate attached to them. The latter was then melted down to make coins.

Simultaneously the royal mints were ordered to reissue the coinage and reduce the silver content by adding copper. The coinage had already been debased in 1543 and there were to be further debasements to 1551, by which time the silver content had been reduced to 25 per cent. Although these measures provided much needed revenue, they created further problems. By increasing the number of coins in circulation the government was adding to inflation. Prices, particularly for grain, rose rapidly, fuelling discontent among the poor.

The Vagrancy Act and public order

That the maintenance of public order was very much in the mind of the administration is shown by the Vagrancy Act of 1547. The harshness of this legislation shows little concern for the poor and needy. The earlier **Poor Law of 1536** did recognise that the able-bodied were having difficulty in finding work, and ordered parishes to support the **impotent poor**.

The 1547 Act was a savage attack on vagrants looking for work, who were seen by the government as a cause of riots and **sedition**. Under the new law, any able-bodied person out of work for more than three days was to be branded with a V and sold into slavery for two years. The children of vagrants could be taken from their parents and set to work as apprentices in useful occupations. The new law was widely unpopular, and many of the county and urban authorities refused to enforce it. Although it also proposed housing and collections for the disabled, this measure does little to support Somerset's reputation for humanitarianism.

It is clear that the level of popular discontent had risen by the middle of 1548 because the Privy Council was forced to take measures to appease public agitation. It has been suggested that this legislation formed part of a reform programme put forward by **John Hales** at the Treasury and the so-called '**commonwealth men**', supported by Somerset. In the light of the evidence now available there are increasing doubts about whether such a group ever existed. It seems more likely that growing discontent over rising prices and local food shortages forced the government to take some piecemeal action. Here again Somerset's reputation as a reformer and a friend to the people is very much open to question.

Enclosure

The trouble was that the government blamed all the economic problems on enclosure. It was felt that the fencing-off of common land for sheep pasture and the consequent eviction of husbandmen and cottagers from their homes were the major cause of inflation and unemployment. Proclamations were issued against enclosures, and commissioners were sent out to investigate abuses. The main effect of these measures was to increase unrest. Hopes were raised among the masses that the government would take some decisive action, which it did not. At the same time, fear grew among the landed élites that the authorities would actually prevent this form of estate improvement. Further measures limiting the size of leaseholds and placing a tax on wool only made the situation worse by increasing these fears. In any case, many of the élites evaded the legislation, which consequently fell most heavily on the poorer sections of society it was supposed to protect.

Key question
What was the link between vagrancy and public order and how effective was the Vagrancy Act in solving public disorder?

Key terms

Poor Law of 1536
This required the better off members of each parish to collect money to support the impotent poor.

Impotent poor
Those who were too old, too young or too sick to work.

Sedition
Action or speech that incites rebellion.

John Hales and the commonwealth men
Hales was an MP and government minister who is thought to have been part of a group concerned with the economic and social welfare of the citizens of the State, especially its poor.

Law and order

It reasonable to suggest that the government was more concerned with avoiding riot and rebellion than with helping the poor and solving economic problems. This suspicion is supported by three proclamations issued in 1548 aimed specifically at maintaining law and order. A ban on violent sports was rigorously enforced on the grounds that they might end in riots and disorder. It also became an offence to spread rumours, as they were likely to create unrest. Finally, all unlawful assemblies were forbidden. Anyone found guilty of these offences was to be sent for varying periods to the galleys – royal warships propelled by oars. These seem like emergency measures passed by a government which realised that the economic position was getting out of hand, and which feared the consequences.

Key question
How and why did Somerset fall from power?

Key date
Rebellion in East Anglia and the West Country: 1549

Key term
Mercenary army
Professional troops who serve for pay.

Fall from power

It appears that these attempts to control the situation were ineffective because in 1549 the country drifted into what was potentially a major crisis. Somerset seemed unable, or unwilling, to take decisive action to suppress well-supported popular uprisings in the West Country and East Anglia (see pages 134–40). His unwillingness to act has traditionally been interpreted as showing sympathy for the rebels.

It seems more likely that the initial delays in action were caused by the reluctance of the local ruling élites to intervene without government support. Lack of money made it difficult to raise a new **mercenary army**, and Somerset, as Commander-in-Chief, was reluctant to withdraw troops from his garrisons in Scotland and France. It was only when the Privy Council realised the seriousness of the situation and provided additional troops that

Contemporary illustration showing Protector Somerset's execution at Tower Hill. Why was the execution of Somerset recorded by a contemporary illustrator?

Lord Russell in the West Country and John Dudley, Earl of Warwick, in East Anglia were able to defeat the rebels.

A major consequence of the rebellions was the fall of Somerset, whose colleagues quickly abandoned him as a man who had failed to prevent anarchy and revolution. When his chief rival, Northumberland, fresh from his victory in Norfolk, engineered Somerset's arrest in October 1549 there was no opposition. Although Somerset was released early the following year and rejoined the Privy Council, within a year he was accused of plotting against the government. He was executed in January 1552.

Key dates

Fall of Somerset: October 1549

Execution of the Duke of Somerset: January 1552

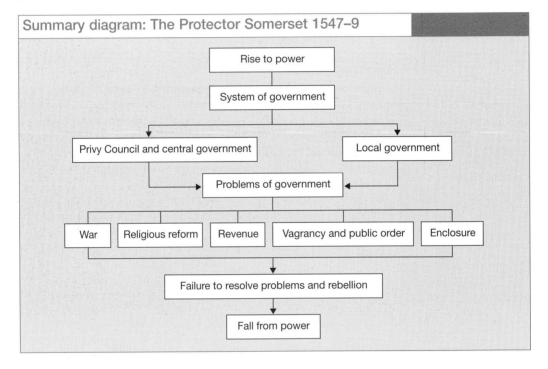

Summary diagram: The Protector Somerset 1547–9

Rise to power

System of government

Privy Council and central government

Local government

Problems of government

War | Religious reform | Revenue | Vagrancy and public order | Enclosure

Failure to resolve problems and rebellion

Fall from power

5 | The Lord President Northumberland 1550–3

Northumberland was the son of a Sussex gentleman, Edmund Dudley, and so came from the middle or gentry class. His lawyer-father had been an MP and Speaker of the House of Commons. He became one of Henry VII's chief councillors and was among the king's most trusted and efficient tax-collecting officers. This made him very unpopular and Dudley was executed for treason by Henry VIII in 1510.

Northumberland's rise to prominence began with his knighthood in 1523 for military service in France under the Duke of Suffolk. He continued to serve in the army and navy of Henry VIII becoming Lord High Admiral in 1543 (a post he held until 1547) and General in command of the army that took Boulogne in 1544. He also held the posts of Deputy Governor of Calais in 1538, Warden of the Scottish Marches in 1542 and Governor of Boulogne in 1544–6. He was rewarded by the king

John Dudley, Duke of
Northumberland,
c1504–53.

for his service by being made Viscount Lisle and a member of the
Privy Council. In the will of Henry VIII Northumberland was
instructed to work with Somerset in ruling the kingdom on behalf
of Edward VI. The two worked closely together until 1549 when
Northumberland arrested and imprisoned Somerset and took
power for himself.

Northumberland was as able a soldier as he was a politician. He
was intelligent and well educated and although prone to greed
and ruthlessness, was probably one of the most gifted politicians
and one of the ablest rulers of his day. On the other hand, he was
not a man of strong convictions or principles as may be seen from
the way he used Lady Jane Grey for his own political purpose and
by his hasty decision to renounce Protestantism in favour of
Catholicism in order to save his life when Mary swept to power
in 1553.

Rise to power 1549–51

Key question
How did
Northumberland rise
to power?

Even before his arrest it was clear that Somerset was discredited and had lost control of the political situation. Many members of the Privy Council were offended by his aloofness and arrogance. He had undermined the confidence of the aristocracy and the gentry because of his inept handling of the popular uprisings, while his religious reforms (see Chapter 3) had alienated even moderates among the conservative faction.

Power struggle

A power struggle soon developed in which Northumberland was a leading contender. Northumberland crushed the rebel army in Norfolk on 26 August 1549 and returned to London on 14 September. This gave him a distinct advantage because as the commander of the main army in England, he controlled the capital. Almost immediately he began to negotiate with Lords Arundel and Wriothesley, leaders of the conservative party. In desperation, on 30 September, Somerset issued a proclamation ordering all troops in England to return to their duties in Scotland and France. On 5 October he issued another proclamation for the recruitment of loyal troops for the defence of the realm. There was no response, and Somerset removed the Royal Household from Hampton Court to Windsor Castle for security.

Meanwhile the Privy Council protected its own position by issuing a proclamation blaming Somerset for the rebellions. All parties were anxious to avoid civil war. On 8 October Somerset agreed to negotiate and was arrested three days later.

Northumberland the politician

Northumberland, like Somerset, had risen to political prominence during the last years of Henry VIII's reign. He, too, had gained a good military reputation in the Scottish and French wars. He was a member of the Council named in Henry's will and was ambitious for more power. The events of 1549 gave him his opportunity to take advantage of Somerset's political isolation. By mid-September he had emerged as the major rival for power, and had contrived to have Somerset arrested. At this point Northumberland showed his considerable ability as a politician. By pretending to be a Catholic sympathiser, he successfully conspired with the conservatives. This gave him control of the Council. However, the conservatives – the Earls of Arundel and Southampton and Lords Russell and St John – were secretly planning to seize power and have Northumberland arrested along with Somerset.

Northumberland the tactician

Northumberland plotted too with the reform party, particularly Archbishop Cranmer, who had considerable influence in the Royal Household. With Cranmer's help he gained control over the administration of the Royal Household, which gave him

Key dates

Emergence of John Dudley, Earl of Warwick, as the most powerful man in England: January 1550

John Dudley created Lord President of the Council: February 1550

John Dudley created Duke of Northumberland: October 1551

Key question
How did Northumberland maintain control?

immediate access to Edward VI. This enabled him to win the confidence of the king, and by February 1550 he was in a strong enough position to have the conservatives, Arundel and Southampton, expelled from the Council.

To secure his position he became Lord President of the Council. In April he was made General Warden of the North, which gave him military command. However, he only achieved complete power in October 1551 when he had Somerset re-arrested, and assumed the title of Duke of Northumberland. In spite of his continuing reputation for greed and ruthlessness, historians are beginning to recognise Northumberland as an ambitious, but able, politician. In marked contrast to Somerset he introduced a series of significant and lasting reforms.

Maintaining control

Northumberland had learned from Somerset's mistakes, and saw that control of the Council was the key to political power. As Lord President he was able to appoint and dismiss councillors at will, and had complete control over procedure. Able supporters of Somerset, such as Paget and William Cecil, who had been arrested, were released and allowed to return to their posts. Under their guidance the Council and its procedures were restored to the pattern established in the period 1536–47.

In order to increase his authority, Northumberland enlarged the membership of the Council to 33, selecting councillors upon whose loyalty he could rely. Whenever possible he chose men of military experience, so that in the event of further rebellions, he, unlike Somerset, could be sure of immediate armed support. To make the Council more efficient and stable Northumberland created a smaller, inner committee with a fixed routine to conduct business. Seeing the danger arising from Somerset's frequent by-passing of the Privy Council, Northumberland restored it to the centre of government. For similar reasons he made less use of proclamations, preferring to use parliament to confirm legislation.

Northumberland and the problems of government

The political difficulties facing the new government were the same as those that Somerset had failed to resolve. Unfortunately for Northumberland, they had become more acute. The most pressing problems were:

- the diplomatic position
- the short-fall in revenue.

Key question
Why was England's diplomatic position such a problem?

The diplomatic position

The war situation had deteriorated because the French, taking advantage of England's domestic problems, had declared open warfare in August 1549. This placed Boulogne under serious threat. Although many of the ruling élites were eager to continue hostilities, Paget and other leading members of the Privy Council had been advocating a peace policy to avoid economic disaster.

Possibly it had been Somerset's obsession with continuing the war that had turned influential Privy Councillors against him. Northumberland, very sensibly and in contrast to Somerset, realised that England was in an impossible military and financial position. He ended the war with France and withdrew many of the garrisons from Scotland.

While this eased the immediate difficulties, diplomatic relations with Charles V became strained as the Emperor mistrusted England's new position of neutrality towards France. Northumberland was still in the process of gaining supreme power so he allied himself with the more extreme Protestant reformers, such as Bishops Ridley and Hooper. In return for their political support Northumberland had to allow the Church of England to swing towards Calvinism (see page 89). This still further antagonised Charles V, who favoured moderation in the English Church, and England became diplomatically isolated.

The short-fall in revenue

Revenue remained a serious problem. The government was bankrupt in 1549. Somerset had spent £1,356,000 on the war, and sold crown lands to the value of £800,000. The government even had to borrow to raise the £50,000 a year needed to maintain the Royal Household. Ending the war drastically reduced expenditure, but a number of expedients had to be adopted to keep the government solvent. In May 1551 the coinage was debased for the last time. Although inflation rose still further, the government made a profit of £114,000 to pay immediate expenses and short-term loans. Even so, a further £243,000 had to be borrowed from continental bankers.

> **Key question**
> Why was there a short-fall in revenue?

William Cecil, restored as Secretary of State, was put in charge of financial planning. He was assisted by Sir Thomas Gresham from the Treasury. They recommended the sale of chantry lands and Church goods to start paying off loans. The London trading companies agreed to support government debts and more money was raised from the mints and Crown lands. Gresham was sent to the Netherlands with £12,000 a week to manipulate the stock market, restore the value of sterling against continental currencies and pay off loans.

In March 1552 the coinage was called in and reissued with the silver content restored to that of 1527. This helped to slow the rise in inflation and restore confidence in sterling. Strict economies were made in government spending, and Northumberland paid off the remainder of his mercenary troops. By these means most of the overseas debts were paid off and a 'privy coffer', an emergency fund, was established.

By 1553 the financial situation had been stabilised. Even so, another £140,000 worth of Crown lands had to be sold to replace taxes, voted unwillingly by parliament, which were not collected because they were so unpopular. However, Northumberland had shown considerable political skill in resolving a serious financial crisis. Unlike Somerset, he had displayed the ability to delegate authority, and in selecting the right people for the task.

At the same time there was a concerted effort to improve the efficiency of the financial machinery. The most pressing need was to streamline the collection of revenue and to find ways of increasing government income. In 1552 a commission began to investigate the five revenue courts that carried out the work of the **Exchequer**. The report recommended that to avoid corruption and inefficiency the number of courts should be reduced to two – the Exchequer and the **Office of Crown Lands**. Alternatively all the courts should be merged into the Exchequer. It was also suggested that **custom and excise** rates should be revised. Although these constructive proposals had to be postponed because of Edward VI's death, they were introduced in the reign of Mary.

Economic and social problems

The government was faced by equally pressing economic and social problems, for example:

- Population, and with it inflation, was still rising. This meant that the living standards of the masses continued to decline, and that work was more difficult to find.
- By 1550 the growing instability of the Antwerp cloth market was causing widespread unemployment among textile workers in East Anglia and the West Country.
- The debasement of the coinage in 1551 raised inflation still further.
- Grain prices rose rapidly; a situation worsened by poor harvests.
- In 1550 the country was still simmering after the recent popular uprisings and was further unsettled by the political power struggle among the privy councillors.

Consequently, the administration had to act carefully and skilfully if further serious disorder was to be avoided, for example:

- The unpopular 1547 Vagrancy Act and the sheep tax of 1548 were repealed in 1550, and this helped to dispel unrest.
- In the same year a new Treason Act was passed, which restored censorship and gave the authorities more power to enforce law and order.

Initially these measures helped to prevent the widespread popular discontent from turning into actual revolt. Northumberland benefited from the fact that the 1549 rebellions had badly frightened the government, aristocracy and gentry, who drew closer together to avoid further disorder among the masses. At the same time the administration introduced further measures in 1552:

- It tried to improve the economic situation and relieve poverty and distress.
- The existing anti-enclosure legislation was rigorously enforced, and the unpopular enclosure commissions were withdrawn.

Key question

How serious were the economic and social problems facing Northumberland and how did he deal with them?

Key terms

Exchequer
The centre of the Crown's financial administration since the twelfth century. It had two functions: to receive, store and pay out money, and to audit the Crown's accounts.

Office of Crown Lands
Department set up to manage the estates (most of which had been inherited from previous monarchs) that belonged to the reigning monarch.

Custom and excise
Taxation imposed on the import of goods.

- The revaluation of the coinage halted inflation and reduced prices.
- Acts were passed to protect arable farming, and to stop the charging of excessive interest on debts.
- A new poor law was passed. Although it did nothing to help the able-bodied find work, it did make it easier for the parish and town authorities to support the aged, infirm and crippled.

Again, Northumberland's administration showed a much more positive approach than that adopted by Somerset and although he did little to resolve the underlying economic problems, he did check inflation, and ease some of the worst of the social distress.

The succession

By 1552 Northumberland seemed to be firmly in control but his power depended upon the support of Edward VI. By the end of the year the king's health was deteriorating quickly, and the problem of the succession became a central issue once again. In accordance with Henry VIII's will, Mary was to succeed if Edward died childless. However, it was feared that because of Mary's strong Catholic sympathies she might replace Northumberland and renounce the Royal Supremacy (see pages 101–2).

To prevent a return to Catholicism, and to retain power, Northumberland, with the full support of the king, planned to change the succession. Lady Jane Grey, the protestant granddaughter of Henry VIII's sister Mary, was chosen to succeed.

Unfortunately for Northumberland, Edward VI died before the plans for the seizure of power could be completed. Queen Jane reigned for only nine days before being removed by Mary. A potential political crisis had been avoided.

Key question
Why did the succession become a serious issue?

Key date

Death of Edward VI, brief reign of Lady Jane Grey, and succession of Mary I: July 1553

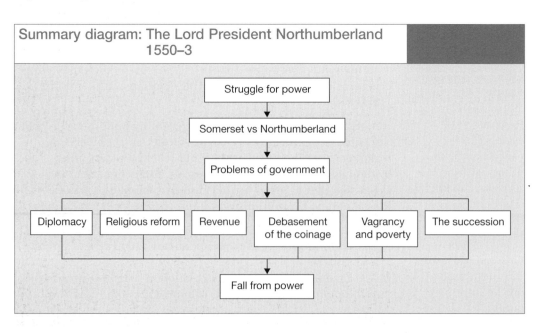

Summary diagram: The Lord President Northumberland 1550–3

Struggle for power
↓
Somerset vs Northumberland
↓
Problems of government
↓
Diplomacy | Religious reform | Revenue | Debasement of the coinage | Vagrancy and poverty | The succession
↓
Fall from power

6 | Mary Tudor 1553–8

Mary (1516–58), the daughter of Catherine of Aragon, was 37 years of age when she came to the throne. During Edward VI's reign she had resisted Protestant reform just as strongly as she had under her father. While Somerset was in power she had been allowed to follow her Catholic religion in private, and she had remained on good terms with the Protector and Edward. With the swing towards Calvinism under Northumberland, increasing pressure had been put on Mary to abandon Catholicism and to conform to the Protestant doctrines of the Church of England.

During this difficult period she had received constant support and advice from her Habsburg cousin, Emperor Charles V. It was fear of the Habsburgs that had prevented the reformers taking extreme measures against her. Mary was a proud woman, who resented the pressures put on her and was embittered by the treatment of her mother who had been exiled from the Court and sent away into the country. This made her mistrust her English councillors when she became queen, and lean heavily on advice from the Habsburg's imperial ambassador, Simon Renard.

Mary Tudor 1516–58.

When Mary proclaimed herself queen on 11 July 1553, even Renard and Charles V had thought it a futile gesture. Yet when she entered London at the end of the month she was greeted with enormous enthusiasm. Political prisoners such as the Duke of Norfolk and Stephen Gardiner were released. Following the advice of Charles V, she showed leniency towards her opponents. Only Northumberland and two of his closest confederates were executed. Although some members of Northumberland's Council, like Cecil, were imprisoned, others, such as Paget, were allowed to join the new Privy Council.

Execution of the Duke of Northumberland: August 1553 — Key date

As a devout Catholic, Mary was insistent that England should return to the Church of Rome. At the same time, she was convinced that national safety depended on a close alliance with the Habsburgs. Her policy rested on the achievement of these two aims. Until 1555 this strategy appeared to be prospering, but thereafter Mary's popularity steadily declined until her death in 1558.

Assessments of Mary's character

Key question
What was Mary like?

The cause of this unpopularity has generally been attributed to Mary's own character. Simon Renard's assessment that she was 'good, easily influenced, inexpert in worldly matters and a novice all round' was scarcely a flattering tribute. Elizabethan propagandists were eager to depict Mary as a weak and unsuccessful pro-Spanish monarch in order to highlight the achievements of their own queen. Protestant reformers reviled her as a cruel tyrant trying to enforce Catholicism through torture and burnings. This has produced a popular picture of 'Bloody Mary' – a stubborn, arrogant, Catholic bigot, who burned Protestants and lost Calais to the French because of her infatuation for Philip of Spain.

In a modified form, this has been the view of many historians, but recently there have been attempts to revise this critical appraisal. It has been pointed out that she showed skill and resolution in defeating Northumberland's attempted *coup d'état* (see pages 140–1). Mary has been criticised for indecision in the negotiations over the restoration of Catholicism to England and her marriage to Philip of Spain. This, it has later been suggested, was in fact masterly political inactivity and pretended weakness, designed to win greater concessions from the Papacy and the Habsburgs, similar tactics to those that her sister Elizabeth used so successfully.

Indeed, it is suggested that Mary had the broad support of the majority of the people until 1555. The problem was not the weakness of Mary's character and policies, but her failure to produce an heir to consolidate her position. This, the outbreak of war with France and the declining economic position, was the real cause of Mary's growing unpopularity. On the basis of the existing evidence it is difficult to assess Mary's true character, and the present consensus of opinion lies somewhere between the two extremes.

System of government

Key question
How well did the system of government operate under Mary?

The system of central and local government remained fundamentally unchanged during Mary's reign. The Privy Council continued to be the centre of the administration. One of the main criticisms of Mary's Privy Council has been that it was too large to conduct business effectively. Certainly, at times the membership did reach 43. In addition it has been claimed that the Council contained a few members of no real political ability and administrative experience. The reason for this was that in the first few weeks of her reign Mary was forced to choose councillors from her own Royal Household, and from among leading Catholic noblemen who had supported her. By October several moderate members of Northumberland's Council had been sworn in as councillors, although they were never fully in the queen's confidence. However, they supplied a nucleus of political ability and administrative experience previously lacking. Apart from this making the Council too large caused strong rivalry between the Catholics, led by the Chancellor, Gardiner, and the moderates, led by Paget.

Although there was disagreement, these two very able politicians co-operated closely to restore effective government. In any case, affairs of State were soon largely handled by an 'inner council' consisting of those experienced councillors who had reformed the Privy Council under Northumberland. Much of the original criticism of the Privy Council came from Renard, who was jealous of the queen's English advisers and wished to maintain his own influence with Mary. The main problem was that Mary did not appear to exert any leadership, or show any real confidence in her Council. Frequently she did not consult the Privy Council until she had already decided matters of policy in consultation with Renard.

It has been maintained that parliament was strongly opposed to Mary's policies. This view has been modified by recent research. There seems to be little evidence that Mary controlled the House of Commons by packing it with Catholic supporters through rigged elections. She had strong support from the higher clergy in the House of Lords, especially after the imprisonment and execution of Thomas Cranmer, Archbishop of Canterbury, Nicholas Ridley, Bishop of London and Hugh Latimer, Bishop of Worcester. Apart from the dislike of the Spanish marriage, both Houses seem to have co-operated with the administration throughout Mary's reign. As was the case in the Privy Council, there were lively debates and criticism of policy, but these were generally constructive. Like previous parliaments, the main interest of the members centred on local affairs and the protection of property rights.

The marriage issue

Key question
Why was royal marriage such a serious issue during Mary's reign?

Mary's political inexperience and stubbornness is shown in the first major issue of the reign – the royal marriage. The Privy Council was divided on the matter. There were two realistic candidates for Mary's hand:

- Edward Courtenay, Earl of Devon, who was favoured by Gardiner
- Philip of Spain, who was supported by Paget.

Courtenay was a descendant of earlier English kings and such a marriage would have strengthened the Tudor dynasty, but Mary favoured a closer link with the Habsburgs through Philip. It was not until 27 October that Mary raised the matter in Council, and then only to announce that she was going to marry Philip. This disconcerted Gardiner, who was blamed by Mary for the petition from the House of Commons in November, asking her to marry within the realm. Mary disregarded all opposition to her plans.

On 7 December a marriage treaty, drafted by Mary, Paget, Gardiner and Renard, was presented to the Council. It was ratified at the beginning of January 1554. Mary had achieved her objective of forming a closer alliance with the Habsburgs. The terms of the treaty were very favourable to England. Philip was to have no regal power in England, no foreign appointments were to be made to the Privy Council, and England was not to be involved in, or pay towards the cost of any of Philip's wars. If the marriage was childless, the succession was to pass to Elizabeth.

In spite of these safeguards Mary's popularity began to ebb, as many people still thought that England would be drawn into Philip's wars and become a mere province of the Habsburg Empire.

By the end of January 1554, anti-Spanish feelings led to rebellion. The rebellion was led by Sir James Croft, Sir Peter Carew and Sir Thomas Wyatt. These men had all held important offices at Court under both Henry VIII and Edward VI. Although they had supported Mary's accession, they feared that the growing Spanish influence would endanger their own careers.

Wyatt Rebellion: January 1554

Marriage of Mary I and Philip of Spain: July 1554

Key dates

The restoration of Catholicism

Once the rebellion was defeated, the restoration of Catholicism (see page 103) became a political issue. Gardiner had lost Mary's favour over the Spanish marriage. In an attempt to regain it he pressed for religious change. He was opposed in the Council by Paget, who feared that such a policy would cause further unrest. Paget raised the matter in parliament to try to block Gardiner's proposals.

This introduced a serious constitutional issue. Mary thought that religion was still part of the royal prerogative (see page 103). However, she was forced to concede that doctrinal changes could only be made through parliament. In fact there was only minor opposition in the House of Commons to the restoration of Catholicism, and this was mainly caused by fears over property rights.

Such worries were removed by guarantees that there would be no attempt to take back monastic and chantry lands already sold by the Crown. By 1555 all Henrician and Edwardian religious legislation had been repealed. There was comparatively little opposition to the actual religious changes. However, many

Key question
Why was the restoration of Catholicism such a serious issue during Mary's reign?

Profile: Stephen Gardiner c1483–1555

c1483 – Born
1520 – Educated at Cambridge University and became a doctor of civil law
1521 – Became a doctor of canon law. Appointed tutor to Duke of Norfolk's son
1524 – Appointed secretary to Lord Chancellor Wolsey, Henry VIII's chief minister (1524–9)
1530 – Appointed Principal Secretary to Henry VIII (1530–4)
1532 – Appointed Bishop of Winchester
1535 – Appointed ambassador to France (1535–8)
1538 – Led resistance to Thomas Cromwell's changes in religion. Fell out of favour with the king
1539 – Promoted Act of Six Articles
1540 – Took part in destruction of Cromwell. With the Duke of Norfolk led the Conservative faction at Court
1542 – Became one of Henry VIII's leading ministers (1542–7)
1548 – Forced out of government and imprisoned in the Tower of London for opposing Somerset
1551 – Stripped of his title as Bishop of Winchester
1553 – Restored to all his offices and titles by Mary, who appointed him Lord Chancellor. Led the Catholic Counter-Reformation and promoted conservative legislation in parliament
1554 – Married Mary and Philip of Spain
1555 – Died

Gardiner was a talented government minister, and respected thinker and theologian. Although he supported Henry VIII's divorce and break from Rome, he opposed any major changes in religion. He was an able leader of the conservative faction at Court which brought about the downfall of Cromwell. His opposition of Somerset in the last years of Henry VIII's reign ensured his downfall after the king's death. Although Somerset was prepared to work with Gardiner the two could not agree on the religious direction the Edwardian government should take. His downfall was the inevitable result of his refusal to compromise. In spite of his strong Catholic beliefs, he tried to save the leaders of the reformist party, Cranmer and Northumberland, from execution. The accession of Mary rescued his career and although he had supported the break with Rome in 1534 he was willing to restore the Pope as Head of the Church in 1554. He served out the remainder of his life as a trusted adviser to the Crown.

historians consider that the policy of Mary and Archbishop Pole of persecuting and burning heretics began to turn even moderate opinion against her (see pages 105–6).

Financial and economic problems
Financial reforms

Key question
What were the main financial and economic problems facing Mary?

The Marian administration was still faced by the financial problems that Northumberland had been trying to solve. To make matters worse, Mary had given away more Crown lands in order to re-establish some monastic foundations. Consequently, it was important both to find new sources of government revenue and to increase the income from existing ones. To achieve this the Privy Council largely adopted the proposals put forward by the commissions in 1552 (see page 98).

In 1554 drastic changes were made to the revenue courts:

- The Exchequer, as the main financial department, took over the work of the Court of First Fruits and Tenths, which had dealt with clerical taxation, and the Court of Augmentations, which had administered income from monastic and chantry lands.
- The Court of Wards, which collected feudal taxation, and the Duchy of Lancaster, administering lands belonging to the monarch as Duke of Lancaster, retained their independence.
- It was planned to remove the large number of debased coins in circulation and to continue the restoration of the silver content of the coinage, but Mary's death meant that the scheme was not put into effect until 1560.
- The 1552 proposal to revise the custom rates, which had remained unchanged since 1507, was implemented. In 1558 a new Book of Rates was issued, which increased custom revenue from £29,000 to £85,000 a year.
- In 1555 a full survey of all Crown lands was carried out. As a result rents and entry fines, a payment made by new tenants before they could take over a property, were raised in 1557.

Mary died before these measures had any real effect, and it was Elizabeth I who benefited from the increased revenue brought about by these reforms.

The economy

Key question
How healthy was the economy during Mary's reign?

During Mary's reign the general economic situation grew worse, with a series of very bad harvests and epidemics of sweating sickness, bubonic plague and influenza. Towns were particularly badly hit, with high mortality rates and severe food shortages. The government's reaction was to continue the policy, started under Henry VIII, of restricting the movement of textile and other industries from the towns to the countryside. This, it was hoped, would lessen urban unemployment and reduce the number of vagrants seeking work. This, however, was short-sighted because what was really needed was an increase in the number and variety of industries in both town and country, which would provide jobs for the growing number of unemployed.

To achieve this the government needed to encourage the search for new overseas markets to replace the trade lost with the decline of the Antwerp market. In 1551 English ships had begun to trade along the north African coast, and between 1553 and 1554 Sir Hugh Willoughby was trying to find a north-east passage to the Far East. However, until after 1558 successive English governments were too anxious to avoid offending Spain and Portugal to encourage overseas enterprise. It was not until the reign of Elizabeth I that any real progress was made in this direction.

Reform of the army and navy

In spite of the assurance that England would not be involved in Spain's wars, Mary's strong emotional attachment to Philip made it likely that England would be drawn into the continental conflict. As early as 1555 the Privy Council was reviewing the condition of the navy, which had been allowed to decline after Northumberland had made peace with France. A new building programme was started, improvements were made to the dockyards, and naval expenditure was increased through a new system of financing.

Equal attention was paid to the army, especially after the outbreak of war in 1557. Arrangements for raising and maintaining the county militias were revised in the Militia and Arms Acts of 1557, which also improved the procedures for supplying arms and equipment. These reforms brought long-term improvements to England's military organisation.

Assessment of Mary's reign

Philip II's visit to England early in 1557, and his success in drawing the country into his war against France, intensified Mary's growing unpopularity. The last two years of her reign saw rising anti-Spanish feelings, mounting opposition to religious persecution, and discontent with the economic conditions. The war with France and the loss of Calais, England's last continental possession united the country against the ailing queen. The enthusiasm which marked her death in November 1558 and the succession of Elizabeth to the throne was even greater than that which had greeted Mary's overthrow of Northumberland five years earlier.

Yet, despite its apparent failings, her reign was not one of complete sterility. Important reforms had been made and the institution of monarchy and the State machinery remained intact. Although the loss of Calais was seen as a national disaster, it can be interpreted as the crucial moment when England turned its attention away from fruitless continental conquest towards exploration opportunities in the New World. Indeed, some historians would go as far as to claim that Mary's failure was her childlessness and her relatively early death, rather than her policies.

Key question
How successful were the reforms in the army and navy?

Key question
How should Mary's reign be assessed?

Key date
Death of Mary I: November 1558

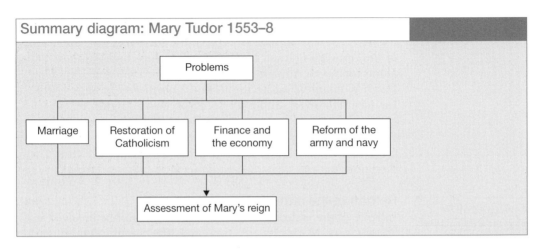

Summary diagram: Mary Tudor 1553–8

Problems

- Marriage
- Restoration of Catholicism
- Finance and the economy
- Reform of the army and navy

Assessment of Mary's reign

7 | Elizabeth I: 1558–1603

Elizabeth, the daughter of Anne Boleyn, was 25 years of age when she came to the throne. During Mary's reign Elizabeth lived a precarious existence partly because of her adherence to the Protestant faith and partly on account of her position as heir to the throne. Unbeknown to Elizabeth, a group of prominent gentry laid plans to mount a rebellion against Mary with the aim of establishing a Protestant regime with her as queen. The failure of the so-called Wyatt rebellion put Elizabeth in peril of her life for she was arrested and imprisoned in the Tower. Suspected of being party to the plot Elizabeth was interrogated and for two months lived with the constant expectation of her death being announced. However, no evidence could be found against her and she was released and banished to an Oxfordshire manor where she was placed under house arrest and kept under surveillance.

Accession of Elizabeth I: November 1558

Key date

Elizabeth I, 1558–1603, shown here in *The Armada Portrait*, attributed to George Gower c1588.

This experience had a profound effect on Elizabeth and shaped her personality and future conduct as queen. She became cautious to the point of being reluctant to take decisions, a fact that irritated and exasperated her ministers and closest advisors. Her unwillingness to sanction the execution of those 'near to the throne' such as Mary, Queen of Scots, has been taken as evidence of her memories of what it was like to be an innocent person around whom a web of lies had been spun. However, the most important lesson she learned from her experience was her unshakable belief that she had been spared by God who had chosen her to be his instrument on earth. This went a long way towards explaining the strong (but uncomplicated) religious faith that she exhibited throughout her reign.

Politics and government

Key question
Was there a crisis in Elizabethan government and politics?

There appeared to be no crisis in politics and government. The most important element in central government was the Privy Council and it is in its composition that Elizabeth achieved her first notable success. Elizabeth made it clear from the outset that she did not intend to repeat Mary's error in having a large Council since it proved difficult to handle and often led to faction fights. As Elizabeth herself said, 'a multitude doth make rather for discord and confusion than good counsel'. Elizabeth expressed her intention to limit the number of councillors and she proceeded to choose her closest advisers wisely and sparingly. Perhaps the most striking feature of her Council was the element of continuity in that she retained some of Mary's councillors while adding those of her own. The two men most prominent in her government were Sir William Cecil (Lord Burghley from 1571), who became her Principal Secretary of State, and Robert Dudley (Earl of Leicester from 1564). Cecil's appointment added to this sense of continuity since he had served in the government of Edward VI. In fact, historian G.R. Elton said of Cecil that he 'took up where Cromwell left off' and that 'the failure of Tudor government between 1540 and 1558 was redeemed by Elizabeth's council' because there was no need for major administrative reforms. The success of Elizabeth's Privy Council was put down to the fact that she put 'fresh energy and drive into the existing institutions'.

Parliament

Key question
What was the Crown's relationship with parliament?

Unlike today, the late sixteenth century parliamentary system did not lie at the heart of the nation's political life; this powerful position was reserved for the monarch. Parliament had been and remained an occasional and peripheral part of the political system. There were only 13 sessions of parliament during more than 44 years of Elizabeth's reign, and no session lasted for more than a few months. It was expected that, in the Commons in particular, any questioning or querying of the queen's intentions would be moderate, cautious and highly respectful. Elizabeth drew a clear distinction between those subjects that touched on her royal prerogative (and were therefore not to be discussed in parliament except by invitation) and those that had to do with the commonweal (which fell within parliament's competence). Naturally there were differences of opinion about what was 'off limits' and what was not but MPs generally were aware that religion, foreign policy, marriage and the succession were matters reserved for the queen and her closest advisors.

It appears that almost without exception Elizabeth had to be persuaded by her ministers to call parliament. In 12 out of 13 parliamentary sessions the argument used by her advisers was the need to arrange for the raising and collection of taxation. When in session parliament was invited to discuss a range of issues such as religious reform and other law-making bills. Debates and discussions were closely controlled by the Speaker and by the queen's representatives in both houses. The monarch retained the final say on all matters by exercising the royal veto. The veto was used sparingly by Elizabeth and when it was used it was usually in response to a poorly drafted bill that required redrafting before the royal assent could be given. Only when a bill received the royal assent could it become law. There is no evidence to suggest that Elizabeth deliberately obstructed parliamentary business. Nevertheless, it is clear from the evidence that Elizabeth regarded parliament as a somewhat inconvenient necessity. Equally, there is no doubt that the times when parliament was in session were periods of stress and strain for the queen, which helps to explain why she was easily irritated and why she sometimes suffered outbursts of ill-temper.

Elizabeth and parliament: the Whig view of history, Neale and revisionism

Key question
How and why has the study of Elizabethan parliaments changed?

The Whig view of history developed during the nineteenth century when Britain evolved from a parliamentary monarchy into a parliamentary democracy. The Whig historians believed that Elizabethan parliaments were happy to accept the queen's dominance and superiority. They acknowledged that Elizabeth's reign witnessed the first tentative steps by MPs to break free from the stifling control of the monarch but, in their view, the real struggle between Crown and parliament only began in earnest after 1603.

This view of parliament's relationship with Elizabeth was challenged by the eminent historian Sir John Neale. His research over 20 years, between the mid 1930s and early 1950s, suggested that the relationship between monarch and parliament was anything but smooth. In his opinion the Elizabethan period witnessed an attempt by an organised group within the House of Commons to increase parliamentary powers and privileges in the face of stout resistance from the Crown. The phrase most commonly used to describe Neale's 'organised group' was the 'Puritan Choir'. Consisting of 43 **Puritan** MPs named in a contemporary pamphlet published in 1566, Neale believed that the aim of this group was to change the laws regulating religion so as to make the Church of England more Protestant. The 'Choir' was credited with forcing Elizabeth in 1559 to adopt a

Puritans
Protestants who wished to purify the Anglican Church and purge the State religion of any Catholic practices.

Key term

more Protestant Religious Settlement than she really wanted, with stirring up trouble in 1563 and 1566 over the queen's failure to marry, with scheming between 1563 and 1571 to bring about further reforms in the Church, and with agitating in 1572 for the executions of the Duke of Norfolk and Mary, Queen of Scots.

To Neale this seemed to be a clear-cut example of MPs starting to flex their collective muscles. To support his interpretation Neale also used the Wentworth brothers, Peter and Paul, as examples of MPs openly criticising the queen. In the parliaments between 1576 and 1593 the brothers attacked Elizabeth for what they saw as her mistaken policies and for not turning the Church into a purely Puritan organisation. The fact that they also called for the right of MPs to discuss whatever they wished in the debating chambers encouraged Neale to see this as part of the wider struggle for power between monarch and parliament.

The 1980s witnessed a radical shift of opinion among historians. To the revisionists, like Norman Jones, M.A.R. Graves and G.R. Elton, Neale's 'Puritan Choir' was a figment of the imagination. In their opinion, Neale not only misunderstood but misinterpreted the evidence. Neale's 'power struggle' between the monarch and parliament was in reality the queen's frustrated ministers using MPs as an additional lever in their attempts to persuade Elizabeth to take action where she was proving reluctant to do so. The Commons were used:

- in the 1560s because of Elizabeth's failure to marry and nominate a successor
- in the 1570s because of Elizabeth's failure to take action against Norfolk and Mary, Queen of Scots
- in the 1580s because of Elizabeth's failure to lend effective support to the Dutch rebels.

To the revisionists the Puritan Choir simply did not exist while the Wentworth brothers were individuals expressing their personal dissatisfaction with the system. Where there were attempts made by parliament, in particular the Commons, to defend, and even extend, its privileges these were temporary knee-jerk reactions to events over which MPs felt powerless to act. In the opinion of the revisionists the relationship between the Crown and parliament was, in the main, one of co-operation.

Marriage and the succession

Key question
Why was the prospect of Elizabeth's marriage and the issue of her successor a potential crisis?

Elizabeth was expected to marry. As a woman in a male-dominated world it was expected that she, like her sister Mary, would seek the advice and security that marriage to a powerful man could offer. Moreover, the succession was at stake, therefore in the opinion of her ministers Elizabeth had to marry in order to have an heir. However, Elizabeth was unusual in that she refused to bow to pressure and confirm to the social norm. She would not follow her sister's example and be dominated by a man, let alone a Catholic prince. Her marriage and the issue of her successor were matters for her alone, a point made clear by her insistence that they were part of the royal prerogative. In fact, Elizabeth used marriage as a tool in her foreign policy, holding out the prospect of marriage with foreign princes without ever committing to any of them. As the diplomat Thomas Challoner put it, Elizabeth's hand was the 'card of our negotiations'. This delicate balancing act proved effective until the mid to late 1570s when she passed the age of childbearing.

Nevertheless, Elizabeth remained vulnerable, a fact made clear in the succession crisis of 1562 when she succumbed to smallpox. Without a named successor her death might have plunged the nation into conflict and it was only her recovery from the deadly disease that averted the crisis. Her natural successor was her cousin Mary, Queen of Scots, but she was a devout Catholic. Mary's succession would not only imperil the establishment of the Anglican Church but would likely be opposed by the largely protestant nobility. If, on the other hand, Elizabeth married a foreign prince in order to have a son, then England would likely be dragged into the European power-struggle. Marriage with a member of the English nobility was also out of the question because it might lead to envy, bitter rivalry and the growth in dangerous factions. Whereas Elizabeth's infatuation with Robert Dudley, Earl of Leicester, caused envy and rivalry, her dalliance with Robert Devereux, Earl of Essex, led to faction and eventually rebellion.

In reality Elizabeth had few options but one of the safest was to remain unmarried and when the time was right to nominate a successor. Only when the Scottish (Mary, Queen of Scots) and Spanish (**Armada**) threats had disappeared, did Elizabeth finally name James VI, King of Scotland, as her heir.

Mary, Queen of Scots

Mary Stuart was directly descended from Henry VII and as such was Elizabeth's closest living relative. In the opinion of historian M. Levine, Mary was Henry Tudor's 'only living descendant whose lineage could not be challenged with a charge of bastardy by alleging a doubtful marriage'. Elizabeth was reluctant to recognise her cousin as her heir because she might yet marry and have a son of her own. Mary was viewed with suspicion because she was a Roman Catholic with strong ties to France. So long as she remained in Scotland she could be largely ignored by both Elizabeth and her leading councillors.

This changed in 1568 when Mary was forced to abdicate her throne and flee south to England in search of shelter and protection. Mary's rule in Scotland had been a disaster and her arrival on English soil began a political crisis that would not be resolved for nearly 20 years. She was considered a dangerous threat to Elizabeth and the Tudor regime because English Catholics who distrusted Elizabeth and opposed her Protestant reform of the Church saw Mary as a realistic candidate for the English Crown. In 1569 a group of northern Catholic nobles, led by the Earl of Northumberland, rose in rebellion. They failed in

Key date

Succession crisis: 1562

Key term

Armada
The Spanish invasion fleet of 1588.

Key question
Why was Mary, Queen of Scots, seen as a threat to Elizabeth?

their aim to put Mary on the throne but the shock of rebellion frightened Elizabeth and her ministers.

Elizabeth faced a number of options on what to do with Mary. She could either release her or keep her prisoner in England:

- If Mary was released Elizabeth could either send her back to Scotland or help her get to France. The dangers posed to England by a civil war in Scotland and/or a French-led military expedition in support of Mary meant that release was not a realistic option.
- If Mary remained under house arrest in England she could be watched and her movements controlled. The danger here was the possibility of plots being laid to free her and/or the Catholic powers uniting against Elizabeth demanding Mary's freedom.

Although this second option was not without its dangers it was the one chosen by Elizabeth and her ministers. Some of her leading advisers, Sir William Cecil and especially Sir Francis Walsingham, preferred a third option – the execution of the troublesome Scottish queen. They worked for nearly two decades to achieve their aim.

The danger posed by Mary's imprisonment increased year on year:

Key term

Excommunicate
To cast a sinner out of the Roman Catholic Church. When dead, an excommunicate could not be buried on consecrated ground and the soul would go to hell.

Key dates

Pope excommunicated Elizabeth: 1570

Execution of Mary, Queen of Scots: 1587

- In 1570 the Pope **excommunicated** Elizabeth and issued a pardon to all English Catholics who dared rebel against the heretic queen of England.
- In 1571 the Ridolfi Plot was discovered, which involved the Duke of Norfolk. Norfolk planned to marry Mary Stuart and raise the standard of rebellion in collaboration with Spain. Norfolk was executed in 1572.
- In 1583 (Throckmorton), 1585 (Parry) and again in 1586 (Babington) a series of plots to free Mary and remove Elizabeth from the throne was discovered and put down. The plotters were executed.

It was not until 1587 that Elizabeth reluctantly agreed to the execution of Mary, Queen of Scots. She did so only on account of evidence presented to her that revealed her cousin's involvement in the Babington Plot. With her death it was hoped the crisis surrounding Mary would be ended. However, it proved to be the excuse Philip of Spain needed to launch his Armada against England in 1588. The failure of the Armada finally put paid to the Mary, Queen of Scots affair.

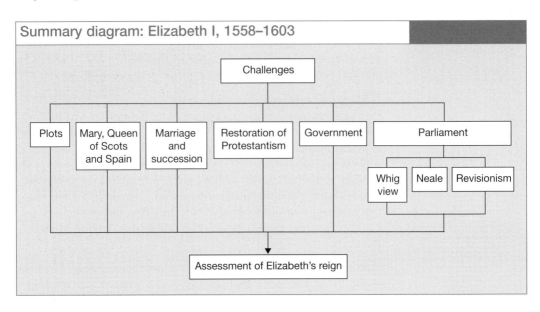

Summary diagram: Elizabeth I, 1558–1603

8 | Concluding Assessment: Was there a Political Crisis?

Great importance has been attached to the potential constitutional and political crisis arising from Henry VIII's failure to leave an adult male heir. With the anarchy of the Wars of the Roses (1455–85) still very much a living memory there were obvious fears that the Tudor State would collapse into chaos. The following key points show why such worries proved to be groundless:

- The permanent machinery of State continued to function without a break after 1547, showing that the overhaul of government under the first two Tudor monarchs had achieved a firm basis. The main beneficiary of this stability in government was Elizabeth in whose reign the Privy Council evolved into a versatile and effective institution.
- At the same time the ruling élites provided great support and loyalty to the legitimate monarchy. At no time, even in 1569 with the rebellion of the Northern Earls, was there a crisis in the élites. The majority remained loyal and rallied round the monarch in times of crisis.
- Although there was considerable rivalry between the political factions under Edward VI, it was no greater than it had been during the reign of Henry VIII. In the opinion of one contemporary, Sir Robert Naunton, Elizabeth 'ruled by faction' meaning that she was able to skilfully manipulate the competing groups and bend them to her will.
- At no time, even in 1549 with the fall of Somerset, was there a real political crisis. The most dangerous moment came in 1553 with the death of Edward VI, when Northumberland tried to bar Princess Mary from the succession. Once again the ruling

élites were solid in their support for the legitimate descent, and the incident passed without crisis.

- It is true that the political leadership was often inept and indecisive between 1547 and 1558. Even so the administration continued to function without a check, and some useful measures of bureaucratic reform were passed. When Mary I died in 1558 the Crown was offered peacefully to her sister Elizabeth, a tribute to the strength and continuity of Tudor government.

Although there is general agreement that there was no serious mid-century political or constitutional crisis, opinions about the political leadership continue to vary:

- The 'good' Duke of Somerset is now seen in a much less favourable light, while the 'bad' Duke of Northumberland is credited with being a much more able politician than has traditionally been thought.
- Mary I is still regarded as a monarch without any real ability, but her reign is now thought to have achieved some significant advances. Speculation about the true nature of Mary's personality continues, and she is now regarded as having been unfairly compared with her more glamorous sister Elizabeth.
- Elizabeth's posthumous reputation has never been greater – 'Gloriana never so glorious' – but most historians now temper their admiration of her by pointing out her weaknesses and mistakes. In short, she is no longer seen as infallible.

Yet, great interest continues to be shown in the nature of the ruling élites in general. Fresh analyses of the nobility and the gentry, at both national and county levels, are being produced. New works on the House of Lords and Stephen Gardiner throw more light on the workings of central government. Particular attention is being paid to the study of individual families and their circle of friends and associates, to reveal the part they played in local and central government. Such research continues to lead to a much greater understanding of the complex motives and ambitions behind the political factions of mid-Tudor England.

Summary diagram: Politics and the State

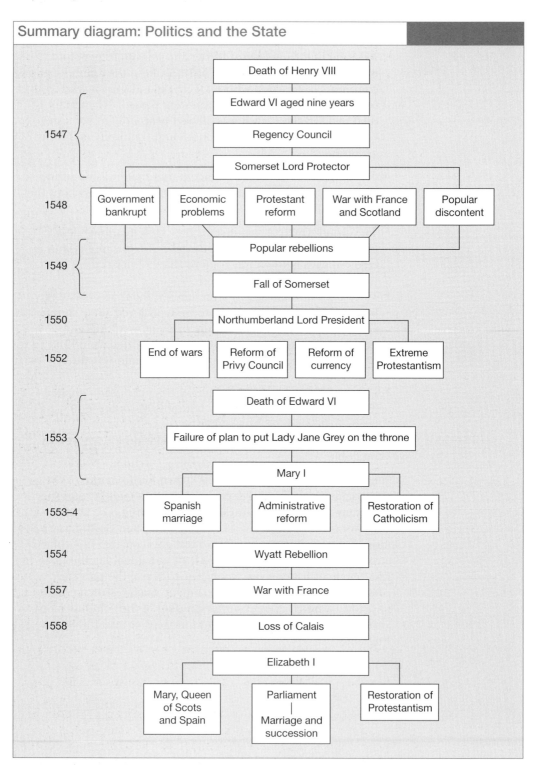

Study Guide: AS Question

In the style of OCR

Study the five sources on royal servants 1538–60, and then answer both sub-questions. It is recommended that you spend two-thirds of your time in answering part (b).

(a) **Study Sources A and D.**
   Compare these sources as evidence for criticisms of royal servants.

(b) **Study all the sources.**
   Use your own knowledge to assess how far the sources support the interpretation that the actions of royal servants undermined good government between 1538 and 1560.

Royal servants 1538–60

Source A

Commission of investigation, report, 1538. Comments said to have been made about Thomas Cromwell by George Paulet, who appeared before a Royal Commission to answer charges of slandering the minister.

The King has six times the revenue of his predecessors, but it is all spent by Cromwell. No gentleman supports Cromwell because of his extortion. I would not be in his place for all his wealth. Twice a week the King calls him 'villain' and 'knave', and sometimes slaps him hard. He is well pummelled about the head and shaken up, as if a dog, then thrown out of the Privy Chamber. But he still enters the Great Chamber looking merry as though he rules the roost. I laugh at his faction and ruffs, and then have to reconcile him with the King again.

Source B

Richard Grafton, Chronicle, entry for 1549. A contemporary relates the early stages of the successful plot against Protector Somerset in October 1549. The 'Earl of Warwick' mentioned here is the future Duke of Northumberland.

After these revolts were pacified, many lords and councillors, disliking the government of the Lord Protector, started to plot to replace him. They assembled at the house of the Earl of Warwick. Then they published a proclamation against him, as follows:

   The Lord Protector by his malicious and evil government was the occasion of all the recent uprisings that so disturbed the realm. He was ambitious and sought his own glory, as appeared by his lavish buildings. He did not value the wise advice of the other councillors. He sowed sedition between the nobles, gentlemen and commons.

Source C

Francis Bourgoyne, letter to John Calvin, 22 January 1552. A contemporary, based in London, relates the events leading to the execution of the Duke of Somerset in January 1552.

Somerset was the head of a conspiracy against the whole Council, and more particularly against the Duke of Northumberland, whom Somerset pursued with a deadly hatred, since Northumberland had been foremost among those who deprived him of the rank of Lord Protector. Somerset obtained some supporters from among the Council itself. They agreed that Northumberland should be murdered and they should take over the government of the kingdom. Somerset should lead the government, or even be restored to the office of Protector.

Source D

Elizabeth, letter to the Duke of Northumberland, July 1553. The Princess Elizabeth writes to the Lord President of the Council concerning his attempt to place Lady Jane Grey on the throne after the death of Edward VI.

My sister and I were unwilling to believe reports of your recent plot to advance your own family by excluding us from the succession. We had seen you as a gentleman defending law and justice. We could not conceive you capable of such a scandalous act as to persuade an innocent and infirm king, by foolish suspicions and lies, to exclude his lawful heirs recognised by Will and Act of Parliament. Your Lordship used your power to exclude the rightful daughters of King Henry VIII, in favour of the daughter of the Duke of Suffolk, whose only claim is to have married one of our aunts. We hope parliament and the judges free us from the oppression in which your ambition has cast us.

Source E

Richard Rex, The Tudors, published in 2002. A modern historian observes an occasion when William Cecil persuaded Elizabeth I to follow his advice, against her instincts.

The Scottish crisis of 1559–60 was the first of many episodes in which we can see policy emerging from the complex relationship between Elizabeth and her trusted chief minister and other advisers. Where William Cecil had a real breadth of strategic vision, Elizabeth's approach was cautious and frugal. When her instincts and Cecil's did not immediately converge, the result was hesitation. Cecil was not yet established in his dominant position on the Privy Council. She only agreed to follow his advice when he asked to be relieved of the burdens of office.

Exam tips

The OCR Enquiries unit (AS Unit F963) is a source-based paper which requires two approaches: first, a comparative analysis and judgement on two primary sources as evidence for a specific issue; secondly, an assessment of the validity of an interpretation by analysis, evaluation and judgement of a set of sources (four or five) integrating relevant knowledge to develop, confirm or qualify their content and provenance.

The skills required for this unit are:

- gaining knowledge and understanding of the historical evidence
- making links within the evidence to answer a specific question
- using knowledge as context and as a basis for judgement in comparative source analysis, and in assessing the relative reliability and utility of sources
- assessing possible interpretations arising from sources
- analysing and evaluating an individual source or a set of sources with discrimination
- integrating knowledge and analysis to reach a substantiated judgement on the validity of an interpretation.

Time management is essential. There are 30 minutes available for part (a) and one hour for part (b), including reading and planning time. It is important to plan carefully as answers are assessed by individual assessment objectives:

- AO1a Use of clearly expressed historical context and understanding.
- AO1b Explanation, organisation, analysis and judgement.
- AO2a Use and evaluation of the sources.
- AO2b Bringing all the threads together to answer an interpretative question.

(a) First of all make sure you are comparing the correct two sources, Source A with Source D. Then take account of the following in your answer:

- Focus: here the focus is on 'criticisms of royal servants'. This should be kept clearly in mind throughout, as the purpose of the comparison.
- Links: similarities and differences should be cross-referenced point by point and linked to the question, 'criticisms of royal servants'. In planning, highlight aspects of source content that link to these key terms.
- Avoid a formulaic approach. Think about the sources in the light of their historical context, and show your understanding of their significance in answering the question.
- Provenance: it is important to start by focusing on *who, what, when, why* and *to whom* the source was written and its tone. Not all of these aspects may be relevant to this particular question, so avoid a formulaic approach. Concentrate on the most significant aspect(s).

- Content: try to balance similarities and differences of content in the light of their provenance, integrating content with provenance.
- Analyse: the detail, sentence by sentence, cross-referencing in the light of the question. Compare the reliability or usefulness of the two sources in answering it.
- Judgement: decide which of the two sources provides the better evidence of 'criticisms of royal servants' and give convincing support for your decision. This may be based on usefulness, reliability, whether the view is typical, more complete, better informed, written at a significant date or some other relevant criterion.

The provenance (nature) of Source A is an official report of a slander being investigated by a Royal Commission, whereas Source D is a private letter, so the criticisms have different levels of authority. Source A is an investigation on behalf of King Henry VIII whereas Source D is from Elizabeth, Mary's heir, on behalf of herself and the rightful queen. The context is Northumberland's *coup* which recently placed Lady Jane Grey on the throne, ignoring the 1544 Act of Succession.

In the source content, both ministers are criticised for their ambition, and in both cases wealth is involved, but the criticism is politically far more serious in D and the criticism in Source A seems to arise from factional or personal jealousy. It portrays Cromwell as an upstart of low birth, whereas the tone of Source D is almost deferential in parts, 'a gentleman defending law and justice', though the purpose is to show in stark relief the 'scandalous acts he had committed' and therefore lose him popular support. In both cases, the writer of the source is someone acting on behalf of the Crown, but while Henry VIII seems to be supporting Cromwell by investigating criticism of him, Mary and Elizabeth are exposing Northumberland's treason. Both ministers were to lose power and be executed not long after these criticisms were made.

In your judgement you might view Source D as the better evidence for *criticisms of ministers*, as it is a genuine royal criticism of a traitorous minister, despite slightly selective contents. Although the inside knowledge of Henry's Court makes Source A valuable, the implication of slander makes its contents of dubious reliability.

(b) In order to answer this part of the question:

- The sources should be grouped by their point of view: sometimes a source contains more than one point for cross-reference.
- The significance for the question, of the views in the content of the sources, should be developed using accurate historical context and terminology.

- Relevant aspects of the provenance of the sources should be linked to answering the question. This 'provenance' might be authorship, date, nature, purpose, audience, tone.
- Accurate knowledge and terminology should be integrated into the answer to verify, qualify or evaluate the views in the sources as well as their provenance
- A judgement should be reached on the 'value' of the sources in linking to the interpretation in the question, where 'value' might be judged by:
  - reliability and/or usefulness of content and provenance
  - completeness of content or aspects deliberately ignored
  - limitations of the sources as a set.

Things to avoid:

- Do not use the sources as illustrations of an essay style answer.
- Do not merely *describe* or *paraphrase* source content, but always use it to argue.
- Do not use the sources as a mine for extracting *references*. Their purpose is to validate or qualify the interpretation in the question, enabling you to use them in effective argument.
- Do not make 'stock' comments about the provenance of sources, especially common with secondary authors, e.g. 'he is an eminent historian so we can trust his view'. Always link comments on provenance to the focus of the question.

Sources A–D suggest that royal ministers were personally ambitious, undermining good government. A and B refer to ministers squandering the royal income and serving their own glory, while Sources C and D refer to Somerset's and Northumberland's political ambitions. Content, provenance and context should be integrated to develop this idea and a judgement reached on how far Cromwell, Somerset and Northumberland undermined good government by serving their own self-interest. A judgement should be reached evaluating how far good government was undermined.

Sources A–C suggest factional rivalry among ministers, in Source A shown by the tone of ridicule of Cromwell, in Source B the charges of 'sowing sedition', and in Source C by the spitefulness of the report on Somerset. Content, provenance and context should be integrated to develop this idea. An example of good use of provenance in evaluating the reliability of Sources B and C might be to use the religious bias of Bourgoyne to Calvin in comparison with the more objective tone of Grafton's chronicle. Again, a judgement should be reached evaluating how far good government was undermined by factional jealousies among ministers.

On the other hand, Sources D and E suggest that sometimes ministers' actions produced good government. In Source D, Elizabeth concedes that Northumberland was perceived as a defender of law and justice and that she and Mary found it hard to believe he would plot to overthrow the succession. In Source E, Cecil is described as Elizabeth's 'trusty minister' and it was Elizabeth's hesitation which undermined good government, making Cecil offer to resign to force her to take necessary action. Content, provenance and context should be integrated to develop the idea. The likely evaluation here is that Source E suggests that good government depended to a large extent on Cecil at the start of Elizabeth's reign.

A judgement should be reached evaluating how far the sources support the interpretation overall. This is likely to reflect the reliability and use of the sources as well as changing historical context and the qualities of individual royal servants.

Final tips:

- The limitations of the set of sources should be supplied from relevant own knowledge, not merely suggested less appropriately, e.g. 'The sources would be more useful if they told us what Mary herself thought about Northumberland'. This comment adds little to the evaluation.
- The grouped sources should drive the answer, and an evaluative argument should be created by integrating context with source content and provenance.
- Marks are awarded for synthesis, bringing together all the elements of the answer. Therefore the final paragraph of conclusion is *very important* and will play an important part in gaining marks. It should bring together all the threads of the argument and judge how far the sources, as a set, support the interpretation in the question. If the sources are limited or unreliable, they will not support the interpretation effectively.

Study Guide: A2 Question

In the style of Edexcel

'Co-operation secured by skilful intervention.' How far do you agree with this view of Elizabeth's relationship with her parliaments in the years 1566–88? Explain your answer, using Sources 1–3 and your own knowledge of the issues related to this controversy.

Source 1

From: A.G.R. Smith, The Government of Elizabethan England, *published in 1967.*

Ordinary MPs regarded parliaments as occasions when they could discuss the great questions of the day, questions such as religion and the succession to the throne. The government's attitude was clearly very different. On only one occasion was parliament summoned to consider a major political issue: that was in 1586 when it was asked to discuss the position of Mary Queen of Scots. From the government's point of view, parliament was essentially an assembly for granting taxes and passing laws, with the emphasis on the former function. Subsidy bills and other important public enactments would, however, have passed less smoothly than they did if the government had not been very conscious of the need for effective management of the House of Commons.

Source 2

From: John McGurk, Tudor Monarchies 1485–1603, *published in 1999.*

Parliament met occasionally and for brief sessions at a time. The government's need for money largely explains why they were summoned at all. It can no longer be maintained that the queen and council members used crude electoral engineering to 'pack' parliaments. But there was a powerful nucleus of officials, and many MPs gained their seats from the patronage of peers and courtiers. The crown could normally rely on their support. The queen could interfere directly and sometimes did, especially when she considered a bill or a discussion to be a matter in her own prerogative, such as religion, her marriage and the succession. Her usual combination of tact and influence meant that she got her way. Elizabeth therefore controlled the workings of parliament by use of the royal veto, direct interventions to stay bills being discussed, and drastically the imprisonment of members. However some see in her speeches and messages to both Houses a charm and rapport that worked.

Source 3

From: M. Graves, Elizabethan Parliaments 1559–1601, *published in 1987.*

The Crown's removal or imprisonment of a member for an offence committed in the House was likely to provoke uproar. This happened when the Privy Council ordered William Strickland to say away during the 1571 session after he had introduced a bill to revise the book of common prayer contrary to the queen's command not to meddle in such matters. The case concerned two related problems: Elizabeth's novel restraints on what parliament might discuss and uncertainty about what she could legitimately do when someone breached those restraints. The Queen was compelled to back down and restore Strickland. Thereafter she prepared the ground more thoroughly: so Presbyterian agitators in 1586–7 were arrested for extra-parliamentary activities which were not covered by privilege.

Exam tips

This question provides you with sources that relate to Elizabeth's relationship with her parliaments. You should use them, together with your own knowledge, to discuss the statement. It is important that you treat questions of this type differently from the way you would plan an essay answer. If you ignore the sources, you will lose more than half the marks available. The sources raise issues for you. Make sure you have identified all the issues raised by the sources, and then add in your own knowledge – both to make more of the issues in the sources (add depth to the coverage) and to add new points (extend the range covered). In the advice given below, links are made to the relevant pages where information can be found. Two aspects of the statement require assessment: whether Elizabeth's relationship with her parliaments can be characterised as cooperative and whether that co-operation was secured by effective management.

The sources indicate that:

- management of parliament was directed at the limiting of discussion while, at the same time, securing co-operation since parliament was necessary for the passage of legislation and the granting of taxation (pages 67–8)
- tensions arose over parliament's freedom to discuss matters of religion, marriage and the succession (page 68)
- Elizabeth secured co-operation with the use of patronage and appointments to create a 'nucleus of support', and also by effective royal intervention and the use of charm (pages 67 and 72)
- there were some instances of confrontation when royal control was exercised, and Elizabeth in these cases was not always successful in securing co-operation (pages 68–9).

You should use your own knowledge, in combination with the sources, to explore these issues, particularly the reference in

Source 2 'it can no longer be maintained that the queen and council members used crude electoral engineering to "pack" parliaments'.

Your answer will be stronger if, when discussing these issues, you cross-refer between the sources rather than treating them singly. For example, in dealing with the nature of royal intervention you could note that while McGurk emphasises Elizabeth's tact and charm, Graves is examining an incident mishandled by Elizabeth. However they both acknowledge that she was prepared to imprison recalcitrant MPs. Graves notes 'thereafter she prepared the ground more thoroughly'. These incidents indicate royal control and discipline of members rather than co-operation and management. You should use your own knowledge to assess the extent to which these were the exception. You should reach an overall judgement on the extent to which parliament presented a challenge and the extent to which it was skilfully handled or effectively managed, using your knowledge of the period as well as the evidence of the sources.

3 Religious Change 1536–88

POINTS TO CONSIDER

This chapter examines the main religious changes during the reigns of Henry VIII, Edward VI, Mary and Elizabeth. A major point of debate is: 'Were most people still Catholic during this period or did they just conform to the religion of the monarch?' In order to understand and enter into this debate you will need to consider the following key points:

- What religious legacy did Henry VIII leave his successors?
- How successful were the reformers in introducing Protestant doctrines into the Church of England during the reign of Edward VI?
- Would Mary have succeeded in permanently returning England to the Church of Rome if she had lived long enough?
- Did Elizabeth's Religious Settlement succeed in firmly establishing the Protestant faith in England?

These issues are examined as six themes:

- Henry VIII's religious legacy 1536–47
- The Edwardian Church under Somerset 1547–9
- The Edwardian Church under Northumberland 1550–3
- The Marian Church 1553–8
- The Elizabethan Church and the Religious Settlement, 1558–88
- Was there a religious crisis?

Key dates

1534	November	Henry VIII became Head of the Church in England
1536	July	The Ten Articles introduced some Lutheran doctrines
1539	June	The Six Articles restored full Catholic doctrine
1547	November	Repeal of the Act of Six Articles
	December	Act for the Dissolution of the Chantries
1548	December	First Book of Common Prayer
1549	January	Act of Uniformity
1552	January	The Second Book of Common Prayer introduced some Calvinistic doctrines
	April	Second Act of Uniformity

1553	September	Catholic Mass re-introduced
1554	November	England and Rome reconciled
1555	October	Bishops Ridley and Latimer burnt at the stake
1556	March	Archbishop Cranmer burnt at the stake
1558	November	Death of Mary and Cardinal Pole. Elizabeth became queen
1559	May	Act of Supremacy restored Henrician anti-papal laws
		Act of Uniformity enforced the use of the Second Book of Common Prayer
1563		Thirty-Nine Articles set out Protestant beliefs
1570		Pope excommunicated Elizabeth

1 | Henry VIII's Religious Legacy 1536–47

In order to see the significance of the religious changes which took place after 1536 it is necessary to understand:

- The reasons why religion had become a political issue and the problems this caused for Henry VIII and his successors.
- The impact religious change had on foreign affairs after 1536.
- The doctrinal position in the Church of England at the death of Henry VIII.

Religion as a political issue

There is wide agreement that Henry VIII's motives in breaking away from Rome were much more political than religious. The English Reformation put the Church firmly under the control of the State. It also removed England from the authority of the Pope, a source of outside interference which was highly resented among the English ruling élites. The resulting Royal Supremacy made Henry VIII more independent and more powerful perhaps than any monarch in English history. It enabled him to rule an undivided kingdom where Church and State were merged into a single **sovereign State**. Henry VIII was able to reduce the political power of the Church and exploit its vast wealth. Church wealth replenished the Exchequer for a time, which had been almost bankrupted by Henry VIII's unsuccessful wars of the 1520s.

Somerset

On the surface, the Crown was the main beneficiary of the English Reformation. Yet, once religion had come to the forefront of politics, it created problems for the monarchy. Religious differences deepened the rift between political factions at Court. Henry VIII had to tread a cautious path between the conservative Catholic and reforming Protestant parties. By 1547 he had decided that the safest way to protect the succession and the Royal Supremacy was to give control of the Privy Council to Somerset and the reformers. However, the fall of Somerset in 1549 (see pages 51–2) triggered a renewed power struggle for

---

Key question
Why had religion become a political issue and what problems did this cause?

Key date
Henry VIII became Head of the Church in England: November 1534

Key term
Sovereign State
A country in which the monarch has supreme power over the State: government, law, the economy; and the Church: doctrine, appointments and property.

political power between the Catholic conservatives and the Protestant reformers. Some of the leading Catholic conservatives, principally the Earls of Southampton and Arundel, were able briefly to influence events in the Privy Council. However, once Northumberland had consolidated his position, they were expelled.

Northumberland

The power struggle between the conservatives and reformers resurfaced again in 1553 when Northumberland attempted to change the succession. Northumberland's action was prompted not only by personal ambition, but also by the desire to prevent the Catholic faction regaining power under Mary Tudor. Even so there was still a great deal of toleration and Catholic politicians were not excluded from government purely for religious reasons. Stephen Gardiner, the leading Catholic bishop, spent most of Edward VI's reign in prison, but this was largely because he refused to co-operate with the Privy Council. Unlike the hard-line Gardiner, a majority of the ruling élites favoured moderate reform.

Mary Tudor

When Mary Tudor came to power in 1553 there was no great purge of Protestant politicians. Indeed, men like Paget were given high office. It is true that Mary did not trust such men, but neither did she have great confidence in her English Catholic councillors. Given that among the ruling élites moderate reformers were in a majority, the fact that Mary came to the throne at all is a sign of the toleration in England. She was supported as the legitimate heir in spite of her religion. During her reign most politicians and civil servants were prepared to conform to her religious views. It was not her religion, but the ending of the Royal Supremacy and her marriage to Philip II of Spain that provoked most opposition.

Elizabeth I

When Elizabeth succeeded her sister she realised that the main danger areas were religion and faction. She inherited a kingdom divided and confused in its religion and in its politics. In order to avoid faction and religious tension Elizabeth moved quickly to settle both. There was no purge of Marian politicians, 11 of whom were appointed by Elizabeth to serve on her Privy Council. To these the new queen added seven new appointments to create a balanced Council of 18 members. Two of the most prominent casualties of the new reign were Sir William Paget and Mary's Lord Chancellor, Archbishop Heath, both of whom were sacked from the Council.

The doctrinal position in the Church of England during the 1530s and 1540s

From the time Henry had made himself Head of the English Church in 1534 he had been under pressure to formulate an acceptable doctrine. The reform party led by Cranmer had advocated the introduction of moderate Lutheran ideas. On the

Key question
What was the doctrinal position in the Church of England at the death of Henry VIII?

Key dates

The Ten Articles introduced some Lutheran doctrines: July 1536

The Six Articles restored full Catholic doctrine: June 1539

Key terms

Act of the Ten Articles
Passed in 1536, the Act was intended to promote Protestant religious ideas in England and Wales by stripping away many of the traditional festivals, relic-cults, shrines and parts of the Church service.

Consubstantiation
The belief that the sacramental bread and wine given by the priest to parishioners in church were a symbolic representation of the body and blood of Christ and therefore remained unchanged at communion.

Eucharist
The Christian Sacrament commemorating the Last Supper, in which bread and wine are consecrated and consumed.

other hand, the pro-Catholic, conservative faction led by Gardiner had favoured a policy of minimum change to the basic Catholic doctrines.

During the period 1534–46 royal favour swung between the two groups. The first major statement of doctrine, the **Act of the Ten Articles**, came in 1536. This Act was passed when the reformers were in the ascendancy. They introduced a number of Lutheran doctrines into the Church of England, for example belief in **consubstantiation**. Three years later the conservatives regained royal favour and the Act of the Six Articles (see page 47) was passed to remove many of the Lutheran beliefs. Such shifts of policy meant that by 1547 the doctrines of the Church of England were a compromise and contained many inconsistencies that were unacceptable to reformers and conservatives alike.

Catholic doctrines in the Church of England

When Henry VIII died the main articles of faith in the Church of England were in line with traditional Catholic orthodoxy:

- The **Eucharist** was clearly defined in the Catholic form of **transubstantiation**. The Lutheran form of consubstantiation was no longer accepted in the Church of England.
- Only the clergy were permitted to take communion in both the bread and the wine, while the laity were again restricted to taking only the sacramental bread.
- The Catholic rites of confirmation, marriage, holy orders and **extreme unction** had been reintroduced, alongside the previously recognised sacraments of the Eucharist, penance and baptism.
- The laity were still required to make regular confession of sins to a priest, and to seek **absolution** and penance.
- English clergy were no longer allowed to marry, and those who had married before 1540 had to send away their wives and families, or lose their livings.
- Although there was no specific statement on the existence of **Purgatory**, the need for the laity to do 'good works' for their salvation had been reinstated.
- The singing of masses for the souls of the dead was held to be 'agreeable also to God's Law'. It was for this reason that the chantries, where a priest sang masses for the souls of the founder and his family, were not closed down at the same time as the monasteries.
- Paintings and statues of the saints were still allowed in the churches, although the laity was instructed not to worship them.

Many of the processions and rituals of the Catholic Church were still practised, because it was maintained that they created a good religious frame of mind in those who witnessed them.

Protestant practices in the Church of England

Although the Church of England remained fundamentally Catholic in doctrine, it had adopted a number of Protestant practices by 1547:

- Services were still conducted in Latin, but Cranmer's prayers and responses of the **Litany** in English had been authorised in 1545.
- Greater importance was attached to the sermon, and the Lord's Prayer, the Creed and the Ten Commandments had to be taught in English rather than Latin by parents to their children and servants.
- Similarly the Great Bible of 1539 was the authorised English translation which replaced the Latin Vulgate Bible. Moreover, the élite laity was allowed to read the Great Bible in their own homes, unlike on the continent where often only the Catholic clergy were allowed to read and interpret the Bible.
- The practice of the Church of England with regard to some Catholic doctrines was ambiguous. Saints could be 'reverenced for their excellent virtue' and could be offered prayers, but the laity were forbidden to make pilgrimages to the shrines of saints or to offer them gifts, because it was maintained that grace, salvation and absolution of sins came only from God.
- At the same time, the number of Holy Days – days on which, like Sundays, the laity was expected to attend church and not to work – had been reduced to 25.
- Finally, in sharp contrast to Catholic countries, there had been no monasteries in England since 1540. They had been closed by royal order and their possessions had been transferred to the Crown.

Attempts between 1534 and 1546 to establish a uniform set of articles of faith for the Church of England had succeeded only in producing a patchwork of doctrines that often conflicted. Until 1547 this ramshackle structure was held together by the Henrician treason and heresy laws. Anyone breaking, or even questioning, the statutes and proclamations defining the doctrines of the Church of England was liable to confiscation of property, fines, imprisonment or execution. Similarly the censorship laws prevented the printing, publishing, or importation of books and pamphlets expressing views contrary to the doctrines of the Church of England.

Key terms

Transubstantiation
The belief that, at the moment of consecration the bread and wine change in substance, though not in appearance, into the actual body and blood of Christ.

Extreme unction
The act of being anointed with oils as part of a religious rite or ceremony.

Absolution
Forgiven for committing a sin.

Purgatory
A place between heaven and hell.

Litany
Recital of religious teachings contained in the Book of Common Prayer.

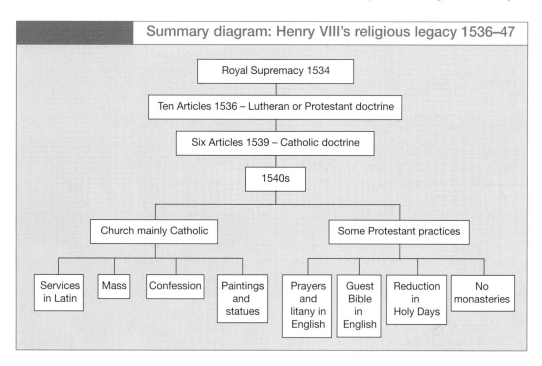

Summary diagram: Henry VIII's religious legacy 1536–47

Royal Supremacy 1534

Ten Articles 1536 – Lutheran or Protestant doctrine

Six Articles 1539 – Catholic doctrine

1540s

Church mainly Catholic

Some Protestant practices

Services in Latin

Mass

Confession

Paintings and statues

Prayers and litany in English

Guest Bible in English

Reduction in Holy Days

No monasteries

2 | The Edwardian Church under Somerset 1547–9

The accession of Edward VI, who had been educated as a Protestant, roused the hopes of English reformers that there would be a swing towards more Lutheran, and possibly Calvinist, doctrines. Somerset's appointment as Lord Protector in 1547 established the reform party firmly in power, as intended under the terms of Henry VIII's will (see pages 39–40).

Attitudes towards reform
The immediate government circle

Key question
Why was the new regime so cautious about introducing religious reform?

Somerset was a moderate Protestant, but although he was devout, he had no real interest in theology. He was religiously tolerant, and favoured a cautious approach towards reform. Although he is reputed to have had Calvinistic leanings, and, certainly, exchanged letters with John Calvin, there is little evidence of such influences affecting him when he was in power. The reformers were in the majority in the Privy Council.

Among the bishops, there was little agreement. Although the majority of them fully supported the Royal Supremacy and the separation from Rome, they remained hopelessly divided on the issue of religious reform:

- Nine bishops led by Archbishop Thomas Cranmer and Nicholas Ridley, Bishop of Rochester, supported reform.
- Ten bishops led by Stephen Gardiner, Bishop of Winchester, and Edmund Bonner, Bishop of London, opposed change.
- Eight bishops were undecided.

The death-bed of Henry VIII together with Edward VI and the Pope c1548. What were the probable aims of the artist in painting this picture? How reliable is this painting as a source of information about what happened at meetings of the Privy Council under Somerset?

With such an even balance of opinion among the bishops, Somerset and the Privy Council moved very cautiously on matters of religious reform.

Outside the immediate government circle

The attitudes towards reform outside the immediate government circle are more difficult to assess:

- A majority of the ruling élites seem to have been in favour of (or at least, not opposed to) some measure of religious reform.
- In general, however, the lower clergy were opposed to religious change. This, it has been suggested, was largely because the English parish clergy were still relatively uneducated, and were anxious to maintain their traditional way of life without any complications.
- The same was true for the great mass of the population, who were very conservative in their outlook. Moreover, as far as they were concerned, both their popular culture, which was based on rituals and festivals associated with the farming year, and their belief in magic and witchcraft, all formed part of the ceremonies of the old Church.

Yet there were exceptions:

- In East Anglia, because of the settlement of large numbers of Protestant refugees from the continent, there was considerable support for religious reform.
- In London and the larger towns, where clergy were better educated, there were very vocal minorities demanding more rapid, and more radical, religious change.

The introduction of some reform

Key question
Why did the Privy Council introduce some moderate Protestant reforms?

In these circumstances the Privy Council decided to review the state of the Church of England, and to introduce some moderate Protestant reforms. Such a policy was opposed by the conservatives, prompted by Gardiner, who maintained that under the terms of Henry VIII's will, no religious changes could be made until Edward VI came of age at 18. In spite of Gardiner's vigorous opposition, royal commissioners were sent to visit all the bishops. They were instructed to compile a report by the autumn of 1547 on the state of the clergy and the doctrines and practices to be found in every **diocese**. To help the spread of Protestant ideas, every parish was ordered to obtain a copy of Cranmer's *Book of Homilies*, and *Paraphrases* by Erasmus.

In July an **injunction** was issued to the bishops ordering them to instruct their clergy to conduct services in English, and to preach a sermon every Sunday. Furthermore, the bishops were to create libraries of Protestant literature and provide an English Bible for each parish, and to encourage the laity to read these books. Finally the bishops were told to remove all superstitious statues and images from their churches.

These modest moves towards religious reform did not satisfy the more vocal Protestant activists. The amount of anti-Catholic protest was increased by the presence of Protestant exiles who had returned from the continent after the death of Henry VIII. The problem for the Privy Council was that, while it did not wish to introduce reforms too quickly for fear of provoking a Catholic backlash, it was anxious not to prevent religious debate by taking repressive measures. As a result, the Henrician treason, heresy and censorship laws were not enforced and a vigorous debate over religion developed.

Radical reformers

The more radical reformers launched a strong attack through a pamphlet campaign on both the Catholic Church and the bishops, who were accused of being self-seeking royal servants and not true pastors. Other pamphlets attacked the wealth of the Church, superstitious rituals, and in particular the Eucharist. However, there was no agreement among the protesters about the form of Protestant doctrine that should be adopted. With the government refusing to take any firm lead there was growing frustration, and some of the more radical protesters took matters into their own hands.

Key terms

Diocese
A district under the pastoral care of a bishop.

Book of Homilies
A book containing a list of sermons and other religious tracts for use in daily worship.

Paraphrases
A book containing a list of religious phrases, meanings and explanations for use in daily worship.

Injunction
A law or decree issued by the Crown to compel the clergy in the Church of England to follow a particular order or practice.

In London, East Anglia, Essex and Lincolnshire, where large numbers of Protestant refugees from the continent were settling, riots broke out. These frequently included outbreaks of **iconoclasm**, in which stained glass windows, statues, and other superstitious images were destroyed. In some cases gold and silver candlesticks and other Church goods were seized and sold, with the money being donated to the poor. Such incidents were often provoked by extreme **millenarianists**, who wished to see a more equal society and a redistribution of wealth to the poor. Although the Privy Council was alarmed by the violence, it refused to take any action against the demonstrators. This inaction enraged the more conservative bishops. Bishop Bonner was particularly vehement in his protests to the government, and was imprisoned for two months.

> **Key date**
> Act for the Dissolution of the Chantries: December 1547

Problems over reform

When parliament and **Convocation** were summoned in November 1547, the question of religious reform was freely discussed. Both assemblies were in favour of reform, and Convocation agreed to reintroduce clerical marriage, although this was not approved by parliament and so did not become law. Yet the Privy Council was still reluctant to make any decisive move towards religious reform. The reason for this was that the new regime still felt insecure, fearing that any major changes to doctrine might provoke even more unrest and possibly lead to the fall of the government.

The two major pieces of legislation, the Chantries Act and the Treason Act, did little to resolve the doctrinal uncertainties:

- The Chantries Act. The main purpose of the Act was to raise money to continue the war with France and Scotland; the reason given was that the chantries were centres of superstition.
- The Treason Act. The Act repealed the Henrician treason, heresy and censorship laws (see pages 48–9). This measure increased the freedom with which the Protestant activists could discuss and demand radical doctrinal reforms. The immediate result was a renewed spate of pamphlets demanding that the Bible should be recognised as the only true authority for religious belief. English translations of the writings of Luther and Calvin were being widely circulated.

In January 1548 the Privy Council issued a series of proclamations to try to calm the situation. However, the proclamations indicated no clear policy, and so only added to the confusion. Justices of the Peace and churchwardens were ordered to enforce the existing doctrines of the Church of England, including transubstantiation. On the other hand, instructions were issued to speed up the removal of Catholic images from churches. Such contradictions infuriated both reformers and conservatives alike. Finally, in September, the Council forbade all public preaching in the hope of stifling debate.

> **Key question**
> Why was there indecision and confusion over religious reform?

> **Key terms**
>
> **Iconoclasm**
> The act of breaking, destroying or defacing religious images such as wall paintings or stained glass, and statues like those depicting Christ and the Virgin Mary.
>
> **Millenarianists**
> Radical thinkers who believed in social reform whereby a kingdom's wealth would be distributed equally to all citizens.
>
> **Convocation**
> An assembly of clergy that discussed Church matters, passed Church laws and regulated the way the Church was run.

Key question
Why was there a more positive move for religious reform after 1548?

Key dates

First Book of Common Prayer: December 1548

Act of Uniformity: January 1549

Moves towards introducing Protestant doctrine

When parliament reassembled in November 1548, Somerset and the Council were in a stronger position after the successful campaign in Scotland (see page 47). For this reason they felt secure enough to take a more positive approach to religious reform. Their objective was to end the uncertainty over religious doctrine. It was hoped that the new law, known as the First Edwardian Act of Uniformity, passed in January 1549, would achieve this.

Protestant practices

The Act officially ordered all the clergy of England and Wales to use a number of Protestant practices which had been allowed, but not enforced, during the two previous years:

- Holy communion, matins and evensong were to be conducted in English.
- The sacraments were now defined as communion, baptism, confirmation, marriage and burial.
- Cranmer adapted the old communion service by adding new prayers, so that the clergy and the laity could take both the sacramental bread and the wine.
- Permission was given once again for the clergy to marry.
- Many of the traditional Catholic rituals, which the Protestant reformers considered to be superstitious, disappeared. The practice of singing masses for the souls of the dead was no longer approved.

Catholic practices

- There was still no really clear statement on the existence, or otherwise, of Purgatory.
- Any form of the worship of saints, although not banned, was to be discouraged, while the removal of statues, paintings and other images was encouraged.
- Cranmer's Book of Common Prayer was a mixture of Lutheran and Catholic beliefs.
- Fast days were still to be enforced and no change was to be made to the number of Holy Days.
- The new communion service followed the order of the old Latin Mass, and the officiating clergy were expected to continue to wear the traditional robes and vestments.
- Most importantly, no change was made to the doctrine of the Eucharist, which was still defined in the Catholic terms of transubstantiation. This was a fundamental point that angered many of the more radical reformers, who continued to urge the government to adopt a more Protestant definition of the sacrament of communion.

The Privy Council hoped that these cautious measures would satisfy the majority of moderate reformers, without outraging the Catholic conservatives. Although any clergy who refused to use the new service were to be liable to fines and imprisonment, no penalties were to be imposed on the laity for non-attendance. This can be interpreted as a hope by the Privy Council that they could coerce the more recalcitrant minority among the parish clergy, while not antagonising the undecided majority among the laity.

The government decided to continue with its policy of educating the laity in Protestant ideas which it had introduced in July 1547. Bishops were instructed to carry out visitations to encourage the adoption of the new services, and to test whether parishioners could recite the Lord's Prayer and the Ten Commandments in English. The effectiveness of either the legislation, or the education programme, depended on whether the bishops and ruling élites would enforce them. There was opposition in Cornwall, Devon, Dorset and Yorkshire. However, most of the country seems to have followed the lead of the aristocracy and gentry in accepting moderate Protestantism.

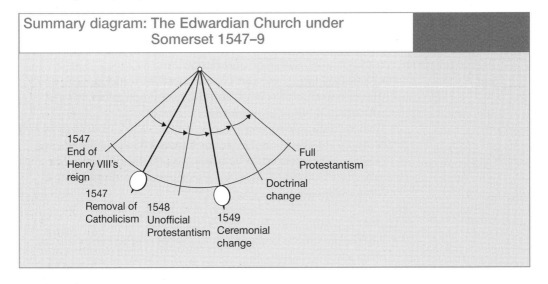

Summary diagram: The Edwardian Church under Somerset 1547–9

3 | The Edwardian Church under Northumberland 1550–3

Key question
How Protestant had the Edwardian Church become under Northumberland?

When Northumberland gained power in 1550 religious reform became more radical. This might suggest that the government thought there was no widespread opposition to religious change, or that they believed the recent suppression of the popular uprisings (see pages 134–40) was sufficient to prevent any further unrest. Possibly, as is thought by many historians, the changes came about because of the political in-fighting in the Privy Council that led to Somerset's fall from power. What is certain is that by 1553 the Church of England had become Protestant.

Struggle over doctrine

Key question
Why was there a doctrinal power struggle between 1550 and 1553?

After the arrest of Somerset in October 1549 it appeared that the conservative faction supported by Northumberland might seize power. They planned, with the help of Charles V, to make Princess Mary regent for the young Edward VI. However, neither

Charles V nor Mary supported the scheme which, in any case, would not have been practical in view of Edward VI's support for Protestantism. Meanwhile, Northumberland, having used the conservatives to strengthen his position on the Privy Council, then switched his allegiance to the more radical Protestant reformers. This political struggle within the Privy Council continued when parliament met in November. Attempts by the conservative faction to repeal the 1549 Act of Uniformity and strengthen the power of the bishops were defeated. In December parliament approved measures to speed up the removal of popish images and old service books from the churches, and set up a commission to revise the procedures for the **ordination** of priests.

By February 1550 Northumberland was firmly in control of the Privy Council, and the conservatives were driven out of office (see page 54). To strengthen his position still further and to prevent a possible conservative backlash, Northumberland moved against the more conservative of the bishops:

- Gardiner, the most able of the pro-Catholics, was already imprisoned in the Tower of London. In July he was ordered by the Privy Council to agree to the doctrines of the Church of England. He refused, and was sentenced to stricter terms of confinement.
- Bishop Bonner of London, already imprisoned by Somerset, was retried and deprived of his diocese. He was replaced by Ridley, then Bishop of Rochester, who was an enthusiastic reformer.

During the next year active reformers were appointed as bishops of Rochester, Chichester, Norwich, Exeter and Durham. These changes cleared the way for more sweeping religious reforms. The Catholic laity and clergy, deprived of their main spiritual leaders, offered little opposition, although some pro-Catholic pamphlets were circulated.

In view of his reconversion to Catholicism before his execution in 1553, many historians do not think it likely that Northumberland was a genuine religious reformer. Other historians feel that his support for such a Protestant enthusiast as John Hooper as opposed to the more moderate Cranmer and Nicholas Ridley, the newly appointed Bishop of London, in the doctrinal dispute during the autumn of 1550 does show that he was interested in religious reform. This is a question that, without fresh evidence, is unlikely to be resolved. Certainly the first moves towards introducing more radical Protestantism seem to have arisen from the political expediencies following Somerset's fall from power.

Key term

Ordination
Ceremony in which holy orders were conferred on priests enabling them to serve in parishes.

More extreme Protestantism

Key question
Why was there a swing towards radical Protestantism?

The first move to introduce more radical Protestantism was initiated by Ridley in London, where he ordered all altars to be removed and replaced by communion tables in line with the teachings of the Calvinists and other reformed Churches. In other dioceses the destruction of altars proceeded unevenly, and depended on the attitudes of the local ruling élites and clergy. At the same time the Parliamentary Commission's proposals to change the form of the ordination of priests were introduced, and instructions were issued to enforce the first Act of Uniformity (see page 93).

The new form of ordination, which was basically Lutheran, soon caused controversy. The major change – which empowered priests to administer the sacraments and preach the gospel instead of offering 'sacrifice and [the celebration of] mass both for the living and the dead' – satisfied moderate reformers. It removed the supposedly superstitious references to sacrifice, Purgatory and prayers for the souls of the dead. However, it did not please some of the more extreme reformers, especially because it made no attempt to remove any of the 16 ceremonial vestments, such as the mitre, cope, tippet or stole, normally worn by bishops and priests while conducting services. These were regarded as superstitious by many of the reformed Churches, whose clergy wore plain surplices.

The figure shows the differences between a Catholic and Protestant Church service. How effective is this modern illustration in highlighting the differences between the two faiths?

John Hooper, who had been invited to become Bishop of Gloucester, complained that the form of ordination was still too Catholic and started a fierce dispute with Ridley over the question of vestments. As a result he refused the offered bishopric, and in July he began a campaign of preaching against the new proposals. At first it appeared that Northumberland was sympathetic and supported Hooper, but in October he was ordered to stop preaching, and in January 1551 he was imprisoned for failing to comply. Finally he was persuaded to compromise and was made Bishop of Gloucester, where he introduced a vigorous policy of education and reform. But he complained that both laity and clergy were slow to respond.

Measures to make the Church of England fully Protestant

During 1551 Northumberland strengthened his position. This cleared the way for a major overhaul of the Church of England. Cranmer was in the process of revising his Prayer Book, to remove the many ambiguities that had caused criticism. Further action was taken against the remaining conservative bishops. Gardiner was finally deprived of the diocese of Winchester in February, and in October reformers were appointed at Worcester and Chichester. These moves ensured that there would be a majority among the bishops to support the programme of religious changes that was being prepared.

Doctrinal changes

Parliament was assembled in January 1552 and the government embarked upon a comprehensive programme of reform. In order to strengthen the power of the Church of England to enforce doctrinal uniformity, a new Treason Act was passed. This made it an offence to question the Royal Supremacy or any of the articles of faith of the English Church. At the same time, uncertainties over the number of Holy Days to be recognised was ended by officially limiting them to 25.

In March the second Act of Uniformity was passed. Under the new Act it became an offence for both clergy and laity not to attend Church of England services, and offenders were to be fined and imprisoned. Cranmer's new Book of Common Prayer became the official basis for church services, and had to be used by both clergy and laity. The new prayer book was based upon the scriptures, and all traces of Catholicism and the Mass had been removed. The Eucharist was clearly defined in terms of consubstantiation (see page 87), although there are some suggestions that Cranmer was moving towards a more **Zwinglian** or Calvinistic definition of the Eucharist as commemorative of Christ's sacrifice or the Last Supper.

Extreme reformers did not approve of the new service because communicants were still expected to kneel, and this was considered to be idolatrous. Some historians attribute such objections to the Calvinism of Hooper and another extreme reformer, John Knox, the leader of Scottish Protestantism. It is

Key question
What measures were introduced?

Key dates

The Second Book of Common Prayer introduced some Calvinistic doctrines: January 1552

Second Act of Uniformity: April 1552

Key term

Zwinglian
Huldrych Zwingli was a Swiss Protestant religious reformer who believed that local religious communities should have the right to control their own affairs without interference from either the Church authorities or State officials.

also suggested that the influence of Hooper and Knox was behind the instructions sent to bishops to speed up the replacement of altars by communion tables, and to stop their clergy from wearing vestments when conducting services.

Further attacks on the wealth of the Church

While these measures were being introduced, the government began a further attack on Church wealth. In 1552 a survey of the **temporal wealth** of the bishops and all clergy with parishes worth more than £350 a year was undertaken. The resultant report estimated that these lands had a capital value of £1,087,000, and steps were taken to transfer some of this property to the Crown.

> **Temporal wealth** Church wealth that is calculated in land, property and goods.
>
> **Key term**

The bishopric of Durham provides a typical example of this secularisation. Bishop Tunstall of Durham was arrested in October 1552 and imprisoned in the Tower of London. It was then proposed that his diocese should be divided into two parts. Durham itself was to be allocated £1320 annually, and a new diocese of Newcastle was to be given an annual income of £665. This left an annual surplus of £2000 from the income of the original diocese, which was to be transferred to the Crown. In the event, this proposal did not come into effect because of the death of Edward VI.

At the same time, commissioners had been sent out to draw up inventories and to begin the removal of all the gold and silver plate still held by parish churches, and to list any items illegally removed since 1547. The commissioners had only just begun their work of confiscation when the king died and the operation was brought to an end, but not before some churches had lost their medieval plate.

Historical opinion

- Some historians have seen the attack on Church wealth as yet another example of the greed of Northumberland.
- Others maintain that it was necessary if the Church of England was to be thoroughly reformed.
- Recently these actions have been interpreted as an expedient to improve royal finances after the bankruptcy resulting from the wars against France and Scotland.
- To Marxist historians it is clear evidence of the growing commercialism of the aristocracy and gentry, who were pressurising the government for a further redistribution of ecclesiastical wealth.
- Yet another explanation is that it was a political move to strengthen the control of the Church by the State.

Without fresh evidence and research it is difficult to decide which one, or whichever combination of these explanations, is nearest the truth.

Key question
How Protestant was the Edwardian church by the time of Edward VI's death in 1553?

Key term

Forty-Two Articles A list of essential doctrines drawn up by Cranmer and intended to form the basis of the new Protestant Church of England.

Assessment of the Edwardian Church

What is certain is that the death of Edward VI and the fall of Northumberland brought this part of the English Reformation to an abrupt end. The **Forty-Two Articles** that had been drawn up to list the doctrines of the new Protestant Church of England never became law. It is generally agreed that by 1553 the Edwardian Reformation had resulted in a Church of England that was thoroughly Protestant. There is less agreement over whether its doctrines were basically Lutheran, or to what extent they were influenced by Zwinglian or Calvinist ideas.

However, it is clear that, although the doctrines of the Church of England had been revolutionised, the administrative structure of the Church had remained unchanged. There is equal agreement that there is insufficient evidence at present to decide whether the people of England had wholeheartedly embraced the Protestant religion. Research at a local level has so far provided conflicting evidence. Although a majority of the landed élites and

Contemporary illustration showing Catholics being banished from England. Why did the government believe it necessary to exile some Catholics?

Profile: Thomas Cranmer 1489–1556

1489	– Born in Nottinghamshire, the younger son of a lesser gentry family
1520s	– Studied at Cambridge University where he joined the 'White Horse' group to discuss the new ideas coming from Europe such as Lutheranism
1526	– Became a doctor of divinity
c1529	– Became chaplain to Thomas Boleyn, Earl of Wiltshire, father of Anne. Supported the case for Henry VIII's divorce
1530	– Appointed ambassador to Charles V (1530–3)
c1532	– Secretly married the niece of the Lutheran church leader of Nuremberg in Germany
1533	– Chosen by Henry VIII to succeed William Warham as Archbishop of Canterbury
1533–4	– Presided over Henry VIII's divorce from Catherine of Aragon, promoted the marriage with Anne Boleyn and declared Henry VIII Head of the Church in England
1536	– Presided over Henry VIII's divorce from Anne Boleyn, promoted marriage with Jane Seymour
1536–8	– Worked with Cromwell in government and in turning England towards Protestantism, e.g. responsible for the 'Bishops' Book' of 1537
1539	– Unsuccessfully opposed the conservative Act of Six Articles. Forced to separate from his wife but refused to resign his offices
1540	– Took no part in the destruction of Cromwell
1541–7	– Became leader of reformist party at Court. Henry VIII's support enabled him to survive conservative attempts to destroy him
1547	– Took leading part in the Edwardian regime both in government and in the Church. Issued Protestant Book of Homilies (see page 91)
1549	– Issued the blandly reformist First Book of Common Prayer
1552	– Issued the more extreme Second Book of Common Prayer
1553	– Stripped of his title as Archbishop of Canterbury
1554	– Arrested and imprisoned for heresy
1556	– Burnt at the stake when he withdrew an earlier promise to accept some key Catholic doctrines

Arguably, Cranmer played a greater role than any other single churchman in establishing and shaping the Church of England. He was fiercely loyal to the Crown and he proved to be an able government minister and churchman. His greatest strength lay in his refusal to support religious extremism; he was willing to accept gradual change in the Church, advocated toleration and preached against persecution.

those in government circles seemed to favour moderate Protestantism, only a few of them found it impossible to conform under Mary I.

Many of the lower clergy and a majority of the population seem to have been largely indifferent to the religious debate. Only in London and the surrounding counties does there appear to have been any widespread enthusiasm for the Protestant religion. A study of the county of Essex indicates more enthusiasm among the authorities in enforcing Protestantism than among the general public in accepting it. Earlier interpretations which indicated wild enthusiasm for either Protestantism or Catholicism are now treated with caution. It is considered that Protestantism, if not widely opposed, received only lukewarm acceptance.

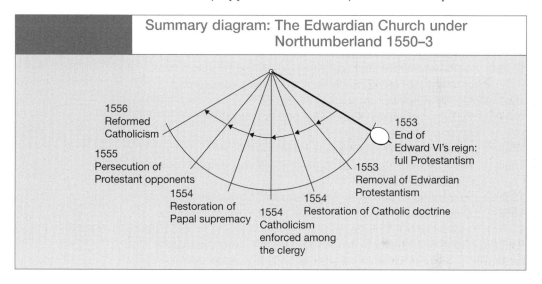

Summary diagram: The Edwardian Church under Northumberland 1550–3

4 | The Marian Church 1553–8

While it is difficult to assess Northumberland's religious views, there is no doubt about those of Mary I. Some historians have described Mary as courageous, gentle and sympathetic. Others see her as being proud, arrogant and stupid. These views have not been greatly altered by recent research. However, it is agreed that she was passionately attached to the Roman Catholic religion.

The religious situation in 1553

Key question
What was the religious situation in 1553?

In 1553 few in England doubted that Mary, after her 20 years of resistance to the Royal Supremacy for the sake of her religion, would restore Roman Catholicism. It was just as much Edward VI's wish to preserve Protestantism, as Northumberland's personal ambition, that led to the attempt to exclude Mary from the throne. Mary and her Catholic supporters saw the failure of the scheme as a miracle, and she was determined to restore England to the authority of Rome as quickly as possible. What Mary failed to realise was that her initial popularity sprang, not

Profile: Reginald Pole 1500–58

1500 – Born a younger son of Sir Richard Pole and Margaret, Countess of Salisbury

1515 – Educated at Oxford University where he received his degree in divinity

1521 – Went to study on the continent (1521–7)

1527 – Became Dean of Exeter Cathedral

1529 – Went to study in Paris (1529–30)

1530 – Became Dean of Windsor but refused the king's offer of the Archbishopric of York

1531 – Opposed king's divorce policy

1532 – Went abroad to study

1536 – Criticised in print Henry VIII's supremacy of the Church in England

1537 – Summoned to Rome by the Pope who made him a cardinal and Papal Legate to England

1538 – A furious Henry VIII had his mother and brother arrested and charged with treason. Brother executed

1541 – His 68-year-old mother was executed

1547 – Failed to persuade Somerset to return England to Roman Church

1549 – Narrowly failed to get elected as Pope

1554 – Returned to England as Papal Legate and helped restore the Church to Rome

1555 – Succeeded Cranmer as Archbishop of Canterbury

1558 – Died same day as Mary I

Pole was a dedicated Catholic who risked his life, and the lives of his family, to oppose Henry VIII's break with Rome. He spent most of his life abroad and was out of touch with the feelings and attitudes of his compatriots when he returned in 1554. His impact on English religious thinking was limited and he failed to turn the clock back to the 1520s. The restoration of the Pope as head of the English Church lasted only three years and did not survive Pole's death. His greatest achievement was to maintain an English presence at the Papal Court.

from a desire for a return to the Roman Catholic Church, but from a dislike of Northumberland, and respect for the legitimate succession.

Her main supporters in England and abroad urged caution. Both Charles V and Pope Julius III warned her not to risk her throne by acting too rashly. Cardinal Reginald Pole, appointed as Papal Legate to restore England to the authority of Rome, stayed in the Netherlands for a year before coming to England. Whether this was because Charles V refused to allow the Cardinal to leave until the planned marriage between Philip and Mary had come to fruition, or whether it reflected Pole's natural caution about returning to his native land and a possibly hostile reception, is difficult to decide. Even Gardiner, Mary's most trusted English adviser, who had consistently resisted reform, was unenthusiastic about returning to papal authority.

Mary failed to appreciate the political implications of restoring Roman Catholicism to England. A return to papal authority would mean an end to the Royal Supremacy, which was strongly supported by the ruling and landed élites. Even the most ardent of the leading conservatives had been firm in their allegiance to the Crown and the Tudor State. It is agreed that the major causes of Mary's widespread unpopularity by the end of her reign, apart from the religious persecution, were the return to papal authority and the Spanish marriage. Many regarded this as interference by foreigners and an affront to English nationalism.

The restoration of Anglo-Catholicism

Key question
How successful was Mary's planned return to the Anglo-Catholicism of her father's reign?

In 1553 there was no doubt about Mary's popularity and the élites rallied to her support. The aristocracy and gentry were initially prepared to conform to Mary's religious views, and the bulk of the population followed their example. But some 800 strongly committed Protestant gentry, clergy and members of the middle orders left the country and spent the remainder of the reign on the continent. Such an escape was less easy for the lower orders, and most of the 274 Protestants executed during Mary's reign came from this group. At the beginning of the reign even the most zealous of the urban radicals were not prepared to go against the mainstream of public opinion, and waited to see what would happen. Certainly, when Mary, using the royal prerogative, suspended the second Act of Uniformity and restored the Mass, there was no public outcry.

Key date
Catholic Mass reintroduced: September 1553

Parliament

This lack of religious opposition was apparent when parliament met in October 1553. Admittedly, the arrest and imprisonment of Cranmer, Hooper and Ridley, along with other leading Protestant bishops, removed the major source of opposition in the House of Lords. After a lively, but not hostile debate, the first step towards removing all traces of Protestantism from the Church of England was achieved with the passing of the first Statute of Repeal. This Act swept away all the religious legislation approved by parliament during the reign of Edward VI, and the doctrine of the Church of England was restored to what it had been in 1547 under the Act of the Six Articles (see page 47).

Although Mary had succeeded in re-establishing the Anglo-Catholicism of her father, her advisers had managed to persuade her into some caution. There had been no attempt to question the Royal Supremacy, or to discuss the issue of the Church lands which had been sold to the laity. Both these issues were likely to provoke a more heated debate.

Marriage to Philip II

Opposition to Mary's proposed marriage to Philip II of Spain and the consequent rebellion (see pages 142–6) meant that further religious legislation was postponed until the spring of 1554. Gardiner, anxious to regain royal favour after his opposition to Mary's marriage (see pages 61–2), tried to quicken the pace at which Protestantism was removed by persuading parliament to pass a bill to reintroduce the heresy laws. He was successfully opposed by Paget, who feared that such a measure might provoke further disorder.

The Protestant clergy

Thwarted, Gardiner proceeded to turn his attention to Protestant clergy. The Bishops of Gloucester, Hereford, Lincoln, Rochester and the Archbishop of York were stripped of their offices, and were replaced by committed Catholics. In March 1554 the bishops were instructed to enforce all the religious legislation of the last year of Henry VIII's reign. Apart from ensuring a return to 'the old order of the Church, in the Latin tongue', these injunctions demanded that all married clergy should give up their wives and families, or lose their livings. The authorities largely complied with these instructions, and some 800 parish clergy were so deprived. Although some fled abroad, such as Richard Davies, vicar of Burnham in Buckinghamshire, the majority were found employment elsewhere in the country.

Return to the Church of Rome

Cardinal Pole's return to England in November 1554 marked the next decisive stage in the restoration of Roman Catholicism. Parliament met in the same month and passed the second Act of Repeal. This Act ended the Royal Supremacy, and returned England to papal authority by repealing all the religious legislation of the reign of Henry VIII back to the time of the break with Rome. However, to achieve this Mary had to come to a compromise with the landed élites. Careful provision was made in the Act to protect the property rights of all those who had bought Church land since 1536. This demonstrates that Mary had to recognise the authority of parliament over matters of religion. It meant that she had to forgo her plans for a full-scale restoration of the monasteries. Instead she had to be content with merely returning the monastic lands, worth £60,000 a year, still held by the Crown.

Key question
How did Mary restore Roman Catholicism to England and Wales?

England and Rome reconciled: November 1554

Key date

Religious persecution

At the same time, parliament approved the restoration of the old heresy laws. This was the beginning of religious persecution:

- The first Protestant was burnt at the stake for heresy on 4 February 1555, and Hooper suffered a similar fate five days later in his own city of Gloucester.

Key dates

Bishops Ridley and Latimer burnt at the stake: October 1555

Archbishop Cranmer burnt at the stake: March 1556

- In October, Ridley and Hugh Latimer, the former Bishop of Worcester, were executed at Oxford, where they were followed by Cranmer in March 1556.

The death of Gardiner in November 1555 had removed a trusted and restraining influence, and thereafter the regime became more repressive. Although Gardiner had started the persecution on the grounds that some executions would frighten the Protestant extremists into submission, he was too astute a politician to fail to see that the policy was not working. Far from cowing the Protestants, he realised that the executions were hardening the opposition to Mary and encouraging the colonies of English exiles on the continent. He counselled caution, but his advice was ignored.

After his death, Mary, and Pole, who had been made Archbishop of Canterbury in December 1555, felt that it was their sacred duty to stamp out heresy, and stepped up the level of persecution. It is now estimated that the 274 religious executions carried out during the last three years of Mary's reign exceeded the number recorded in any Catholic country on the continent over the same period. This undermines the claim by some historians that the Marian regime was more moderate than those on the continent.

Popular reactions against religious persecution

Gardiner's unheeded warnings were soon justified, and Mary's popularity waned rapidly. There was widespread revulsion in the south-east of England at the persecution, and to many people Catholicism became firmly linked with dislike of Rome and Spain.

The Martyrdom of Cranmer and the burning of bishops Ridley and Latimer (1556), from John Fox's *Book of Martyrs* (published in 1563). How are Cranmer, Ridley and Latimer depicted in the illustration? In your opinion was Fox a Catholic or a Protestant author?

Many local authorities either ignored, or tried to avoid enforcing, the unpopular legislation.

The number of people fleeing abroad increased, reinforcing the groups of English exiles living in centres of Lutheranism and Calvinism on the continent. They became the nucleus of an active and well-informed opposition, which began to flood England with anti-Catholic books and pamphlets. The effectiveness of this campaign is shown in the proclamations issued by the Privy Council in 1558, ordering the death penalty by martial law for anyone found with heretical or seditious literature. If before 1555 the English people were generally undecided about religion, the Marian repression succeeded in creating a core of highly committed English Protestants.

Attempts to consolidate the Marian Church
Restoring stability

Key question
How successful were the measures to strengthen the Marian Church and eradicate Protestantism?

Although Pole actively tried to eradicate Protestantism, his first priority appears to have been to restore stability after 20 years of religious turmoil. It is widely considered that, in view of his lack of administrative experience and ability, such a formal and legalistic approach was a mistake. The reduction in Church revenues meant that there were insufficient resources available to reorganise the Marian Church effectively. Indeed, a great part of Pole's three years in office were spent in the virtually hopeless task of trying to restore the Church of England's financial position.

Reconciliation with Rome

Pole's attempts to reorganise and reconcile the Church of England to Rome were not helped by the death of Pope Julius III in 1555. The new Pope, Paul IV, disliked Pole and hated the Spanish Habsburgs. He stripped Pole of his title of Legate and ordered him to return to Rome. Pole refused to comply, and continued his work in England as Archbishop of Canterbury, but the Papacy would not recognise his authority. This further hindered his work because he could not appoint bishops, and by 1558 seven sees were vacant. Such quarrels, and the blatant papal intervention in English affairs, did little to convince anyone except the most zealous Catholics of the wisdom of returning to the authority of Rome.

Certainly, such events did not help the government in its task of winning the hearts and minds of English men and women to the Roman Catholic faith. Pole hoped that, while he struggled with his administrative tasks, the re-establishment of the old religion would lead to wholehearted acceptance of Roman Catholicism were not to be realised.

Pole was fully in favour of the educational programme that was being adopted on the continent. He appointed capable and active bishops, all of whom subsequently refused to serve in the Elizabethan Protestant Church of England.

Westminster synod
Also known as the
London Synod, this
was a meeting of
the important clergy
under Cardinal Pole
who wished to
consolidate and
promote Roman
Catholicism in the
kingdom and to
plan the future of
the Church.

Key question
How Catholic was the
Marian Church by the
time of Mary I's death
in 1558?

Twelve Decrees
Term used to
describe the key 12
points drawn up by
Pole at the
Westminster Synod.
They included the
need for every
parish priest to be
properly trained,
educated and
permanently
resident. To help the
hard-pressed clergy,
Pole commissioned a
newly edited
Catholic New
Testament and a
new Book of
Homilies to replace
Cranmer's
Protestant edition.
However, they were
never used.

Seminaries
Religious
institutions of
learning designed
to educate and train
priests.

The Twelve Decrees

In 1555 the **Westminster synod** approved the passing of the
Twelve Decrees that included the establishment of **seminaries**
in every diocese for the training of priests, but shortage of
money limited the programme to a single creation at York. This
meant that the majority of the parish clergy remained too
uneducated, and lacking in evangelical zeal, for the new laws to
have any immediate impact on the laity. Mary's death in
November 1558 came too soon for Catholic reform to have
had any lasting effect. That is not to say that if Mary had lived
longer, Catholicism would not have gained wider support.
But the fact remains that only a significant minority clung
to their faith after the establishment of the Elizabethan
Church.

Assessment of the Church of England in 1558

It is just as difficult to assess the state of religion in England in
1558 as it is to measure the advance of Protestantism by 1553. It
is impossible to decide whether the bulk of the population were
Protestant or Catholic. While it is easy to trace the changing
pattern of official doctrine in the Church of England through
the acts and statutes passed in parliament, what the general
public thought about religion is difficult to determine. At present
the consensus among historians is that the ruling élites accepted
the principle of the Royal Supremacy, and were prepared to
conform to whichever form of religion was favoured by the
monarch.

Although the lower orders are generally considered to have
had a conservative affection for the traditional forms of worship,
it is thought they were prepared to follow the lead of the local
élites. Whether the religious legislation passed in parliament
was put into effect very much depended on the attitudes of
the local élites, and to a lesser extent those of the parish
authorities.

For this reason detailed research into parish and county
communities is being undertaken in the hope of revealing the
religious attitudes among the laity. Such research uses the
evidence of wills, parish registers, churchwardens' accounts and
court records to delve into local religious attitudes. Although such
sources can be helpful, they are often difficult to use. For
example, the sources show clearly that religious legislation was
being enforced in many parishes, but the problem is to decide
what this reveals about the attitudes of the local people. It might
be assumed that, because some parishes had complied with
generally unpopular pieces of legislation for setting up
communion tables and surrendering church plate, the
parishioners were in favour of Protestantism. On the other hand,
the record of religious changes might merely indicate that the
local authorities were conforming to government policy, and show
nothing about popular attitudes.

Selected local case studies

Despite the detailed research of local studies, gaining an insight into the religious attitudes among the non-élite is proving hard to piece together. For example:

- Lancashire élites are shown to have actively resisted the introduction of reformed religion.
- In Essex, Protestantism is seen to have been enthusiastically enforced.

In neither case is much revealed about the views of the general public. Nor are historians confident that the findings for one county are typical for the surrounding region, far less for the whole country.

One recent study, based on Devon and Cornwall, does seem to have succeeded in finding out more about popular attitudes. This is an area where, because of the Western Rebellion of 1549 (see pages 134–7), historians expected to find strong religious conservatism. However, the study, while revealing no zeal for Protestantism, uncovered equally little enthusiasm for Catholicism. Indeed, by 1558 passivity and indifference seem to have replaced religious fervour in the West Country.

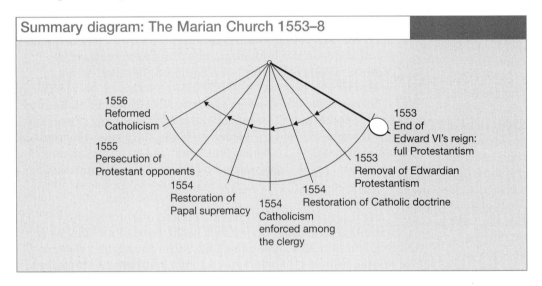

Summary diagram: The Marian Church 1553–8

1556 Reformed Catholicism

1555 Persecution of Protestant opponents

1554 Restoration of Papal supremacy

1554 Catholicism enforced among the clergy

1554 Restoration of Catholic doctrine

1553 Removal of Edwardian Protestantism

1553 End of Edward VI's reign: full Protestantism

5 | The Elizabethan Church and the Religious Settlement 1558–88

Key question
What was the religious situation in England in 1558?

The religious situation in 1558–9

Elizabeth inherited a turbulent situation in which the nation was confused and divided. Elizabeth was a Protestant but, in general, it appears that by 1558 the majority of her subjects were still undecided about religion. Among the élites there was strong support for the Royal Supremacy and they were willing to follow the religion of the legitimate monarch. The mass of the population do not appear to have had strongly held convictions, and in most cases they were prepared to follow the lead of their

Key date

Death of Mary and Cardinal Pole. Elizabeth became queen: November 1558 social superiors. Although there were small minorities of committed Protestants and Catholics, neither religion seems to have had a strong hold in England when Mary I died.

Although the majority of the population occupied the middle ground between Catholicism and Protestantism, largely ignorant and unsure of which way to turn, on the fringes there were groups of deeply religious people who were committed to either one side or the other. These relatively small groups evolved into the **Recusants** and Puritans of Elizabeth's later reign. These extremist groups threatened the religious stability of the kingdom, so with unity of the Church in mind Elizabeth opted for the Settlement enacted in 1559.

Religious Settlement

The Elizabethan Religious Settlement is a phrase used by historians to describe the organisation, ritual and teaching of the Church of England as enforced by Acts of Parliament. Drawn up by the queen in conjunction with her ministers and the Archbishop of Canterbury, Matthew Parker, the Settlement of 1559 was intended to clarify, regulate and stabilise religion in the kingdom. In effect, the objective was to reach a compromise acceptable to both Catholics and Protestants.

The terms of the Settlement were thrashed out in the queen's first parliament which sat from January to April 1559. The passing in parliament of the Act of Supremacy abolished papal authority in England and restored the monarch as Head of the Church. In a clever piece of politicking Elizabeth chose to use the title 'Supreme Governor' rather than 'Supreme Head' as adopted by her father, Henry VIII, in the hope that it might:

- please those of her subjects who objected to a woman as 'Head' of the Church
- not offend the Pope by suggesting that the issue was negotiable
- satisfy both Protestants and Catholics by suggesting the possibility of a compromise.

The new title did not diminish her power over the Church because the legal clauses in the Act ensured that she would have the same ecclesiastical authority as her father and brother. Mindful of her duty to God and to her people Elizabeth was determined that the Settlement should appeal to as wide a range of opinion as possible. Her preference for the restoration of the less controversial 1549 First Book of Common Prayer is evidence of this wish to compromise. However, due to the opposition of a few stubborn Marian bishops the Act of Uniformity of 1559 restored the Second Book of Common Prayer (1552). This shows that Elizabeth was prepared to resist her opponents and, if pushed too far, adopt a more radical position. The restoration of the more Protestant Second Book Of Common Prayer was disliked by Catholics.

Key term

Recusants
Catholics who refused to conform to the State religion and refused to attend church services.

Key dates

Act of Supremacy restored Henrician anti-papal laws: May 1559

Act of Uniformity restored the Second Book of Common Prayer of 1552: May 1559

Supremacy and uniformity

Elizabeth informed the Spanish ambassador that she intended to restore the form of religion as practised in the final years of her father's reign. Not fully understanding what the queen meant by this statement the ambassador chose to think that she intended to adopt a more conservative approach to religion: something like her father's Anglo-Catholicism but with trace elements of Protestantism. In leaving the ambassador to make up his own mind Elizabeth aimed to avoid confrontation. In reality her aim was to establish an Anglican Church that was essentially Protestant but with trace elements of Catholicism. By being deliberately vague on matters of minor religious controversy Elizabeth hoped her subjects too might make up their own minds rather than confront the Crown with their grievances both real and imagined.

In opting for a 'middle way' in religious matters Elizabeth hoped to pacify and satisfy both Catholics and Protestants. For example, knowing that some Catholics might object to the adoption of the Second Book of Common Prayer as the legal form of service, Elizabeth compromised on the question of the real presence. The 1552 Prayer Book implied that communion was a symbolic commemorative act but this was supplemented by words taken from the 1549 Prayer Book, which suggested that Christ's Body was really present in the Eucharist. Thus the form of words used in holy communion was capable of either a Catholic or Protestant interpretation.

Enough of the old Church remained – bishops, the wearing of clerical vestments and certain aspects of ritual in worship – to keep Catholics happy. On the other hand, the innovations in religion – adoption of the Edwardian Prayer Book, restoration of the Supremacy and the rejection of the Mass – were sufficient to satisfy Protestants. In the opinion of historian Conrad Russell the Elizabethan Church 'looked Catholic but sounded Protestant'.

Injunction and visitation

In 1559 a set of Injunctions was issued by the Crown with a view to establishing the pattern of worship that must be followed in church. Although it was largely Protestant in character some Catholic practices were retained. The following list gives some idea of the terms of the Injunctions:

- Catholic style religious processions and pilgrimages were banned.
- Monuments associated with miracles were removed.
- Recusants (those who refused to attend the services of the Anglican Church) were to be reported to the authorities.
- Clergy were to teach the Royal Supremacy.

Whereas these points would have satisfied most Protestants the following terms would not:

- Churches were allowed to keep some of the more popular religious images.
- Protestant preaching was restricted to those who obtained a license issued by the authorities.
- Parishioners were required to bow their heads at the name of Jesus and kneel at prayer.
- Clergy were required to wear distinctive clerical dress.

The majority of both Catholics and Protestants would have found the following points acceptable:

- Each parish was required to obtain a copy of the Bible in English and a copy of Erasmus's *Paraphrases* of the Gospels.
- Clergymen were allowed to marry but only with the permission of their bishop and two Justices of the Peace.

To ensure that the terms of the Injunctions were being enforced a series of Visitations (inspections) was ordered to be carried out. Acting on the instructions of individual bishops the Visitors had the power to question the parish clergy about their beliefs and to punish those who refused to abide by the terms of the Acts of Supremacy, Uniformity and the Royal Injunctions. Between 1559 and 1564 some 300 parish clergy either resigned or were ejected from their livings.

The Settlement: success or failure?

If the Settlement had been designed simply to avoid religious conflict and possible civil war (as happened in France) then it must be hailed a success. It lasted almost intact for some 10 years, until 1570, during which time the Church had the opportunity to establish itself, evolve and refine its clerical and doctrinal position. As early as 1563 Archbishop Parker, working through Convocation, adopted a revised version of Cranmer's Forty-Two Articles, the **Thirty-Nine Articles**. The Articles avoided a direct attack on Catholic belief but Article 17 sanctioned the Protestant belief in **predestination**.

In political terms the Settlement may also be considered a success. Elizabeth had succeeded in establishing a State Church under the domination of the Crown. This meant that religious opposition to the Settlement would be regarded in the same way as political opposition to the State. The laws of treason could be applied to stamp out opposition. This fact, allied to a misunderstanding of the queen's role in the Church, caused some continental Catholic critics to describe the Church of England as a mere parliamentary religion devoid of any truly spiritual

Key date

Thirty-Nine Articles set out Protestant beliefs: 1563

Key terms

Thirty-Nine Articles
Articles that set out Protestant beliefs and the method of worship in church services.

Predestination
Belief that a person's life has been mapped out by God before birth and cannot be changed.

conviction. This was unfair and untrue since Elizabeth had, from the beginning, ensured that the bishops would retain their responsibility for the administration and supervision of the Church and its clergy.

In religious terms the Settlement had mixed success. It largely succeeded in establishing a broadly based national Church which excluded as few people as possible. Until at least 1570 the Settlement made conformity as easy as possible without provoking opposition or disagreement. In theological terms the Thirty-Nine Articles were widely accepted and remained at the doctrinal heart of the Church. On the other hand, the Settlement failed not only to attract the Puritans but also to harness their evangelical enthusiasm. Devout Catholics were likewise marginalised with the consequence of encouraging opposition and non-conformity.

Religion in crisis: Puritans and Recusants

The compromise enshrined in the Settlement came to a premature end in 1570 with the crisis caused by the appearance of Mary, Queen of Scots in England (1568), the Catholic rebellion in the north (1569) and the Pope's excommunication of Elizabeth (1570). Thereafter, the Settlement would be rigorously enforced and fines for non-attendance at Church would be progressively raised. The authorities became less tolerant of dissident Protestants (Puritans) and recusants (Catholics), and displayed a greater degree of ruthlessness in their pursuit of **seminary priests**, **Jesuits** and **evangelicals**.

Key terms

Seminary priests
Priests who were trained in the seminary college of Douai and sent across Europe to educate people in the Roman Catholic faith.

Jesuits
Set up in 1540 by the Spaniard Ingatius Loyola, the specially trained order, known as the society of Jesus, spearheaded the Catholic Counter-Reformation in Europe.

Evangelicals
People who recruit followers to their particular brand of religion.

Key date

Pope excommunicated Elizabeth: 1570

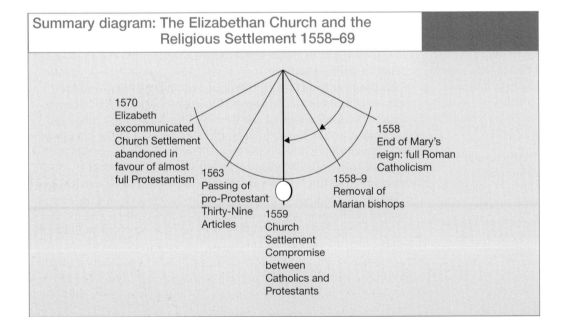

Summary diagram: The Elizabethan Church and the Religious Settlement 1558–69

1570
Elizabeth
excommunicated
Church Settlement
abandoned in
favour of almost
full Protestantism

1563
Passing of
pro-Protestant
Thirty-Nine
Articles

1559
Church
Settlement
Compromise
between
Catholics and
Protestants

1558–9
Removal of
Marian bishops

1558
End of Mary's
reign: full Roman
Catholicism

6 | Concluding Assessment: Was there a Religious Crisis?

Views among historians about the significance of religion in mid-Tudor England have changed during recent years. It is now felt that there was a much greater degree of religious compromise in England than on the continent, and that as a result religion itself was not a cause of crisis. Certainly there was religious compromise among the élites, and apathy, or even indifference, among the mass of the population towards religious change between 1547 and 1570. However, religion is regarded as having a considerable influence on the political, social and economic changes that were taking place at the time. Consequently, religion can be seen as contributing directly, or indirectly, to potential crises:

- the Western Rebellion of 1549 (see pages 134–7)
- the attempt by Northumberland to stop Mary Tudor succeeding to the throne in 1553 (see pages 140–1)
- the Northern Rebellion of 1569 (see pages 146–50).

Assessing the impact of religious reform

Assessing the impact of religious reform is difficult because the English Reformation was too close for either its long- or even short-term effects to be really felt by the middle of the century. Clearly religion had immediate consequences for politics and foreign policy, but in neither case can it be said to have caused a crisis. The longer term influences of social and economic change were only to become apparent over the next century.

In the past, historians such as W.K. Jordan saw the Edwardian Reformation as a period of remarkable toleration during which reformed religion became firmly established in the country. They considered it to have been followed by five years of Catholic repression and persecution, which failed to stamp out English Protestantism.

Such views are no longer widely held. Historians like Christopher Haigh increasingly doubt whether Protestantism had taken much of a hold in England by 1553. Indeed, it is now suggested by historians such as David Loades that Catholicism had wide popular support among the lower orders in both the towns and the countryside and that, had Mary lived longer, England would probably have remained Roman Catholic.

Some historians like Penry Williams think that there was much less animosity between English Catholics and Protestants than was previously believed. It is true that there were extremists on both sides, just as there were individuals prepared to die for their faith. However, the vast majority of people are seen as being very moderate in their outlook, and prepared to accept whatever doctrine was held by the ruling regime. It is this that is regarded as being the basis for religious compromise in England. The whole of the period between 1547 and 1570 is held to be one of marked toleration. To some historians, even the Marian religious repression is regarded as very mild in comparison with the persecution on the continent.

Summary diagram: Religious change 1547–59

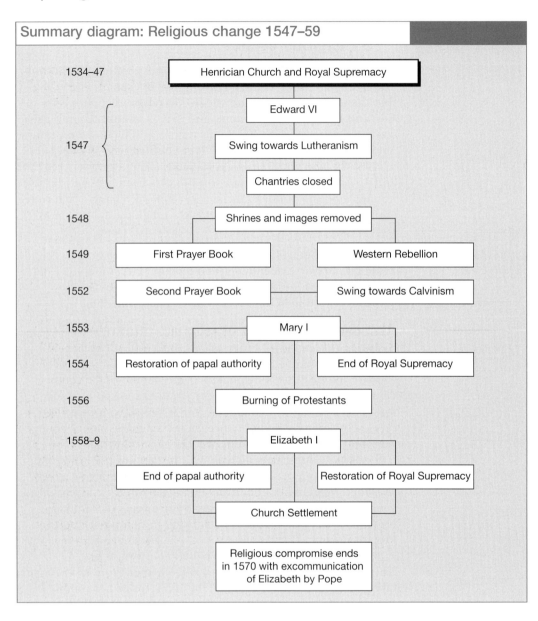

Study Guide: AS Question

In the style of OCR

Study the five sources on government policies towards the Church 1550–8, and then answer both sub-questions. It is recommended that you spend two-thirds of your time in answering part (b).

(a) **Study Sources B and C.**
Compare these sources as evidence for the ways in which rulers dealt with religious opponents.

(b) **Study *all* the sources.**
Use your own knowledge to assess how far the sources support the interpretation that successive rulers faced similar problems in implementing their religious policies between 1550 and 1559.

Government policies towards the Church 1550–8

Source A

Martin Bucer, letter to John Calvin, June 1550. A distinguished German protestant who arrived in England in 1548, and taught theology at Cambridge University until his death in 1551, sends news of religious events in England to one of the leading European Protestants.

The Bishops have not yet agreed on Christian doctrine, let alone the rules of the Church, and very few parishes have qualified clergymen. Sometimes the clergy read the service rapidly, so that the ordinary people have no more understanding of it than if it were still in Latin rather than English. When these problems are presented to the bishops, they say they cannot correct them without an Act of Parliament. Though parliament meets every year, the number of secular matters stops Church affairs being discussed. When you next write to the Duke of Somerset, you must urge him to reform the Church.

Source B

Second Act of Uniformity, 1552. An Act of Parliament of 1552 condemns the absence of people from church and imposes the Second Book of Common Prayer.

In spite of the introduction of the First Common Prayer Book by Parliament, a great number of people in this realm wilfully and damnably refuse to come to their parish churches on Sundays and holy days. In future those who are absent shall be punished by the Church courts. The First Common Prayer Book has produced doubts about the form of worship, so the King has ordered a Second Book of Common Prayer to replace it. Anyone who uses another form of worship shall be imprisoned for six months.

Source C

Proclamation on Religion, 16 August 1553. At the beginning of her reign Mary I sets out her intentions on religion.

Her Majesty will observe the Catholic religion she has professed all her life, and desires that all her subjects would quietly follow suit. However she will not compel any to this until further decisions are made. She commands her subjects to live together in Christian charity, avoiding the new and devilish terms of papist and heretic, and trying to live peaceful Christian lives. Any man who stirs up the people to disorder will be severely punished. Printers have published books and ballads written in English which discuss controversial religious teaching. Let nobody do so in future without the Queen's express permission.

Source D

Simon Renard, report to Philip of Spain, 5 February 1555. The Imperial ambassador comments on the hostility in London to the burnings of Protestants.

The people of London are murmuring about the cruel enforcement of the recent acts of parliament against heresy which has now begun, as shown publicly when a certain Rogers was burnt yesterday. Some of the onlookers wept. Others prayed to God to give them strength, persistence, and patience to bear the pain and not to convert back to Catholicism. Others gathered the ashes and bones and wrapped them up in paper to preserve them. Yet others threatened the bishops. The haste with which the bishops have proceeded in this matter may well cause a revolt. If the people got the upper hand, not only would the cause of religion be again menaced, but the persons of your Majesty and the Queen might be in peril.

Source E

Venetian Ambassador, report, 1558. The Venetian ambassador to London reports the religious confusion there a few weeks after Elizabeth I came to the throne.

Queen Elizabeth often promised to continue the Catholic religion. But on Christmas Day, Her Majesty told the Bishop that he was not to elevate the host during mass. He replied that this was the only way he knew, so Her Majesty rose and departed. On the same day, two individuals, a mechanic and a cobbler, followed by a very great mob, entered by force into the church of St Augustine, breaking the locks of the doors. Both leaped into the pulpit and preached uttering rude jokes about the blessed Queen Mary and Cardinal Pole. Queen Elizabeth forbade such preaching, fearing riots.

Exam tips

(a) First of all make sure you are comparing the correct two sources: Source B with Source C.

- Focus: here the focus is on 'ways of dealing with religious opponents'. This should be kept clearly in mind throughout, as the purpose of the *comparison*.
- Links: similarities and differences should be cross-referenced point by point and *linked* to the question, '*ways in which rulers dealt with religious opponents*'. In planning, highlight aspects of source content which link to these key terms.
- Avoid a formulaic approach. Think about the sources in the light of their historical context, and show your understanding of their significance in answering the question.
- Provenance: it is important to start by focusing on *who, what, when, why* and *to whom* the source was written and its *tone*. Not all of these aspects may be relevant to this particular question, so avoid a formulaic approach. Concentrate on the most significant aspect(s).
- Content: try to balance similarities and differences of content in the light of their provenance, integrating content with provenance.
- Analyse: the detail, sentence by sentence, cross-referencing in the light of the question. Compare the reliability or usefulness of the two sources in answering it.
- Judgement: decide which of the two sources provides the better evidence of 'ways in which rulers dealt with religious opponents' and give convincing support for your decision. This may be based on usefulness, reliability, whether the view is typical, more complete, better informed, written at a significant date or some other relevant criterion.

The *provenance* (*nature*) of Source B is an Act of Parliament establishing by law a uniform Protestant form of worship in the Second Edwardian Prayer Book 1552, whereas Source C is a proclamation requesting peace and co-operation among religious opponents. Northumberland is the ruler at the time of Source B, in the final year of a minority rule ('the King has ordered'), when a previous ambiguous attempt to gain religious uniformity had failed, whereas Source C is within the first month of the reign of the first female ruler of England, succeeding after Northumberland's challenge to her Catholic rule. There is no parliament in session in August 1553, and the sale of monastic land might make one uncooperative in restoring Catholicism. Religious unrest is the historical *context* of both sources, and brief evidence of this might be used to explain the difference in *ways*.

The *content* of Source B lays down penalties of imprisonment for active opponents, enforceable in the law courts, whereas Source C merely says that further decisions will be made later and merely threatens 'severe punishments' should persuasion fail. Mary may have misread her popularity as a legitimate successor and perceived widespread support for Catholicism, so might feel persuasion may be all that is needed. Source B defines lesser punishments, in Church courts, for those passively disobeying but suggests that there are wilful opponents who have not been persuaded, especially implying clergy 'who use another form of worship'. This may support Mary's reliance on persuasion early in her reign, though Source C too defines two types of religious opponent. She suggests that abusive words are stirring up disorder and requests peace, but specifically mentions publishers of religiously controversial 'books and ballads', who will in future have to obtain a royal licence. This shows that Protestants have issued propaganda in Edward's reign and have become more formidable opponents, so new ways may have to be found to deal with them.

Judgement might view Source B as the better evidence for 'rulers' ways of dealing with religious opponents, as it establishes an official and uniform religion with clear, legally enforceable penalties. Following the break with Rome, this was to be the pattern for later Church Settlements. Source C shows Mary acting tentatively at the start of her reign, and we know from hindsight that this was not typical of her dealings with religious opponents later in her reign.

(b) This question requires the grouping of the sources into two or more sides to an argument. The starting point should be the interpretation in the question: 'rulers faced similar problems in implementing their religious policies'. The alternative argument will focus different *problems* within a changing historical context. Links within the sources will discuss small phrases and evaluate how similar or different these problems were:

- The sources should be grouped by their point of view: sometimes a source contains more than one point for cross-reference.
- The significance for the question, of the views in the content of the sources, should be developed using accurate historical context and terminology.
- Relevant aspects of the provenance of the sources should be linked to answering the question. This 'provenance' might be authorship, date, nature, purpose, audience, tone.
- Accurate knowledge and terminology should be integrated into the answer to verify, qualify or evaluate the views in the sources as well as their provenance.
- A judgement should be reached on the 'value' of the sources in linking to the interpretation in the question, where 'value' might be judged by
  - reliability and/or usefulness of content and provenance
  - completeness of content or aspects deliberately ignored
  - limitations of the sources as a set.

Things to avoid:

- Do not use the sources as illustrations of an essay style answer.
- Do not merely *describe* or *paraphrase* source content, but always use it to argue.
- Do not use the sources as a mine for extracting *references*. Their purpose is to validate or qualify the interpretation in the question, enabling you to use them in effective argument.
- Do not make 'stock' comments about the provenance of sources, especially common with secondary authors, e.g. 'he is an eminent historian so we can trust his view'. Always link comments on provenance to the focus of the question.

Sources A, D and E suggest that the bishops caused a problem for rulers, Content, provenance and context should be integrated to develop this idea and a judgement reached on how similar a problem they posed to Northumberland/Edward, Mary and Elizabeth at the times in their reigns when the sources were written.

Sources C–E refer to active religious revolt and disorder being a problem or potential problem feared by rulers. Source B is an attempt to quell opposition *three* years after the Western Rebellion, which might be supplied by own knowledge, though Wyatt's Rebellion is less relevant. An evaluation should be made, and a judgement should be reached on how similar the problem was for the various rulers.

On the other hand, lack of education and understanding in Source A could be cross-referenced with Source E, 'the only way he knew how'. In contrast, Source C refers to outspoken opinions and propaganda, and Source B hints at apathy, with congregations unwilling to attend the new Protestant Church services. The frequent swings in the official religion during this period provide useful context which should be used in evaluation of the views, in the light of context and provenance. Again, a judgement should be reached on how similar the problem was for the various rulers.

Source D suggests that Mary faced a different problem from the other rulers, by allowing her bishops to create martyrs and associating the official religion with unpopular foreign influence. This might be linked to Source E, which might be seen as lessening the problems for Elizabeth in establishing Protestantism. A judgement should be reached evaluating how different the problem was for these rulers.

Final tips:

- The limitations of the set of sources should be supplied from relevant own knowledge, not merely suggested fancifully, e.g. 'the sources would be more useful if they told us what an ordinary yeoman felt about religion'.
- The grouped sources should drive the answer, and an evaluative argument should be created by integrating context with source content and provenance.
- Marks are awarded for synthesis, bringing together all the elements of the answer. Therefore the final paragraph of conclusion is *very important* and will play an important part in gaining marks. It should bring together all the threads of the argument and judge how far the sources, as a set, support the interpretation in the question. If the sources are limited or unreliable, they will not support the interpretation effectively.

Study Guide: A2 Question

In the style of Edexcel

'A triumph of compromise.' How far do you accept this judgement on Elizabeth I's Religious Settlement in the years 1559–66?

Exam tips

The cross-references are intended to take you straight to the material that will help you to answer the question.

This question requires you to examine how far the Elizabethan Settlement represented a compromise and whether it can be called a triumph. To deal with 'compromise' you should examine the way in which it dealt with those matters of church organisation, doctrine and public worship over which there was division in 1558 (pages 109–10):

- Royal Supremacy
- transubstantiation/real presence
- episcopacy
- use of vestments and images
- the Prayer Book and Bible
- preaching
- clerical marriage.

To deal with 'triumph' you should consider how far the settlement was:

- the limited overt Catholic challenge in this period (pages 112, 134–7)
- the extent of the Puritan challenge (pages 68–9, 109, 112).

However you should note the accompanying powers of enforcement (pages 110–12):

- the oath of supremacy
- the use of visitations and the ejection of non-compliant clergy
- recusancy laws
- the association of religious opposition with treason.

In coming to an overall conclusion you should examine how far, in spite of the State's powers of enforcement and the vocal Puritan challenge, the Settlement was a triumph as a compromise which avoided widespread or serious challenge in this period.

4 Disorder and Rebellion: A Crisis in Authority?

Key dates

1536	October	Lincolnshire Uprising
	November	Yorkshire Rebellion
1549	June	Introduction of First Book of Common Prayer
	June	Western or Prayer Book Rebellion
	July	Ket's Rebellion in East Anglia
	October	Fall of Somerset
1553	May	Guildford Dudley married Lady Jane Grey
	July	Death of Edward VI, Lady Jane Grey proclaimed queen
	July	Northumberland's military expedition against Mary Tudor Failed
	July	Mary Tudor proclaimed queen
	August	Northumberland executed
	December	Marriage proposal between Mary and Philip of Spain presented to the Royal Council
1554	January	Wyatt Rebellion
	February	Wyatt entered London

	February	Elizabeth arrested for supposedly being involved in the rebellion
	February	Lady Jane Grey and Guildford Dudley executed
	July	Marriage of Mary and Philip
1568	May	Mary, Queen of Scots arrived in England
1569	November– December	Northern Rebellion
1569–70		Dacre Rebellion

1 | Challenging Authority

Although the idea of a mid-Tudor crisis has been challenged in recent years, it is difficult to escape the fact that the period between 1547 and 1554 saw a large number of disturbances. In particular, 1549 has been singled out as a notable period of crisis because it witnessed two serious rebellions – the Western and Ket Rebellions – and numerous other minor disturbances, which one historian, John Guy, believes brought England close to **class war**. This idea, that there was a genuine class war between the élites and non-élites, is a controversial one and stems from the belief there was a general drift from respect for authority, towards the challenging of authority. Certainly, there were tensions in both town and country as social and economic problems reached new levels of intensity. Changes in central government and religion had not only loosened loyalty to the regime but also fuelled a growing disrespect for the clergy and the Church.

To concentrate on the idea of a class war being at the root of disorder and rebellion between 1547 and 1554 is to risk ignoring those challenges to authority which came from within the ruling class. Unlike the uprisings in 1549, the *coup d'état* surrounding Lady Jane Grey, Wyatt's Rebellion and the Northern Rebellion (see pages 146–50) were political conspiracies among the ruling élites, and there was little popular support. Factional tensions at Court and rivalry in central government surfaced at times of crisis as in:

- 1549, when Somerset was removed by Northumberland due to his ineffective handling of the rebellions in the West Country and East Anglia
- 1553, when Edward VI's death and Mary's accession threatened to destroy Northumberland's rule
- 1554, when Mary's marriage to Philip of Spain became the focus for opposition by men who resented their exclusion from both the Court and government
- 1569, when Mary, Queen of Scots became a focus for opposition by the Catholic Earls of Northumberland and Westmorland, who disagreed with the Religious Settlement and resented their exclusion from the government of the north.

Therefore, in order to understand the root causes of crisis and the challenging of authority, it is necessary to appreciate what constituted the forces of authority and explore the problems that affected those at the bottom of society as well as those at the top.

Key question
What lay behind the challenges to the authority of the Crown, government and Church?

Key term

Class war
Used by some historians to help explain the causes of the disorder and rebellions that occurred during the reign of Edward VI. The resentment of the poor and economically vulnerable was directed towards the wealthy and powerful élites.

Key date

Fall of Somerset: October 1549

The forces of authority

Ruling class views of the poor had hardened in the sixteenth century. Where once paternalism had informed the attitudes and guided the actions of the élites, now the poor were viewed with a degree of detachment that often bred disdain and fear. Casual violence and crimes of theft among the common people were thought by the élites to be on the increase while riot was an ever-present threat. The rise in poverty and its associated evil vagrancy, caused alarm and led to an overreaction on the part of the authorities who enthusiastically enforced harsh measures such as the so-called **'Slavery' Act of 1547**. Coercion and persuasion were the twin means by which the Crown and government attempted to keep control but the forces of authority available to maintain law and order were limited.

Formal authority

Tudor England had no police force or a standing army. The monarchy relied on its God-given power to govern and make laws. This **divine right** to rule enabled the monarch to command the respect of the people who were constantly reminded of the Crown's privileged status by the Church. The people were expected to abide by the law but for those who disturbed the **'king's peace'** there was arrest by the Crown's officers, trial in the royal courts of justice and punishment either by fine, imprisonment, or death.

Fear of what the Crown could do was a potent weapon in the struggle to maintain law and order. The monarchy communicated its orders by means of royal proclamations that were carried by royal messengers to various parts of the kingdom. Although not everyone would be able to read these proclamations, word soon spread and the monarchy thus made its will known to a great number of people.

Royal officials

The monarchy also relied on the unpaid services of the local gentry and nobility who were expected to uphold and enforce the law by means of the powers vested in them through the offices of **Lord Lieutenant**, Sheriff and Justice of the Peace. The holders of these offices had no supporting forces but relied on their standing and influence in the community to exert their authority.

Only the Lord Lieutenant had the power to call musters and assemble an armed militia recruited from among the local community in times of danger such as that posed by insurrection at home or invasion from abroad. Another method employed by the monarchy to enhance its prestige and, indirectly, to reinforce the power and status of its officials in the regions was to be seen on **royal progresses**.

Yeomen of the Guard

Unlike its counterparts on the continent, the English monarchy did not have the financial means to maintain a regular, professional army. Nor could the Crown rely on the armed retainers maintained by the nobility since Henry VII had passed

Key question
What forces were available to the State to keep order?

Key terms

'Slavery' Act of 1547
Described as 'the most savage of all Tudor poor laws', the statute stated that sturdy or able-bodied vagrants should be branded with the letters V and S and subjected to forced labour or slavery for repeat offenders.

Divine right
Belief that monarchs were chosen by God to rule the kingdom and that their word was law.

King's peace
The idea that as the king was appointed by God his law was the highest authority which brought order and protection to the people.

Lord Lieutenant
Local military officer with the power to call musters and assemble an armed militia.

Royal progresses
Royal visits served to overawe those who witnessed them and to remind the people of the might and majesty of the monarch.

laws to prevent the keeping of private armies. This was done as a result of the Crown's experiences in the Wars of the Roses when private armies had been used to defy the law. The only professional force available to the monarch was the 400 men that made up the royal bodyguard, known as the Yeomen of the Guard.

Mercenaries

In times of crisis, the monarch often employed mercenaries hired from the continent to stiffen the resistance of those forces mustered in each county by the Lord Lieutenants. However, if a county was in the grip of rebellion, as occurred in Norfolk, Cornwall and Devon in 1549, then troops had to be mustered from other counties and deployed in the affected areas of the kingdom. This is why the Crown feared a nationwide revolt such as the one planned by Sir Thomas Wyatt in 1554 which involved four simultaneous rebellions in Kent, Devon, Leicestershire and on the Welsh border (Herefordshire and Shropshire).

Informal authority

The Crown also exercised its authority in more informal but equally effective ways. Royal imagery was used to impress both people and visitors alike. For those wealthy and influential enough to be invited to attend the monarch in one of the many palaces owned by the Crown, the sheer scale and size of the buildings themselves would have been impressive, let alone the paintings and portraits that hung within. Even the majority of the population who might be fortunate enough to view the palaces from afar would have been impressed. But if they needed reminding of the power of the Crown they had only to reach for their coins, every denomination of which carried pictures of the ruling monarch.

The Church

The most visible symbol of authority in the kingdom after the monarch was the Church. The Church exercised formal authority over its clergy and non-clerical employees, and its influence over the population at large was such that the voices of its clergy commanded respect. The Church's rituals and its moral authority helped to enforce discipline and obedience. The Church was also an effective means of reaching the people because the vast majority were expected to attend their local church on a regular basis. The Crown was well aware of the importance of the Church's role in maintaining social stability and in ensuring people's loyalty and obedience.

The Royal Supremacy ensured that, as Head of the Church, the monarch had a captive audience willing to believe what the parish priest had to tell them. Therefore, preaching was used to guide and inform people of royal policy. For those priests who opposed the Reformation or were unwilling to preach propaganda on behalf of the Crown, the Edwardian government issued homilies (see page 91) or printed sermons to be read in all churches.

Contemporary representation of the Great Chain of Being. This shows God and the angels at the top, descending through nobility, gentry and common people down to animals and plants. What was the purpose in having the Great Chain of Being depicted in this way?

Those clerics who refused to comply with government orders were expelled from the Church.

Although the changes brought about by the Reformation weakened the spiritual authority of the Church, there is no doubt that the pulpit remained the most powerful instrument of control. The Church was able to exert so much authority over the people because of a concept known as the 'Great Chain of Being'. This conveyed the contemporary idea of God punishing those who rebelled against their monarch. It emphasised that those in authority held their power for the good of those below them, and subject to those above them.

Key question
What were the root causes of crisis and how did they contribute to the challenging of authority?

The root causes of crisis and the challenging of authority

The non-élites

The mass of the people who made up the non-élites were not prone to violent rebellion. For them it was usually the last desperate act when all other attempts to resolve their grievances had failed. They were generally uninterested in politics and reacted only to those social, economic and sometimes religious forces that affected their everyday lives. Theirs was a precarious existence living on the edge of subsistence where a drought, a bad harvest or a price rise might push them into despairing poverty. Predictably perhaps, rising crime and destitution coincided with bad harvests and hunger, which often provided the spark for riot and rebellion. Consequently, the causes of non-élite disorder and rebellion can be found mainly in the social and economic changes that occurred in mid-Tudor England.

The standard of living

There were clear links between living standards and popular discontent in the middle of the century. Even if the standard of living of the mass of the population had not fallen as dramatically as was once assumed, it had certainly not improved. For example, the rebels in Norfolk clearly felt that their economic position had declined since the end of the fifteenth century, and blamed it largely on rising rents. The groups which had generally gained from increased rents and prices were the élites, the yeomen, merchants, industrialists, and some husbandmen. Consequently, part of the problem in 1549 was the general economic resentment of those who felt they were the losers, against those groups which they felt were gaining. However, it must be remembered that it is too simple to make such a clear-cut distinction. Within each grouping there were both winners and losers. Unrest in 1549 (see pages 134–40) was very localised, and a riot or rebellion might have been sparked off by one individual who thought that his neighbour had cheated him or was becoming unduly prosperous.

Rents and wages

The levels of rents and wages are regarded as another possible contributor to popular unrest, because they too had a direct effect on the standard of living. With relatively sluggish population growth up to 1540, rents and wages would remain comparatively stable.

As far as wages were concerned this is exactly what happened. In the south of England the wages for rural workers remained at 4d a day and for building workers at 6d a day until the 1550s. This meant that the level of wages obtained in the fifteenth century when population was very low was maintained in spite of the increase in population. However, because of the considerable increase in inflation, the standard of living of all wage-earners fell.

The evidence of the level of rents is less conclusive. In some areas, especially around London, rents had risen by the 1530s, and had more than doubled from 6d per acre to 13d per acre. In other areas, away from south-eastern England, they remained static, and in some places fell slightly. The pressure was heaviest on pasture land because of the demand for wool and other animal products. Enclosed land commanded higher rents, which affected levels of rent in the surrounding district.

Although the evidence is not conclusive, resentment over the level of rents and wages added to popular discontent, especially in the southern half of the country. The problem is that there is no clear distinction between smallholders and labourers. Although it is estimated that over 40 per cent of the population were wage-earners – 10 per cent working in industry – only a minority were full-time employees. Many smallholders supplemented their incomes by wages, and most workers in cottage and other industries had their own smallholdings. A large number of town labourers spent part of the year working in the countryside, especially at harvest time. This makes it very difficult to select any one particular cause for economic discontent among the lower orders, and large-scale uprisings may have been caused by groups with different grievances coming together for mutual support.

Inflation, rising prices and poverty

During the first half of the sixteenth century the price of most goods rose sharply. However, the most serious rise in prices affected foodstuffs like grain, bread, cheese and meat. This was caused in part by a rising population because it put pressure on agriculture which was not flexible enough to increase production to meet the growing demand. This led to hunger and anger particularly when wages failed to keep pace with rising prices. Hungry people are more inclined to riot or rebel because it is an immediate problem that cannot wait for remedy in the long term.

By 1550 the rate of inflation may have reached 200 per cent, and the very high levels of inflation reached by 1549 contributed to the widespread popular discontent. Inflation contributed to damaging the economy, which led to an increase in unemployment and poverty. Ignorant of the causes of poverty and vagrancy, the government reacted ruthlessly by punishing beggars, which in turn led to resentment against authority.

The élites

The élites did not so much challenge authority as undermine it. By involving themselves in acts of rebellion they not only set a bad example for the common people but contributed to weakening the authority of the State. They did not deliberately set out to do this because their privileged position in society, their economic wealth and political power depended on maintaining the very authority that their rebellious acts were undermining. Therefore, the élites often trod a fine line between maintaining their authority over those below them – the common people –

and challenging the authority of those above them – the monarchy and central government. The dangers posed by élite rebellion were potentially more serious than those posed by popular uprisings. For example, Ket and the Western rebels (see pages 134–40) never set out to destroy the government or change the monarchy, unlike the élites who involved themselves in the *coup d'état* of Lady Jane Grey, Wyatt and Northern Rebellions.

Political changes

The causes of élite rebellion can be found mainly in the political and religious changes that occurred in mid-Tudor England. Political change enabled faction to thrive. The shifts in the balance of power between the rival conservative and reformist factions at Court after 1540 contributed to political instability.

This instability enabled Somerset to engineer a *coup d'état* in which the terms of Henry VIII's last will and testament were ignored so that he could become Lord Protector (see page 43). However, Somerset's position was soon undermined not by a rival faction but by a political ally turned rival. Northumberland took advantage of Somerset's indecisiveness and weak rule to organise another *coup d'état* in which he assumed the leadership of the country. In both coups only a minority of the élites actively participated in the change of leadership, the majority remained passive. This was principally because the position of the monarch remained unchallenged. This changed when the succession became an issue, which helps to explain why the *coup d'état* involving Lady Jane Grey and Wyatt's Rebellion both failed.

Although Northumberland's rule was generally sound and progressive he lacked the authority that a monarch could claim as God's anointed. This meant that his position could more easily be challenged. His attempt to crown Lady Jane Grey failed when the élites at Court and in the government turned on him and offered their support to Mary Tudor. In challenging the dying wish of Edward VI and defying the authority of Northumberland and the Council Mary Tudor's was the only successful rebellion of the sixteenth century. On the other hand, Mary could claim that she and the élites who supported her were championing rather than challenging the authority of the State.

Religious changes

Religion became a factor during Mary's reign because Protestant gentry and nobility feared political exclusion and economic ruin. Economically the élites had nothing to fear because the Crown did not force them to hand back monastic and chantry property. However, politically their worst fears were soon realised when Mary removed from office the majority of Northumberland's supporters and promoted those loyal to her and her faith. For example:

• Archbishop Thomas Cranmer was removed from the Council, arrested and eventually executed

- Bishop Stephen Gardiner, who had been imprisoned under Edward VI, was released, appointed to the Council and promoted to Lord Chancellor.

Within six months of her accession Mary had turned England into a Catholic kingdom. This was reinforced by her marriage to Philip of Spain. However, the Spanish marriage and Religious Settlement were not to everyone's taste and men like Sir Thomas Wyatt, Sir Peter Carew and Sir James Croft plotted to overthrow the government.

Similarly, in Elizabeth's reign the religious compromise of 1559 was not to everyone's liking but simmering resentment did not boil over into open rebellion for 10 years. Pressure of faction, fear of marginalisation at Court and anger at the treatment of Mary, Queen of Scots, combined with a renewed zeal for the Catholic faith, caused the two most powerful earls in the north of England to rebel in 1569.

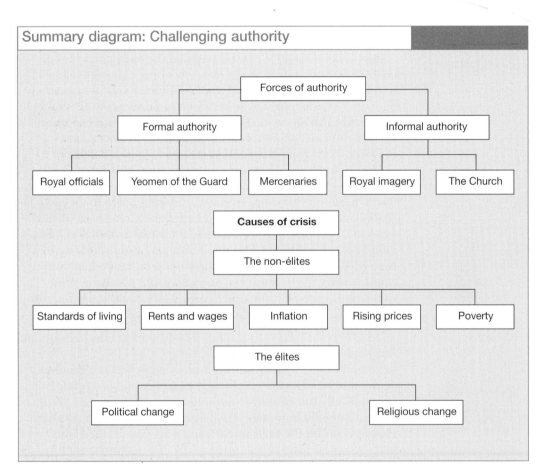

Summary diagram: Challenging authority

Forces of authority

Formal authority

Informal authority

Royal officials | Yeomen of the Guard | Mercenaries | Royal imagery | The Church

Causes of crisis

The non-élites

Standards of living | Rents and wages | Inflation | Rising prices | Poverty

The élites

Political change | Religious change

Key question
What was the
Pilgrimage of Grace?

2 | The Pilgrimage of Grace 1536–7

The Pilgrimage of Grace was a widespread popular revolt that took place between late 1536 and early 1537 in the north of England. Although it is only strictly accurate to use the phrase 'Pilgrimage of Grace' to describe the uprising in Yorkshire between October and December 1536, the term is normally applied to all the rebellions that took place in the north of England including Cumberland, Durham, Lincolnshire and Northumberland. It has been estimated that between 30,000 and 40,000 people took part in these rebellions and they proved to be the largest and, arguably, the most serious outbreaks of violence in the sixteenth century.

Key question
What caused the
Pilgrimage of Grace?

The Pilgrimage of Grace was caused mainly by resentment over the changes in the Church and the dissolution of the monasteries but there were also underlying economic, social and political factors at work. Historians continue to argue over the seriousness of the rebellion and the extent to which it threatened the king but there is no doubt that it did threaten the maintenance of law and order in the north.

Lincolnshire

Key date

Lincolnshire Uprising:
October 1536

The Lincolnshire Uprising of October 1536 was the first stage of the wider rebellion known as the Pilgrimage of Grace. The fact that it lasted a mere fortnight suggests that it was a relatively minor and unimportant uprising but this is not the case. It was dangerous because it was more than simply a disturbance by the common people, it was led, and perhaps organised, by members of the landowning gentry. These are the people the Crown would normally rely on for support in putting down a rebellion. Although many gentry willingly joined the uprising some were forced to do so. Within a few days of the initial outbreak of the rising some 30,000–35,000 people had joined the rebels. Coming mainly from the areas around Louth and Horncastle the Lincolnshire recruits had been encouraged to join by word of mouth, lighted beacons and the ringing of church bells. It was a call to arms and the volunteers gathered as if on an official **muster** for the king.

Key term

Muster
The method by which the Crown mobilised the people for war by calling out the militia. Each county was obliged to raise, train and maintain a militia of able-bodied men for active service.

The fact and the size of the rebellion horrified the king. His initial reaction was predictable: he wanted it crushed and the ringleaders arrested and executed. However, he had to restrain his impulse for vengeance and although he sent the Duke of Suffolk north with an army of 8000 men, Henry let it be known that he was prepared to hear the rebels' complaints. This served to satisfy the majority of the rebels who quietly went home to wait upon their king. The king had no intention of meeting the rebels' demands but he hoped that once they had disbanded he could strike at their leaders.

Yorkshire

Henry's relief soon turned to despair when he was informed that another equally serious rising was under way in Yorkshire. The similarities between the Lincolnshire and Yorkshire risings are striking. Both involved large numbers of commoners, including whole communities, led by gentry landowners, and both were well fed, supplied and organised. The money was raised as donations that came mainly from the churchmen.

Yorkshire Rebellion: November 1536

Key date

The main difference between the two risings was the quality of the leadership: in Yorkshire the rebels had Robert Aske to lead them. An able lawyer with experience of London and a member of an important Yorkshire family, Aske provided the rebels with a clear sense of purpose: to persuade the king, by a show of armed force, to abandon his attacks on the Church, to stop any further monastic closures and to return England to Rome. It was Aske who came up with and made popular the description of their enterprise as a 'Pilgrimage of Grace'. He insisted that all those who took part in the rising swear an oath so as to prevent treachery and ill-discipline among the rebel ranks.

Aske assumed that the king was really a caring monarch who had been misled by his wicked and low-born councillors, especially Thomas Cromwell, and who would change his policy when he realised that the cost of not doing so would be bloody civil war. Although Aske and the other leaders believed they would not need to fight the king's forces they were prepared to resist if forced to do so. It was Aske's efficient arrangement of his men in conventional army formations that turned the Pilgrimage into a potentially threatening uprising.

The vast majority of the Pilgrims behaved themselves and so they were welcomed at York. From York the rebels moved on to Pontefract where they laid siege to the castle. The siege did not last long as the castle, a royal stronghold guarding the main road south, was lightly garrisoned – 300 troops – and in a poor state of repair. The garrison commander, the 80-year-old Lord Thomas Darcy, surrendered the castle and joined the Pilgrims. Henry did not trust Darcy and when the rebellion was over he did not believe him when he claimed that he had been forced to surrender the royal fortress and join the rebels.

Marching south at the head of around 35,000 well-armed and horsed Pilgrims, Aske presented the king with a formidable challenge. Opposing them were two armies led by the Earl of Shrewsbury and the Duke of Norfolk. When the royal forces merged they numbered a little less than 10,000 men, nowhere near enough to challenge the rebels. Fortunately for Henry, Aske clung to the hope that conflict could be avoided and that the king might settle for a negotiated peace. At Doncaster Bridge on 27 October 1536 Norfolk met with Aske and the rebel leadership to discuss terms. Norfolk managed to convince the rebel leaders that the king was grateful to them for opening his eyes to what had been going on. It was suggested by Norfolk that Henry would seriously consider their demands. It was agreed that Norfolk would present the demands to the king and return with his answer. In the meantime a royal pardon was issued to satisfy the rebels of the Crown's good intentions. In the event the king had no intention of meeting their demands so he played for time by delaying his response. After some weeks he required the rebels to renew their demands and set them down on paper so they could be properly considered by him and his Privy Council.

During this time there were further outbreaks of violence across the north such as Cumberland in February 1537. Aske and the Pilgrim leadership condemned these risings claiming they had nothing to do with them. However, it gave Norfolk and the king the excuse to strengthen their forces in the north and to act ruthlessly in putting these various risings and protests down. By May 1537 Henry felt strong enough to strike and as the Pilgrim leaders were commanded to meet with the king in London they were arrested. Darcy, Aske and some 15 other leaders were tried, found guilty of treason and executed. The rebellion was at an end.

The demands of the rebels

The rebels drew up a list of 24 separate articles, also known as the Pontefract Articles, covering a series of complaints. For example, they demanded:

- an end to the dissolution of the monasteries
- the reversal of the religious changes that had taken place
- the repeal of **entry fines** and a reduction in taxation
- that Thomas Cromwell, Sir Richard Rich and monastic inspectors such as Dr Thomas Leigh be punished
- an end to the enclosure (see pages 186–7) of land without consent
- the restoration of Princess Mary to the king's favour.

Key term

Entry fines
A custom by which a fixed sum of money was paid on taking up a tenancy by inheritance or by sale.

Key debate: assessing the Pilgrimage of Grace

How has the Pilgrimage of Grace been assessed by historians?

Historians have tended to judge the Pilgrimage of Grace on how dangerous it was. At the beginning of the twentieth century historians were in no doubt that it posed a serious threat to Henry VIII. The sheer size of the rebellion in terms of both the numbers who took part and the geographical scale of its influence were considered crucial factors. In addition, the fact that members of the gentry and nobility took part in the uprising must add to its seriousness since these were the men charged with keeping the peace and upon whom the Crown depended for support.

However, more recently, historians have moved to disagree with this assessment. They point to the fact that despite Aske's quality leadership and organisational skill he was focused on negotiation rather than confrontation. Aske was no match for Henry VIII when it came to diplomacy and negotiation. As if to emphasise the weakness rather than the strength of the rebellion, historians point out that the gentry and nobility of the north were far from united in the face of the challenges confronting them. For example, Robert Aske's own brother sided with the Crown, as did Lord Darcy's two sons who refused to join the Pilgrimage. The most persuasive argument put forward by historians who regard the Pilgrimage as anything but serious is the fact that it achieved nothing: it was a failure.

Nevertheless, the fact remains the Pilgrimage of Grace was the largest rebellion ever seen in sixteenth century England, and that any uprising, no matter how large or small, was, by its very nature, a threat to law and order and the stability of the realm.

Some key books in the debate
Michael Bush, *The Pilgrimage of Grace* (Manchester, 1996).
M. Dodds and R. Dodds, *The Pilgrimage of Grace and the Exeter Conspiracy* (Cambridge, 1915).
Scott Harrison, *The Pilgrimage of Grace in the Lake Counties, 1536–7* (RHS, 1981).
R.W. Hoyle, *The Pilgrimage of Grace* (OUP, 2001).

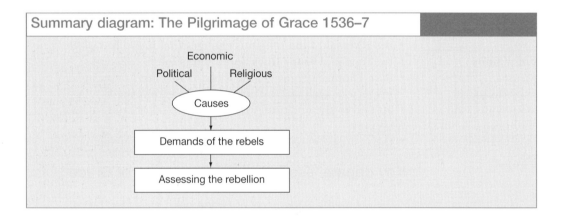

Summary diagram: The Pilgrimage of Grace 1536–7

3 | The Western or Prayer Book Rebellion 1549

It is difficult to judge to what extent underlying opposition to the changes in religion contributed to the rebellions of 1549 and to the fall of Somerset. Certainly, only the Western Rebellion was directly linked with religion, and even there underlying economic and social discontent played an important part in causing the uprising. To a certain extent the rebels in the west were complaining about enclosures and about the gentry, whom they accused of making use of the Reformation to seize Church land for their own enrichment. Such views were held in other areas during the popular uprisings of 1549, but only in the West Country was direct opposition to the new Act of Uniformity (see page 93) the central issue.

Key question
What were the causes of the Western Rebellion?

Cornwall

The popular discontent began in Cornwall in 1547, when the local archdeacon, William Body, who was disliked both for his Protestant views and for his personal greed, began to try to introduce religious reforms. He was mobbed by a hostile crowd at Penryn and fled to London. In April 1548 he returned to Cornwall to supervise the destruction of Catholic images in churches. At Helston Body was set upon, and killed, by a mob led by a local priest. Since the troublemakers dispersed quickly the authorities made only a few arrests. But they hanged the 10 ringleaders.

In 1549 the Cornish lower orders, fearing that the Act of Uniformity was going to be imposed on them, rose in rebellion and set up an armed camp at Bodmin. Because of the hostility expressed by the rebels towards landlords, only six of the pro-Catholic local gentry joined the uprising. However, the West Country élites were very unwilling to take any action against the rebellion on behalf of the government. The main leaders of the rebels were local clergy, and it was they who began to draw up a series of articles listing demands to stop changes in religion.

Devon

In Devon there was an independent uprising at Sampford Courtenay. By 20 June the Devon and Cornish rebels had joined forces at Crediton, and three days later they set up an armed camp at Clyst St Mary. Local negotiations between the authorities and the rebels broke down, and the rebels began to blockade the nearby town of Exeter with an army of 6000 men. Lord Russell, who had been sent to crush the rebellion, was hampered by a shortage of troops and a lack of local gentry support. Crucially, the rebels were led by a prominent local gentleman, Humphrey Arundell, who was a skilled tactician and able commander. As a result it was not until August that the rebels were finally defeated. It has been calculated that the rebels lost as many as 4000 killed.

Key dates

Introduction of First Book of Common Prayer: June 1549

Western or Prayer Book Rebellion: June 1549

Figure 4.1: Map of Western Rebellion.

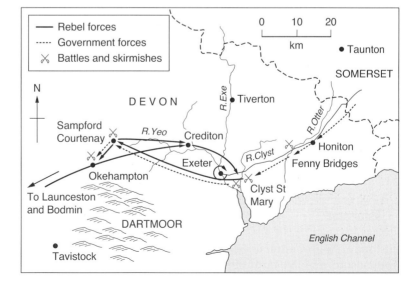

The demands of the rebels

Some of the demands put forward in the final set of articles drawn up by the rebels clearly illustrate their religious conservatism and other grievances felt in the West Country. For example, they wanted:

- to end the changes that they claimed were taking place in baptism and confirmation
- to restore the Act of Six Articles (see page 87)
- to restore the Latin Mass and images
- to restore old traditions like holy bread and water
- to restore the concept of transubstantiation and Purgatory (see page 87)
- the return of Cardinal Pole from exile and for him to have a seat on the king's ruling council.

Government reaction

The government clearly saw these articles as ultra-conservative demands for a return to Catholicism, and they were vigorously repudiated by Cranmer and the leading theologians among the reformers. It was claimed that the rank and file had been misled by, as Somerset put it, 'seditious priests, to seek restitution of the old bloody laws' for their own purposes. It was the manner in which the articles were phrased, just as much as their content, that offended the government. Unlike the usual wording of petitions to the Crown by rebels, such as the 'We pray your grace' used by Robert Ket in the same year (see page 138), each of the Western rebels' articles began 'Item we will'. Such lack of deference and respect, along with denials of the Royal Supremacy in the articles themselves, was seen as a greater threat to the stability of society and the State than the rebellion itself.

Cranmer was particularly enraged by such insubordination, and by the rebel demand that no gentleman should have more than one servant. It was this that enabled the government to accuse the rebels of being dangerous troublemakers, and so distract attention from their attack on religious change. In any case the government found no difficulty in pouring scorn on the lack of doctrinal knowledge in the articles. Their demands for the return of images and the old ceremonies were dismissed as idolatrous, and the old Mass was described as being more like games held during the Christmas season. Even greater scorn was poured on the rebel suggestion that they rejected the new services in English because as Cornish-speakers, it was a language that they did not understand.

Key question
What were the consequences of the Western Rebellion?

Key debate: assessing the Western Rebellion

How has the Western Rebellion been assessed by historians?

Historian Philip Caraman claims that the Western Rebellion was 'the most formidable opposition to the Reformation that England saw'. Historians agree that the rebels showed little knowledge of either Protestant or Catholic doctrines, but suggest that such ignorance in the West Country probably reflected similar confusion among the great mass of the population. Whether this is true or not, these demands do show that, in the West Country at least, many of the laity were still strongly attached to the familiar traditions of the old Church.

Although religion is acknowledged to be a key cause of the rebellion, some historians have drawn attention to the social and economic causes. For example, historian A.F. Pollard suggested that social tension lay at the heart of the rebellion and, according to historians A. Fletcher and J. Stevenson, there is evidence to suggest that the rebels considered the gentry to be their enemies. Even the leader of the royal army, Lord Russell, referred to the unfair exploitation of the common people by the local gentry and nobility, whom he claimed were taxing and raising rents excessively. The rebels were particularly angry at the new sheep tax, which they wanted withdrawn, but they failed to mention it in their list of final demands. Historians tended to ignore the social and economic grievances in favour of the religious. This is no longer the case, for as historian Nicholas Fellows has suggested, it is possible to make a link 'between the rebels' religious grievances and their attack upon the gentry: it was after all the gentry who had gained from the Reformation'.

Some key books in the debate
Philip Caraman, *The Western Rebellion, 1549: The Prayer Book Rebellion* (Halsgrove Press, 1994).
Nicholas Fellows, *Disorder and Rebellion in Tudor England* (Hodder Murray, 2001).
A. Fletcher and J. Stevenson, *Order and Disorder in Early Modern England* (Cambridge, 1985).
A.F. Pollard, *England under Protector Somerset* (London, 1900).

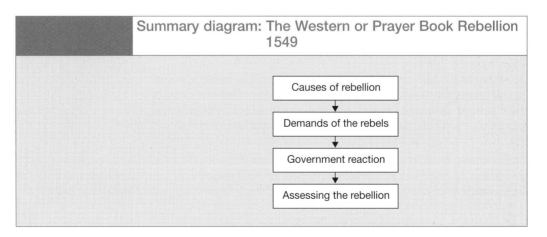

Summary diagram: The Western or Prayer Book Rebellion 1549

Causes of rebellion

↓

Demands of the rebels

↓

Government reaction

↓

Assessing the rebellion

4 | The Ket Rebellion 1549

East Anglia was the most industrialised part of the country. Norwich was the largest town after London, and was a major textile centre. The causes of the rebellion are symptomatic of the confused nature of lower order discontent with the economic changes. The rising was triggered by unrest over enclosures, high rents and unsympathetic local landlords. East Anglia had a large number of independent small farmers, who were being adversely affected by the enclosing of fields and commons by the gentry and yeomen. The collapse of textile exports had thrown large numbers of clothworkers in Norwich and the surrounding countryside out of work. In June there were riots at the neighbouring market towns of Attleborough and Wymondham, and some new fences that had been put up by Sir John Flowerdew were pulled down.

Key question
What were the causes of Ket's Rebellion?

Sir John Flowerdew

Flowerdew was a lawyer who had bought up Church property in the area. This made him unpopular with the locals, who resented him as an outsider. Furthermore, he was in dispute with the townspeople of Wymondham over the local abbey, which he had bought and was demolishing. The townspeople had bought the abbey church for use by the parish, and were incensed when Flowerdew began to strip the lead from the roof. Given the truth of historian Anthony Fletcher's opinion that the gentry were 'detaching themselves in manners and values' from the mass of the people, Flowerdew's apparent insensitivity is perhaps not surprising. This detachment seems to have coloured ruling-class views of the poor and of the danger they posed to society, law and good order.

Robert Ket

Flowerdew was also in dispute with a local yeoman, Robert Ket, over land. Ket was a tanner and small landowner who had enclosed much of the common at Wymondham. Flowerdew tried to turn the rioters against him but Ket turned the tables by offering to act as their spokesman. In fact, Ket showed more organisational skill and decisive leadership than is usually found in the leaders of peasant risings. He quickly gathered an army of 16,000 men, set up camp for six weeks on Mousehold Heath and, in July, was able to capture Norwich. The rebellion is notable for the discipline that Ket imposed, electing a governing council and maintaining law and order. Every gentleman apprehended by the rebels was tried before Ket and his council at the **Tree of Reformation**.

Like the popular uprising in the West Country, the rebellion was eventually crushed when John Dudley, Earl of Warwick (later the Duke of Northumberland), was sent to take command of the Marquis of Northampton's army of 14,000 men. Northampton had succeeded in taking Norwich but had been forced to abandon it after only a day. Unlike Northampton, Warwick was

Key date
Ket's Rebellion in East Anglia: July 1549

Key term
Tree of Reformation
Term used to describe the location of Ket's council of justice which sat under an old oak tree.

Figure 4.2: Map of Ket Rebellion.

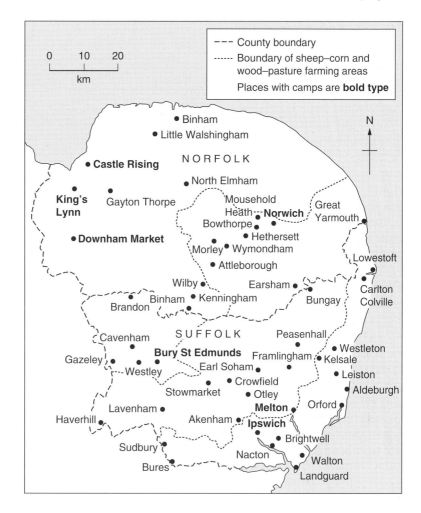

able to bring the rebels to battle at Dussingdale, just outside the city, where nearly 4000 rebels and royal troops were killed. Ket was captured and eventually hanged for sedition.

The demands of the rebels

The rebels drew up a list of 29 articles covering a range of topics. For example, they wanted:

- landowners to stop enclosing common land
- rents to be reduced to the levels they were under Henry VII
- rivers to be open to all for fishing and fishermen be allowed to keep a greater share of the profits from sea fishing
- all **bondmen** be given their freedom, 'for God made everyone free with his precious blood shedding'
- corrupt local officials 'who have offended the commons' to be punished 'where it has been proved by the complaints of the poor'
- incompetent priests to be removed from their churches, particularly those who were 'unable to preach and set forth the word of God to their parishioners'.

Key term

Bondmen
Peasant farmers who had no freedom to choose where they lived and worked. They were tied to the manor on which they were born and brought up.

Assessing the Ket Rebellion

Unlike the West Country rebels who seemed to wish for religion to be returned to the good old days of Henry VIII, the Norfolk insurgents supported the Protestant religious changes. Ket encouraged Protestant ministers to preach to the rebels on Mousehold Heath and to use the new Prayer Book.

Although enclosure has been cited as the primary cause of the rebellion, in truth it was just one among many agricultural demands made by the rebels. Indeed, apart from local examples such as at Wymondham and Attleborough, there had been relatively few enclosures in Norfolk during the previous 50 years. Similarly, the requests that bondmen or serfs should be made free is strange because there is no evidence that there were many unfree tenants in sixteenth-century Norfolk.

The major demands were for commons to be kept open and free for husbandmen to graze their livestock, and that rents should not be increased excessively. The Norfolk rebels appeared to yearn for the favourable economic conditions that had existed under Henry VII. This supports the notion that the major cause of the popular unrest in 1549 was the harsh economic conditions that prevailed in that year.

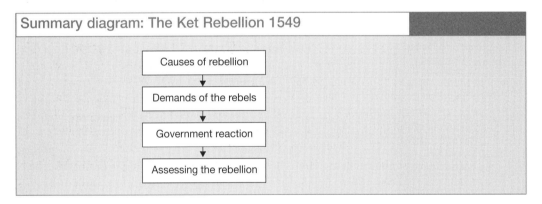

Summary diagram: The Ket Rebellion 1549

Causes of rebellion

↓

Demands of the rebels

↓

Government reaction

↓

Assessing the rebellion

5 | Lady Jane Grey and the Succession Crisis 1553

Key question
What were the causes and consequences of the succession crisis of 1553?

By 1552 Northumberland seemed to be firmly in control. Even the rapid swing towards Calvinism in the Church of England (see page 89) did not appear to be provoking any serious opposition. However, his power depended upon the support of Edward VI. By the end of the year the king's health was obviously deteriorating quickly, and the problem of the succession became a central issue once again. In accordance with Henry VIII's will, Mary was to succeed if Edward died childless. Mary's strong Catholic sympathies made her unpopular with the reform party and with Edward himself. Moreover, it was feared that Mary might renounce the Royal Supremacy.

To prevent a return to Catholicism, and to retain power, Northumberland, with the full support of the king, planned to

Key dates

Guildford Dudley married Lady Jane Grey: May 1553

Death of Edward VI, Lady Jane Grey proclaimed queen: July 1553

Northumberland's military expedition against Mary Tudor ended in failure: July 1553

Mary Tudor proclaimed queen: July 1553

Northumberland executed: August 1553

change the succession. As the Succession Acts of 1534 and 1536 (see pages 39–40) making Mary and Elizabeth illegitimate had not been repealed, it was decided to disinherit them in favour of the Suffolk branch of the family. Frances, Duchess of Suffolk, was excluded as her age made it unlikely that she would have male heirs and her eldest daughter, Lady Jane Grey, was chosen to succeed. To secure his own position Northumberland married his eldest son, Guildford Dudley, to Jane in May 1553.

Unfortunately for Northumberland, Edward VI died in July before the plans for the seizure of power could be completed. Jane Grey was proclaimed queen by Northumberland and the Council in London, while Mary proclaimed herself queen at Framlingham Castle in Suffolk. Northumberland's mistakes were two-fold:

- He failed to arrest Mary and keep her in custody.
- He underestimated the amount of support for Mary in the country.

On 14 July he marched into Suffolk with an army of 2000 men, but his troops deserted him. The Privy Council in London hastily changed sides and proclaimed Mary as queen. Northumberland was arrested in Cambridge, tried, and was executed on 22 August in spite of his renunciation of Protestantism.

Assessing Lady Jane Grey and the succession crisis

The ease with which Mary upheld her right to the throne shows the growing stability of the State and the nation. Potential political crisis had been avoided because the majority of the nation supported the rule of law and rightful succession. The direct line of descent was still considered legitimate in spite of Acts of Parliament to the contrary. A period of dynastic weakness and minority rule had passed without the country dissolving into civil war.

Two Acts were passed, one in 1553 and another in 1554, to resolve the constitutional position. This legislation was designed to confirm Mary Tudor's legitimacy, and to establish the right of female monarchs to rule in England. However, no attempt was made to make Elizabeth legitimate, although she was recognised as Mary's heir in the event of her dying childless.

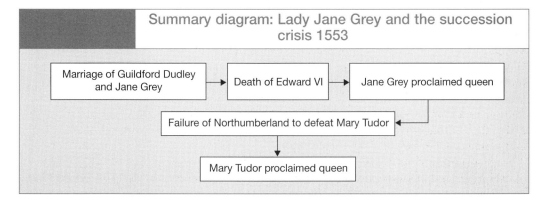

Summary diagram: Lady Jane Grey and the succession crisis 1553

Marriage of Guildford Dudley and Jane Grey → Death of Edward VI → Jane Grey proclaimed queen

Failure of Northumberland to defeat Mary Tudor

Mary Tudor proclaimed queen

6 | The Wyatt Rebellion 1554

Sir Thomas Wyatt was a member of a wealthy and well-connected gentry family from Kent. He succeeded to the family estates on the death of his father, also called Sir Thomas, in 1542. Sir Thomas Wyatt senior had been a courtier and diplomat, and his son was expected to follow suit. He became friendly with the influential Henry Howard, Earl of Surrey, who acted as his **patron**. Wyatt fought in France under Surrey in 1543–4 and in 1545 he was promoted to the English council governing English-controlled Boulogne.

Unfortunately for Wyatt, his career suffered a setback in 1547 when Surrey fell into disfavour with Henry VIII and was executed. As a committed Protestant Wyatt found favour with the Edwardian regime, which he defended in 1549 when riots broke out in Kent. He was trusted by Somerset's successor Northumberland, who appointed him to represent the English government in negotiations with the French in 1550.

Wyatt served the Edwardian regime loyally but he declared his support for Mary when Jane Grey was proclaimed queen. Wyatt's initial support for Mary soon evaporated when he heard of the Spanish marriage. As an MP he became involved in the

Key question
What were the causes of Wyatt's Rebellion?

Patron
A wealthy and powerful individual who uses his influence to promote the career of a supporter.

Key term

Marriage proposal between Mary and Philip of Spain presented to the Royal Council: December 1553

Wyatt Rebellion: January 1554

Wyatt entered London: February 1554

Key dates

Tho: Wiatt Knight.

Sir Thomas Wyatt c1521–54.

opposition to the proposed marriage in parliament but his hopes of persuading the queen to reject the marriage failed.

Conspiracy and rebellion

By the end of January 1554, anti-Spanish feelings led to rebellion. Unlike the uprisings in 1549 this was a political conspiracy among the élites, and there was little popular support. The rebellion was led by Sir James Croft, Sir Peter Carew and Sir Thomas Wyatt. These men had all held important offices at Court under both Henry VIII and Edward VI. Although they had supported Mary's accession, they feared that the growing Spanish influence would endanger their own careers. Wyatt appealed to patriotism by declaring that:

> because you be Englishmen ... you will join with us, as we will with you unto death, in this behalf protesting unto you before God ... we seek no harm to the Queen, but better counsel and councillors.

The conspirators planned to marry Elizabeth to Edward Courtenay, Earl of Devon, whom Mary had rejected. Simultaneous rebellions in the West Country, the Midlands and Kent, were to be supported by the French fleet blockading the English Channel.

The plan failed because the inept Courtenay disclosed the scheme to his patron, Gardiner, before the conspirators were ready to act. In any case, Carew, Croft and the Duke of Suffolk bungled the uprisings in the West Country and the Midlands. Wyatt succeeded in raising an army of 3000 men in Kent, and this caused real fear in the government because the rebels were so close to the capital. The situation was made worse because the troops sent to Kent under the aged and semi-retired Duke of Norfolk deserted to the rebels. Realising the danger, the Privy Council quickly raised forces to protect London.

An over-cautious Wyatt, meanwhile, took his time in making for the capital. He wasted a day besieging Cooling Castle and capturing his enemy Lord Cobham. Wyatt then wasted time by agreeing to consider the queen's offer to discuss his grievances, but this was a calculated plan on Mary's part to gain time. By delaying his advance too long, Wyatt allowed the government time to appeal to the citizens of the capital for support, see to the defence of the city and organise its troops. Although Wyatt enjoyed some initial success as he skirted the city walls, when the main assault on London came, the rebels were trapped and defeated at Ludgate.

Government reaction

The administration had had a bad scare, and Paget suggested leniency for the rebels for fear of provoking further revolts. Fewer than 100 executions took place among the commons and most were pardoned. As for the rebels among the élites, apart from Wyatt and the Duke of Suffolk, only Jane Grey and Guildford Dudley were executed. Croft was tried and imprisoned but his

Key question
What were the consequences of Wyatt's Rebellion?

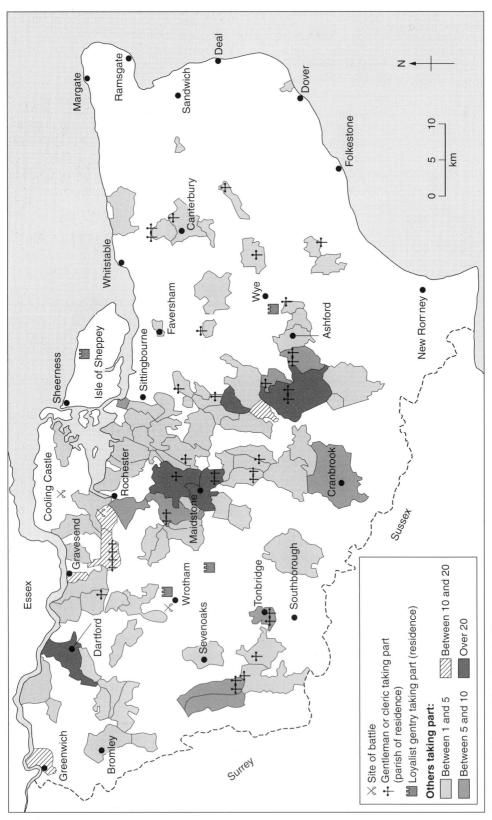

Figure 4.3: Map of Wyatt's Rebellion.

A woodcut showing the execution of Lady Jane Grey. Why has the illustrator referred to the victim as Lady rather than Queen Jane?

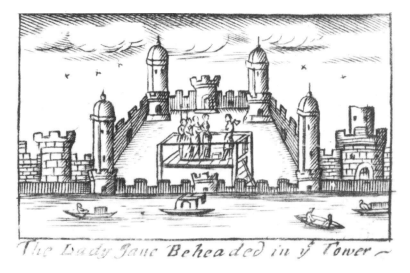

The Lady Jane Beheaded in ẙ Tower ～

Key dates

Elizabeth arrested for supposedly being involved in the rebellion: February 1554

Lady Jane Grey and Guildford Dudley executed: February 1554

Marriage of Mary and Philip: July 1554

release followed after less than nine months in the Tower. Carew fled to France but he was pardoned upon his return in 1556. After a short imprisonment Elizabeth and Courtenay were released, and Elizabeth remained next in line to the throne. Even so, anti-Spanish feelings remained high. Philip's proposed coronation was postponed, and he only remained in England for a few months before returning to Spain.

Key debate: Assessing the Wyatt Rebellion

How has the Wyatt Rebellion been assessed by historians?

The Wyatt Rebellion came as close as any to overthrowing the monarchy. He benefited from the proximity of Kent to the capital and from his own work in improving the muster in the county. A rapid advance on London might have met with success but hesitation and delay gave Mary and the government vital time to prepare. According to historian Paul Thomas 'Mary's new regime was pushing its luck, not so much with a policy of Catholic restoration, as with the Spanish marriage and the provocation of those members of the Court élite who either felt excluded or feared imminent exclusion.' Historian Anthony Fletcher has stated that 'the resort to rebellion by the excluded arose because of the ineffectiveness of the constitutional methods of opposition to the royal marriage policy'. Frustrated and increasingly desperate, men like Wyatt felt compelled to act in a way calculated to end in their deaths unless they succeeded in overthrowing the monarch. In the opinion of historian Diarmaid MacCulloch, the fact that Wyatt failed demonstrates 'the bankruptcy of rebellion as a way of solving' political crises.

Some key books in the debate
Anthony Fletcher and Diarmaid MacCulloch, *Tudor Rebellions*
(Longman, 1997).
David Loades, *Two Tudor Conspiracies* (Cambridge, 1965).
Paul Thomas, *Authority and Disorder in Tudor Times 1485–1603*
(CUP, 1999).

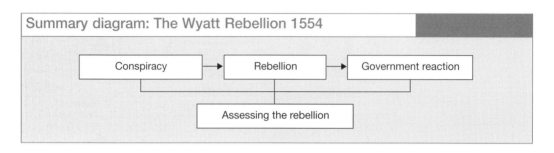

Summary diagram: The Wyatt Rebellion 1554

Conspiracy → Rebellion → Government reaction

Assessing the rebellion

7 | The Northern Rebellion or Rebellion of the Northern Earls 1569

Key question
What were the causes of the Northern Rebellion?

The Northern Rebellion used to be seen as a religious rising but
that is no longer the case. The rebel leaders, the earls of
Northumberland and Westmorland, had genuine religious
concerns but their rebellion was mainly about politics and the
succession. The roots of the rebellion can be found in the politics
and faction of the day and the arrival on English soil of the
fugitive Mary, Queen of Scots, which provided a focus for the
discontented northern nobility.

Mary, Queen of Scots
arrived in England:
May 1568

Key date

Politics and faction

The first few years of Elizabeth's reign witnessed a period of
political unity. This was the time when the regime was being
established. Sir William Cecil enjoyed a close working relationship
with Elizabeth, who relied on him for advice. This gave Cecil
unrivalled political prominence at Court and made him a target
for rival factions. As Elizabeth's chief minister Cecil was
responsible for co-ordinating the implementation of most policy
decisions at home and abroad. In some respects Cecil's position
can be compared to that of Cromwell: both were powerful at
Court, both had the confidence of the monarch and both were
talented and imaginative ministers.

Like Cromwell, Cecil too had rivals at Court but, unlike
Cromwell, they were never outright enemies determined to cause
his death. Faction fighting at the Court of Elizabeth did not
become a serious issue until later in her reign when England went
to war with Spain in the mid-1580s. Self-interest and short-term
aims often pushed rival factions together. Cecil and Leicester
sometimes found themselves on the same side and even when
both were enemies neither wished to see the other executed, only
'cowed' or 'retired'.

Figure 4.4: Map of Northern Rebellion.

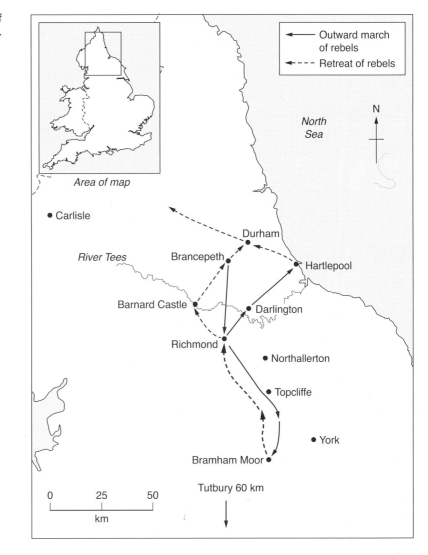

Cecil's rivals included:

- Robert Dudley, Earl of Leicester. Dudley was the son of the former Lord President, the Duke of Northumberland, executed by Mary in 1553. He was a Protestant and a firm favourite of Queen Elizabeth. He was appointed to the Privy Council in 1562 and created Earl of Leicester in 1564. Their relationship was so close that there was talk of their marrying; but this never happened. Elizabeth's emotional attachment to Leicester gave him personal access to the queen, which posed a serious threat to Cecil.

- Thomas Radcliffe, Earl of Sussex. Radcliffe was a talented soldier and administrator. On his return from governing Ireland in 1565 he was appointed to the Privy Council. He was neutral in religion, counting both Catholics and Protestants among his friends and associates. Sussex was an independent who tended to oppose Leicester and support Cecil. But this was not always the case.

- Thomas Howard, Duke of Norfolk. Howard was a religious conservative who leaned towards Catholicism. He was ambitious, arrogant but politically incompetent. He tended to side with Sussex but his lack of courage and honesty made him few friends.

Conspiracy and rebellion

The conspiracy that led to the Northern Rebellion is complex and consists of two overlapping but disconnected strands.

Northern Rebellion: November–December 1569

Key date

Strand 1

A plot was hatched at Court by the Sussex and Leicester factions whereby the Duke of Norfolk would be encouraged to marry Mary, Queen of Scots. The plotters hoped to coerce Elizabeth either into nominating any children of the match as her successor or into marriage whereby she would have children of her own. Part of the arrangement was to be the elimination of Cecil as a political force. He would be replaced by pro-Catholic sympathisers and the traditional friendship with Spain, in the person of Philip II, would be renewed.

The plot failed when rumours of the Norfolk–Mary marriage plan reached the queen. Leicester confessed his part in the affair while Norfolk panicked and left the Court without permission. Racked by indecision Norfolk spent the best part of six weeks on his country estate at Kenninghall, Norfolk. While Elizabeth feared he might rebel, Mary actively encouraged it. Norfolk's supporters in the north, his brother-in-law, Charles Neville, Earl of Westmorland and Thomas Percy, Earl of Northumberland, waited to see what he would do. Westmorland was fully prepared to rise in support of Norfolk but Northumberland was unwilling to 'hazard myself for the marriage'. Eventually Norfolk broke down under the strain: he wrote to Westmorland advising him not to rebel after which he submitted to Elizabeth. Norfolk was promptly put in the Tower.

Strand 2

The second strand of the conspiracy involved the pro-Catholic earls of Northumberland and Westmorland. The earls, along with Lord Dacre, had been sidelined by the Elizabethan regime, which did not fully trust them. Aware of the lingering sympathy for Catholicism that existed in the north, Elizabeth opted to put men she trusted in positions of authority in the region:

- The queen's cousin, Lord Hunsdon, was put in charge of Berwick and the half of the border region.
- The Earl of Sussex was appointed President of the Council of the North in York.
- James Pilkington, an enthusiastic Protestant, was appointed bishop of Durham.

Resentment at being passed over for offices that they considered to be traditionally theirs by right, was turned to outright anger by Pilkington's aggressive evangelical style. News of the failure of the

Norfolk–Mary marriage plan, together with the Duke's imprisonment, added to their frustration. They felt they had no choice but to lead a rebellion against an aggressive, uncaring and, as far as their grievances were concerned, increasingly deaf Protestant regime.

In order to attract as much support as possible, the earls issued a proclamation stating that the reason for their rebellion was to resist the 'new-found religion and heresy'. The pro-Catholic gentry and peasantry flocked to join what they saw as a religious crusade. In all some 6000 joined the rebellion a fair number but nowhere near as many as the earls had hoped. Apart from the capture of Durham, and the restoration of the Mass in the Cathedral, the rebel army did no more than march to and from Bramham Moor near York.

When news came that a royal army of 10,000 men was marching north to meet them, the earls panicked, disbanded their army and fled over the border to Scotland. A rebellion that had begun on 9 November ended without a major confrontation on 16 December 1569. All was not over, for within a few days Lord Dacre rose in rebellion with 3000 men but he was defeated in battle early in January 1570. The Northern Rebellion was over. The government was ruthless in its pursuit of the rebel leaders. Westmorland escaped abroad but Northumberland was captured and executed. Norfolk was eventually tried for treason and executed in 1572.

Key date

Dacre Rebellion: 1569–70

Key debate: Assessing the Northern Rebellion

How has the Northern Rebellion been assessed by historians?

In the opinion of most historians the rebellion failed because of poor leadership: it was incoherent and aimless. As Nicholas Fellows said, the earls did not 'cut a dash; instead their image is one of reluctant rebels, driven into rebellion out of despair, rather than with an iron will'.

There is less consensus on the causes of the rebellion. Writing in the 1930s Sir John Neale saw the rebellion purely in terms of the failed Norfolk–Mary marriage. In his opinion the one led directly to the other. In contrast, recent revisionist studies by David Marcombe and S.E. Taylor have tended to see the rebellion as a distinctly northern phenomenon. To them the rising was part of a regional crisis in which dissatisfied conservative northern gentry and nobility reluctantly rebelled out of frustration and anger at:

- their treatment by southerners planted in the area to run their affairs
- their exclusion from office and power
- the treatment of the Catholic faith.

The defeat of the Northern Earls represented a turning point for the Elizabethan regime. The regime and the largely Protestant

Religious Settlement it had established by Act of Parliament had survived its first test and would never be seriously challenged again.

Some key books in the debate
Anthony Fletcher and Diarmaid MacCulloch, *Tudor Rebellions* (Longman, 1997).
David Marcombe, 'A rude and heady people: the local community and the rebellion of the Northern Earls', *The Last Principality, Religion and Society in the Bishopric of Durham, 1494–1660* (University of Nottingham, 1987).
J.E. Neale, *Queen Elizabeth* (Cape, 1934).
S.E. Taylor, 'The Crown and the North of England 1559–1570'. PhD thesis (Manchester University, 1981).
Paul Thomas, *Authority and Disorder in Tudor Times 1485–1603* (CUP, 1999).

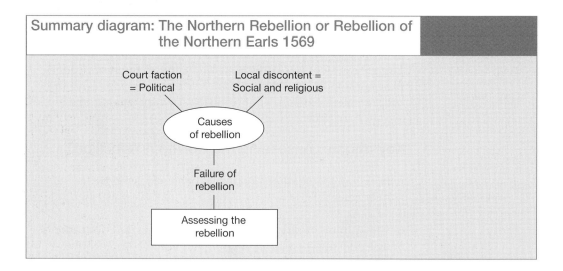

Summary diagram: The Northern Rebellion or Rebellion of the Northern Earls 1569

8 | Conclusion: Was there a Crisis in Authority?

If there was a crisis in authority in the mid-sixteenth century it was in 1549, and was created by a range of misfortunes. For example:

- There was a weak, insolvent government, over-stretching its resources by trying to fight a war on two fronts.
- The government was attempting to introduce drastic religious reforms.
- It aroused the hostility of the élites and non-élites by its social and economic policies.
- Prices, fuelled by currency debasements and increasing population levels, had doubled since the beginning of the century.
- A run of good growing seasons was brought to an end by a wet summer, and the harvest in 1549 was poor. This came at a time

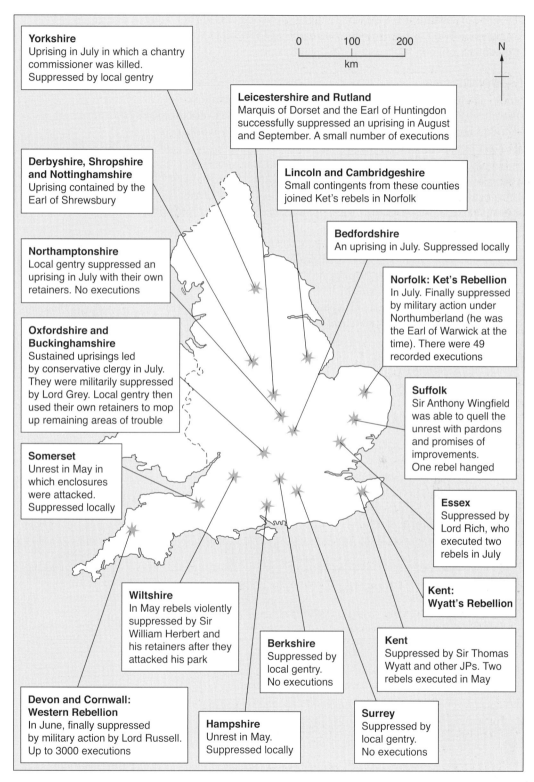

Yorkshire
Uprising in July in which a chantry commissioner was killed. Suppressed by local gentry

0   100   200
km

N

Leicestershire and Rutland
Marquis of Dorset and the Earl of Huntingdon successfully suppressed an uprising in August and September. A small number of executions

Derbyshire, Shropshire and Nottinghamshire
Uprising contained by the Earl of Shrewsbury

Lincoln and Cambridgeshire
Small contingents from these counties joined Ket's rebels in Norfolk

Bedfordshire
An uprising in July. Suppressed locally

Northamptonshire
Local gentry suppressed an uprising in July with their own retainers. No executions

Norfolk: Ket's Rebellion
In July. Finally suppressed by military action under Northumberland (he was the Earl of Warwick at the time). There were 49 recorded executions

Oxfordshire and Buckinghamshire
Sustained uprisings led by conservative clergy in July. They were militarily suppressed by Lord Grey. Local gentry then used their own retainers to mop up remaining areas of trouble

Suffolk
Sir Anthony Wingfield was able to quell the unrest with pardons and promises of improvements. One rebel hanged

Somerset
Unrest in May in which enclosures were attacked. Suppressed locally

Essex
Suppressed by Lord Rich, who executed two rebels in July

Wiltshire
In May rebels violently suppressed by Sir William Herbert and his retainers after they attacked his park

**Kent:
Wyatt's Rebellion**

Berkshire
Suppressed by local gentry. No executions

Kent
Suppressed by Sir Thomas Wyatt and other JPs. Two rebels executed in May

Devon and Cornwall: Western Rebellion
In June, finally suppressed by military action by Lord Russell. Up to 3000 executions

Hampshire
Unrest in May. Suppressed locally

Surrey
Suppressed by local gentry. No executions

Figure 4.5: Major and lesser risings in 1549.

when agriculture was already struggling to feed the higher level of population (this had peaked at three million in 1549), and so grain prices rose.

Lesser risings

Under these circumstances it is not surprising that underlying discontent came to the surface in the form of popular rebellions. Indeed, unrest in 1549 was widespread with some 25 counties affected by disturbances.

The causes of these minor risings were two-fold: enclosure and religious change. Although the majority of these disturbances were local protests or were stopped before they could cause serious harm, taken together they presented the government with a major challenge.

If Somerset had not been so arrogant and unwilling to withdraw troops from Scotland and France, and if there had not been a power struggle developing in the Privy Council, it is unlikely that the situation would have got out of hand. Once the government had mobilised sufficient troops, the rebellions were suppressed with comparative ease.

Study Guide: AS Questions

In the style of OCR

Study the five sources on the 1549 rebellions, and then answer *both* sub-questions. It is recommended that you spend two-thirds of your time in answering part (b).

(a) **Study Sources A and E.**

Compare these sources as evidence for the breakdown of law and order in 1549.

(b) **Study *all* the sources.**

Use your own knowledge to assess how far the sources support the interpretation that government mistakes were the *main* cause of the rebellions of 1549.

The 1549 rebellions

Source A

William Paget, letter, 7 July 1549. William Paget, a trusted adviser to Protector Somerset, writes to him criticising his conduct and its consequences.

I told your grace the truth and was not believed. The king's subjects are out of all discipline, out of obedience, caring neither for protector nor king. And what is the cause? Your own softness, your intention to be good to the poor. Consider, I beseech you most humbly, that society in a realm is maintained by means of religion and law. The use of the old religion is forbidden by a law, and the use of the new is not yet embraced by eleven out of twelve parts of the realm. As for the law, the foot takes on him the part of the head, and the common people are behaving like a king.

Source B

Edward VI, Answer to the Petition of the rebels of Devon and Cornwall, July 1549. In a letter written for him by Protector Somerset, Edward VI lists some of the grievances of the rebels in the South West.

For baptism, you are fearful that your children should now only be christened on holy days. You say certain Cornishmen are offended because they do not have their service in Cornish, since they understand no English.

You object that religious changes were made without my knowledge. But I deny this and affirm that the prayer book is according to scripture and the word of God.

You require the tax granted to me by parliament on cloth and sheep should be cancelled. You complain of the shortage of food and other things.

Source C

Edward VI, letter to the Commons assembled in Norfolk, 18 July 1549. The Privy Council, in the name of Edward VI, writes to the rebels in Norfolk.

We have been informed that you have assembled in large companies in a very disordered fashion. You have forgotten the Bible which teaches obedience to the King. We have always been ready to address your grievances, and have sent commissioners to reform enclosures. You make humble petition to us for further reform and we will ensure that rents are returned to their old levels. Other reforms will be discussed in the next parliament. We urge you now to return quietly to your homes.

Source D

Matteo Dandolo, letter to the Senate of Venice, 20 July 1549. The Venetian ambassador in England reports social and religious unrest, and the government's response.

There is news of major risings against the government in England, and that the King has retreated to a strong castle outside London. The cause of this is the common land, as the great landowners occupy the pastures of the poor people. The rebels also require the return of the Mass, together with the religion as it stood on the death of Henry VIII. The government, wishing to apply a remedy, put upwards of 500 persons to the sword, sparing neither women nor children.

Source E

Protector Somerset, letter to Philip Hoby, 24 August 1549. Protector Somerset writes to a close advisor expressing his view of the rebels.

Some rebels wish to pull down enclosures and parks; some want to recover their common land; others pretend religion is their motive. A number would want to rule for a time, and do as gentlemen have done, and indeed all have a great hatred of gentlemen and regard them as their enemies. The ruffians among them, and the soldiers, who are the leaders, look for loot. So the rebellions are nothing other than a plague and a fury among the vilest and worst sort of men.

Exam tips

(a) First of all make sure you are comparing the correct two sources, Source A with Source E.

- Focus: here the focus is on the *breakdown of law and order in 1549*. This should be kept clearly in mind throughout, as the purpose of the *comparison*.
- Links: similarities and differences should be cross-referenced point by point and *linked* to the question, *the breakdown of law and order in 1549*. In planning, highlight aspects of source content which link to these key terms.

- Avoid a formulaic approach. Think about the sources in the light of their historical context, and show your understanding of their significance in answering the question.
- Provenance: it is important to start by focusing on *who, what, when, why* and *to whom* the source was written and its *tone*. Not all of these aspects may be relevant to this particular question, so avoid a formulaic approach. Concentrate on the most significant aspect(s).
- Content: try to balance similarities and differences of content in the light of their provenance, integrating content with provenance.
- Analyse: the detail, sentence by sentence, cross-referencing in the light of the question. Compare the reliability or usefulness of the two sources in answering it.
- Judgement: decide which of the two sources provides the better evidence of 'the breakdown of law and order in 1549' and give convincing support for your decision. This may be based on usefulness, reliability, whether the view is typical, more complete, better informed, written at a significant date or some other relevant criterion.

The *provenance* (*author and date*): Source A is written by Paget in July 1549, after a series of local rebellions had broken out throughout the country, with a particularly large-scale revolt in Devon and Cornwall and anti-enclosure riots following the renewal of John Hales' Commission. Paget's advice had been ignored by Somerset despite an agreement made between them when Somerset became Lord Protector. Source E, on the other hand, is written by Somerset himself towards the end of August when the rebellions had shown themselves to be extremely serious and difficult to put down. Somerset is unlikely to accept the responsibility for causing the rebellions which is given to him by Paget in Source A.

The *context* of Source E is a crisis of confidence in Somerset's leadership amongst the Council, whose advice he was said to have ignored. So Source E has the purpose of shifting the blame onto the rebels themselves rather than shouldering any responsibility of his own, as suggested in Source A.

The *content* of the sources is similar in that both accept that the common people are overturning the Great Chain of Being and trying to assume power for themselves. They differ in the reasons they give: Source A blames Somerset's softness in dealing with the poor, and his weakness in enforcing law and religion, whereas, in Source E, Somerset blames their hatred for greedy gentlemen who have enclosed the common land. He rejects the claim that the rebels have acted for religious motives and says this is a pretence. The tone of the sources might be used to aid the comparison: Paget is critical but still supportive in July, whereas by the end of August, many of the Council have turned against Somerset and the emotive tone of Source E suggests he is fighting for political survival.

Judgement might view Source A as the better evidence for 'the breakdown of law and order in 1549', as its purpose is merely to let Somerset know he should have listened to his friend, whose advice has proved to be worthy of attention, whereas Source E show Somerset taking a harsh attitude towards the poor, for all his supposed reputation as the 'Good Duke' to try to shift responsibility for the rebellions onto others. Source E is therefore less reliable.

(b) In order to answer this part of the question:

- The sources should be grouped by their point of view: sometimes a source contains more than one point for cross-reference.
- The significance for the question, of the views in the content of the sources, should be developed using accurate historical context and terminology.
- Relevant aspects of the provenance of the sources should be linked to answering the question, where 'provenance' might be authorship, date, nature, purpose, audience, tone.
- Accurate knowledge and terminology should be integrated into the answer to verify, qualify or evaluate the views in the sources as well as their provenance.
- A judgement should be reached on the 'value' of the sources in linking to the interpretation in the question, where 'value' might be judged by:
  - reliability and/or usefulness of content and provenance
  - completeness of content or aspects deliberately ignored
  - limitations of the sources as a set.

Things to avoid:

- Do not use the sources as illustrations of an essay style answer.
- Do not merely *describe* or *paraphrase* source content, but always use it to argue.
- Do not use the sources as a mine for extracting *references*. Their purpose is to validate or qualify the interpretation in the question, enabling you to use them in effective argument.
- Do not make 'stock' comments about the provenance of sources, especially common with secondary authors, e.g. 'he is an eminent historian so we can trust his view'. Always link comments on provenance to the focus of the question.

Sources A–D suggest that mistaken government policies had caused the 1549 rebellions. These included softness in dealing with enclosure riots by proclamation rather than Statute, Hales Commission inquiring into enclosures, an ambiguous First Prayer Book, an unpopular sheep tax and debasement of the coinage amongst others. The provenance of Source B and C are interesting in their unreliability, as Somerset and the Council are the true authors rather than the minor King Edward himself. The back-down apparent in Source D, after the firmer line by

Somerset in Source C, might be used to evaluate the 'softness' mentioned in Source A. Content, provenance and context should be integrated to develop the cause and a judgement reached on the extent to which these sources support the interpretation.

On the other hand, Sources A, C and E blame troublemakers amongst the ordinary people who wish to gain power for themselves. In contrast, Sources C–E suggest that the blame for the rebellions lies with the greedy gentlemen who have enclosed the common land and caused such class tensions. Knowledge of local feuds or regional causes might be used to extend this point, e.g. Flowerdew and Ket in Norfolk, William Body in Cornwall. The rebellions are presented as the result of social change and a breakdown in the Great Chain of Being. Content, provenance and context should be integrated to develop the cause and a judgement reached to answer the question.

The context of minority rule features in the provenance of Sources C–E as a lesser cause of the 1549 rebellions. The content of Source D mentions the withdrawal of the king to a castle outside London. Knowledge might be used of Somerset's action in taking the king to Windsor to avoid factional unrest in London, as context for this source. Political divisions contributed to the tensions that caused the rebellions. An evaluative judgement should be reached on the relative significance of this cause.

A judgement should be reached evaluating how far the sources support the interpretation overall. This is likely to reflect the reliability and use of the sources as well as the changing historical context and the relative importance of the causes of the 1549 rebellions.

Final tips:

- The limitations of the set of sources should be supplied from relevant own knowledge, not merely suggested less appropriately, e.g. 'Somerset is more reliable because he played a part in the events he describes'. This comment adds little to the evaluation.
- The grouped sources should drive the answer, and an evaluative argument should be created by integrating context with source content and provenance.
- Marks are awarded for synthesis, bringing together all the elements of the answer. Therefore the final paragraph of conclusion is *very important* and will play an important part in gaining marks. It should bring together all the threads of the argument and judge how far the sources, as a set, support the interpretation in the question. If the sources are limited or unreliable, they will not support the interpretation effectively.

Study Guide: A2 Question

In the style of Edexcel

How far do you agree with the view that the rebellions of 1549 did not pose a significant threat to the government? Explain your answer, using Sources 1–3 and your own knowledge of the issues related to this controversy.

Source 1

From: N. Fellows, Disorder and Rebellion in Tudor England, *published in 2001.*

Although the concept of a mid-Tudor crisis has been challenged over recent years, it is difficult to escape the fact that the years 1547–53 saw a large number of disturbances. In particular 1549 saw two serious rebellions and numerous other minor disturbances, which some historians believe brought England close to class war.

There were tensions in both town and countryside as economic problems reached new levels of intensity. Changes in central government and religion had loosened loyalty to the regime so that those discontented by the hard times were ready recruits for those who wished to overturn Tudor rule.

Source 2

From: David Rogerson et al., The Early Tudors: England, 1485–1558, *published in 2001.*

By any estimation the uprisings of 1549 were serious. They eventually resulted in the overthrow of the well-established ruler, Protector Somerset, they mobilised tens of thousands of angry commoners across the country and they took the government's resources near to breaking point. The loss of life was very significant, as around 10,000 are known to have died. The rebellions of 1549 were not however threatening in an overtly political way. Their purpose was not to overthrow any member of the government or ruling family. In the case of Ket's rebellion, the rebels appealed to tradition and custom, not to a radical agenda. They remained disciplined and clear-sighted about their objectives. In the Western Rebellion, the rebels did have a more challenging religious agenda that openly rejected the government's Protestant changes. Their articles were written more assertively and they did not display the kind of deference expected in the sixteenth century.

Source 3

From: Edward Towne, The Tudor Years, *published in 1994.*

The crisis theory overlooks the fact that the government never lost control, even in 1549. This may have been partly because the two rebellions in 1549 had limited aims and did not intend to topple the government. The council functioned effectively from 1540 despite undoubted factional turmoil from time to time.

Exam tips

The cross-references are intended to take you straight to the material that will help you to answer the question.

This question provides you with sources that contain differences in their assessment of the seriousness of the rebellions of 1549. You should examine these views in the light of your wider knowledge:

- Source 1 highlights the seriousness of the threat, the tension in town and country and 'loosening of loyalty to the regime' (Chapters 5 and 6).
- Source 2 accepts the seriousness of the rebellions, 'taking the government's resources near to breaking point' but qualifies the extent of the threat with the observation that 'the purpose was not to overthrow any member of government or ruling family' (Chapter 4).
- Source 3 notes both the limited aims of the rebels and the government's ability to maintain control and function effectively (Chapter 4).

Your answer will be stronger if, when discussing these issues, you cross-refer between the sources rather than treating them singly. For example you can link comments in Sources 2 and 3 to explore the significance of the limited aims of the rebels and the implication of this. However, there is evidence in Sources 1 and 2 that can be combined to explore the threat posed by the numbers involved. Using Sources 2 and 3 in combination enables you to qualify the comment in Source 3 that 'the government never lost control' by noting that angry commoners 'took the government's resources near to breaking point'.

Issues emerge when you use the sources in combination that enable you to see that there are differences of view. Remember that you must identify and make use of the issues raised by the sources as an integral part of planning your answer.

In coming to an overall judgement about the seriousness of the rebellions of 1549, your own knowledge should be applied to the exploration of each of these issues. For example you should note that, in the case of the demands of Wyatt's Rebellion, the lack of deference and respect, together with the denials of the royal supremacy, can be seen as greater threat to the stability of society than the rebellion itself (pages 142–5).

A Crisis in Society?

POINTS TO CONSIDER

In order to understand the political and religious changes taking place it is important to know something about mid-Tudor society at all levels. Although political decisions were made by the élites, popular reaction and lower order uprisings were important issues, especially in 1549. This chapter examines the ways in which the social structure changed between the late Middle Ages and the mid-sixteenth century, and assesses whether this process had created a mid-Tudor social crisis. You will need to take note of the various social theories and decide whether they are a useful way to study social changes.

These issues are examined as five themes:

- Theories of social change
- Social structure and social mobility
- Contemporary views of mid-Tudor society
- Mid-Tudor society and the theory of social crisis
- Was there a crisis in society?

Key dates

1349	Black Death and the beginning of recurrent bubonic plague epidemics drastically reduced the population
1390s	Serfdom among the lower orders was coming to an end
1400–1500	Low population, low prices, low rents and high wages created a 'golden age' of lower order prosperity
1470s	Loss of political and economic power by the aristocracy and growth in royal authority
1500s	Increasing population growth and inflation forced up prices and rents and created unemployment
1500s	Growing commerce helped to increase the influence of the gentry and yeomen
1530s	Growing shortage of land created competition among the élites
1536–40	Closure of the monasteries enabled large-scale redistribution of land among the élites
1540	Rapid population growth caused hyper-inflation and rising unemployment

| 1549 | Poor harvest and widespread popular discontent led to Ket's Rebellion in Norfolk |
| 1565 | Sir Thomas Smith published book *The Commonwealth of England* (*De Republica Anglorum*), in which he described English society |

1 | Theories of Social Change

Key question
How do Marxist and revisionist theories of social change differ?

The sixteenth century was a highly significant period because major changes were taking place within English society. However, because social change is usually such a slow, long-term process, it is virtually impossible to measure it over short periods of time such as the period between 1540 and 1558. Instead, historians have to try to assess what stage the series of complicated structural changes which had begun in the fourteenth century (see pages 22–5) had reached by the middle of the sixteenth century. At the same time they have to consider what effects particular events, such as the Reformation, were having on society. Only then is it possible to reach any conclusions about whether there was a mid-century social crisis, or the extent to which social change contributed to any of the problems facing Tudor governments at that time.

It is widely agreed that by the middle of the sixteenth century, although the actual shape of the social structure had altered very little, the changes that were taking place were causing stresses within society. However, the extent to which any such tensions contributed to the popular unrest in 1549 is not clear. This uncertainty reflects the lack of agreement about the nature of the changes taking place.

Alternative theories of social change
Many social and economic historians have stressed the importance of religious change, the variations in population levels, and the effect of inflation or **deflation**, in creating movements within and between social groups.

Key term
Deflation
The reduction of the amount of money in circulation in order to increase its value.

Religion and social change
The Reformation used to be regarded as being particularly important in the process of social change. It was considered that the break from Rome and the introduction of Protestantism were important in promoting the spread of individualism, capitalism and competition. It was suggested that many members of the élites and commercial groups adopted moderate Protestantism so that they could benefit from the increase in prices. Equally the seizure of Church lands was seen as helping the élites to build up their wealth, and to recover from the losses resulting from the breakdown of the late medieval economy. It was claimed that the Western Rebellion of 1549 (see pages 134–7) provides evidence of such developments. Certainly, the rebels were hostile towards the

local gentry who, they claimed, were using the Reformation to enrich themselves.

At the same time, the adoption of Lutheran and Calvinist ideas during the reign of Edward VI was seen as introducing into England the Protestant work ethic, with its stress on thrift, sobriety and hard work. This, along with the attack on superstitious rituals and Holy Days, was considered to have begun to break down the seasonal life of the lower orders. It was the threat to their lifestyle as much as their attachment to the Catholic religion that provoked the rebels in the West Country in 1549.

However, there is considerable scepticism about the whole concept of the Protestant work ethic. It is also pointed out that the Catholic rural and urban élites were just as adept at acquiring confiscated monastic property and money-making as their Protestant counterparts. In any case, the apparent religious apathy of the majority of the population makes it difficult to decide whether religion had any long-term or short-term effects on social change.

Population and social change

Many social and economic historians have not been completely convinced by any of these general theories of social change. They have considered that variations in the levels of population and the consequent inflation or deflation were the major influence on the social structure. For them the deflationary period following the Black Death of 1349, caused by falling population levels, created a period of lower order prosperity. Many smallholders gave up their land and became wage labourers in order to benefit from the high wage levels.

On the other hand, deflation caused economic problems for the landed élites. However, when the population numbers began to recover at the beginning of the sixteenth century the situation was reversed. Landowners now began to benefit from increased prices caused by inflation. They were able to push up rents because more people were looking for land to lease. This forced many of the remaining husbandmen and cottagers from the land because they could not afford the higher rents. As more people were available for work, wages did not increase at the same rate as prices. Consequently, the living standards of both smallholders and wage labourers fell, while most of the élites were prospering. It has been suggested that it was the effect of this change that was being fully felt by 1549, and was a cause of the popular unrest.

New research

Although these ideas still remain a good starting point for thinking about social change in early modern England, they, like all general ideas, are now considered to be far too restrictive. Continued research, particularly at local level, has revealed an English society too varied to be explained by any theory. There were great differences between regions, counties and even neighbouring villages. Equally, convenient labels such as 'capitalism' or 'bourgeoisie' are no longer thought appropriate for the sixteenth century. Similarly, concepts such as 'the Protestant work ethic' are thought to be inappropriate.

While society at all levels was becoming more fluid and individualistic, and there was an increase in commercialism and competition, this is no longer seen as a cause of conflict. Indeed, it can be maintained that popular discontent was always close to the surface in pre-industrial societies where so many people lived near the poverty line. Only in times of severe hardship, such as famine or widespread unemployment, did grievances erupt into violence. So it might well be said that the mid-century problems were more economic than social.

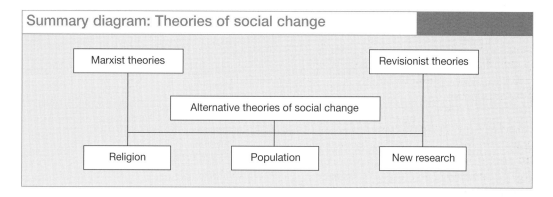

Summary diagram: Theories of social change

2 | Social Structure and Social Mobility

English society underwent an important period of evolution between 1350 and 1550. Mid-sixteenth-century society is regarded as being more competitive and individualistic than it had been during the Middle Ages. Even so, it is considered that it was still overwhelmingly rural, and retained many of the characteristics of feudal society. One of the most important signs of change is thought to be the amount of social mobility existing between the various classes or social groups.

Social mobility

Key question
How significant were the signs of social mobility?

The pace of social change quickened in the century and a half after the Black Death. However, there had been little structural change by the middle of the sixteenth century. The three social hierarchies of monarchy, nobility and gentry stayed broadly unaltered in size and in their relationship to each other. The late medieval economic decline adversely affected both the towns and the Church in economic terms, but had no impact on their social structure. It was rural society that changed both economically and socially.

The rural élites

A consequence of the economic decline of the great landowners was that during the fifteenth century some of them had to sell part of their land, and lease out much of the remainder on long leases

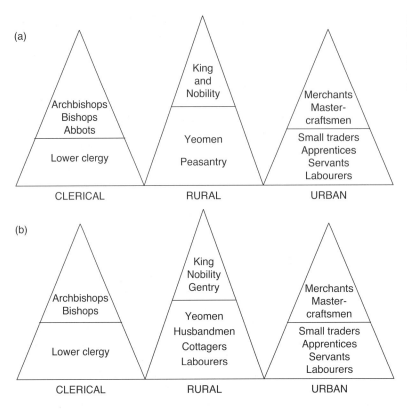

Figure 5.1: Social hierarchy. (a) Feudal social hierarchy c1350. (b) The early Tudor social hierarchy c1550.

of up to 99 years. The immediate impact of this was the temporary lowering of the social prestige of the nobility. They could no longer afford to maintain their great households, and service to the Crown became more attractive to the ambitious among the lesser élites. Likewise, the sale and leasing out of the great estates created a very active land market, which widened the availability of land. This was the beginning of the rise of the gentry.

The major change was that there had been a significant redistribution of land to the new gentry. When prices and rents began to rise after 1500 it was the gentry who benefited from such increases, and from the improving industrial and commercial conditions. The aristocracy were unable to reap any real profit from their estates until the long leases, often 99 years long, ran out towards the end of the sixteenth century and they were able to repossess their land.

The Renaissance

Another highly significant development which is considered to have altered the pattern of social mobility, particularly among the élites, was the spread of the **Renaissance** and **Christian humanism** in England at the end of the fifteenth century. The Renaissance is seen as weakening the influence of the Church. Apart from causing a growth in **anti-clericalism** by attacking the wealth and abuses in the Church, Renaissance thought encouraged the spread of secular education. Previously a clerical career was seen not just as an

Key terms

Renaissance
Rebirth of learning and the arts, which encouraged writers and artists to become part of what was called the spirit of new learning.

Christian humanism
The teaching of the original classical texts in their original Latin and Greek, and the study of the humanities as the basis of civilised life.

Anti-clericalism
Hostility to, and unpopularity of, the Church and its priests.

opportunity to obtain high office in the Church, but as a means of gaining important governmental positions.

Christian humanism

The spread of Christian humanism, with its emphasis on education for the laity, promoted universities, the legal **Inns of Court** and secular schools as an alternative for political careerists. Thomas Wolsey, the son of a Suffolk cattle dealer who rose to become a cardinal, the Archbishop of York, and Lord Chancellor under Henry VIII, is seen as the last of the great English clerical careerists. His successors, such as Thomas Cromwell and William Cecil, came to power through a university and legal education. Increasingly this became the route taken by those aspiring to a political and administrative career.

The rural lower orders

Equally significant changes were taking place among the rural lower orders. The decline in economic and political power among the great landowners is considered to have brought about the disappearance of serfdom and labour services in England during the fifteenth century. All the peasantry were now theoretically free (although there were still serfs in some parts of England until the end of the sixteenth century), and so could move about the country as they chose. This is seen as ending, or at least drastically altering, the structure of peasant society. Peasant smallholders were generally described as husbandmen. Customary tenures were being replaced by a new form of tenancy for the lifetime of the holder called copyhold, for which rent was paid in cash. Many of the former peasants took advantage of the availability of land and amassed holdings of some 200 acres or more. They became commercial farmers, and joined the ranks of the yeomen.

Now that the new copyhold tenancies no longer carried the stigma of being unfree, many of the former yeomen and new gentry were also prepared to acquire this type of land. However, many husbandmen preferred to remain self-sufficient smallholders, with about 30–40 acres of land. At the same time some improved their position by acquiring enough land to become self-sufficient. Others preferred to continue to supplement the produce of their smallholdings by working for wages on the commercial farms and in rural industry. A significant number decided to take advantage of the higher wage levels created by the fall in the size of the labour force, and abandon their land to work full-time for wages. The lower orders enjoyed much greater geographical mobility, so that many more people could take advantage of them.

Assessment

By 1569 it appears that there had been little alteration to the social structure at any level. The monarchy had established its position of social and political superiority. By making good their economic losses the nobility had consolidated themselves as the

Key term

Inns of Court
Located in London, the Inns of Court provided a university-type education for those wishing to study and practise law.

major landowning group below the monarch. The gentry had established themselves as the rank immediately below the nobility. Yeomen were recognised as the most important landowners below the gentry. The urban and clerical hierarchies remained unchanged. Self-sufficient husbandmen were still the most numerous group in the rural communities. The number of wage-earners had increased and they were forming a growing rural and urban working class.

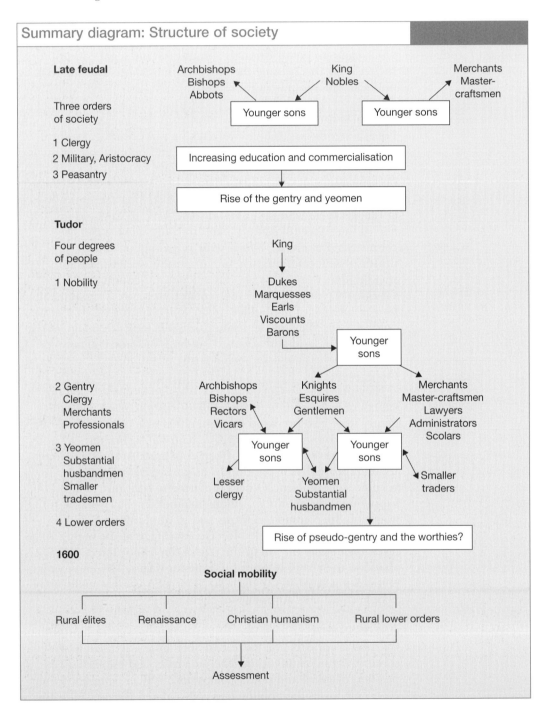

Summary diagram: Structure of society

Late feudal

Three orders of society

1 Clergy
2 Military, Aristocracy
3 Peasantry

Archbishops
Bishops
Abbots

King
Nobles

Merchants
Master-craftsmen

Younger sons

Younger sons

Increasing education and commercialisation

Rise of the gentry and yeomen

Tudor

Four degrees of people

1 Nobility

King

Dukes
Marquesses
Earls
Viscounts
Barons

Younger sons

2 Gentry
Clergy
Merchants
Professionals

Archbishops
Bishops
Rectors
Vicars

Knights
Esquires
Gentlemen

Merchants
Master-craftsmen
Lawyers
Administrators
Scolars

Younger sons

Younger sons

3 Yeomen
Substantial husbandmen
Smaller tradesmen

Lesser clergy

Yeomen
Substantial husbandmen

Smaller traders

4 Lower orders

Rise of pseudo-gentry and the worthies?

1600

Social mobility

Rural élites   Renaissance   Christian humanism   Rural lower orders

Assessment

3 | Contemporary Views of Mid-Tudor Society

Key question
How did the Tudors themselves view their own society?

The idea of a static medieval peasant population with the vast majority of families living for generations in the same village has been disproved; the early Tudor lower orders were more geographically mobile than was once thought. Similarly, it has been shown that not all towns were in economic decline. Some, particularly London, were prospering, while others were passing into obscurity. It is important to stress the localised nature of early Tudor society. The emphasis is now put on the importance and differences between counties and even neighbouring villages. There was a keen sense of local loyalty and interference by the central government was resisted. Tudor MPs were much more interested in matters relating to their own locality than in national events. Similarly, local societies had their own loyalties and interests, which were not necessarily the same as those of their social counterparts elsewhere in the country.

The muster certificates of 1522

A remarkably full picture of English society is provided in 1522. In that year the King's Council ordered a survey to be made of all men fit for military service. At the same time the government used the survey to enquire into the value of land and movable goods held by everyone in the country in order to draw up new tax lists. As a result, the survey provides the most comprehensive census of English society between the Domesday Book of 1086 and the first census in 1801. Unfortunately, the muster returns for 1522 have not survived for all counties. However, sufficient numbers remain for historians to have used them over the past 20 years to analyse the state of early Tudor society.

The picture that emerges from the muster returns is of considerable underlying continuity, but there are clear signs of increasing commercialisation by the 1520s. England was mainly rural, and most of the population lived in small villages. The Church continued to be the largest single holder of land, and there is little evidence of any marked changes in the composition of urban society. However, although the villages were mainly made up of communities of husbandmen, most of them had at least one commercial farmer, or yeoman. It is also clear that the number of servants and labourers had increased noticeably, and it is estimated that 40 per cent of the lower orders were wage-earners. The rise of the gentry as a group was clearly well advanced. By the 1520s they held some 30 per cent of the manors, and were the leaseholders of many more.

Key date
Publication of *The Commonwealth of England*: 1565

The Commonwealth of England 1565

Key question
How reliable is Smith's description of the structure of English society?

In 1565 Sir Thomas Smith, who had been Secretary of State under Somerset, wrote the book *The Commonwealth of England* (*De Republica Anglorum*), in which he described English society as he saw it. According to Smith Tudor society was divided into four groups or classes: gentlemen, urban élite, yeomen and labourers.

The value of lands & property there
The Abbot of Abingdon is chief lord there & his lands are in value by
   the year over all charges £40 0s 0d
Thomas Unton Gent. in lands 6s 8d
John Elyotte in lands 5s 8d
Sir William Craddock Clerk is parson there & his parsonage is in
   value by the year over all charges £13 0s 0d

The value of goods & other movable property there
John Wyse senior householder £22 0s 0d
John White servant 12s 0d
John Yate h. £5 0s 0d
Robert Barteley servant £1 0s 0d
Thomas Abday h. £7 0s 0d
Thomas Seuernake £2 0s 0d
John Bowell H. £4 0s 0d
William Badnoll h. £13 6s 8d
Robert Ryve servant £1 6s 8d
Thomas Carter servant £1 0s 0d
William Browne h. £1 0s 0d
John Cowley h. £2 0s 0d
John Chirchey h. £3 0s 0d
John Tayllor h. £12 0s 0d
William Yate h. £14 0s 0d
Thomas Yate his son £2 0s 0d
William Somner servant 10s 0d
Harry Harne h. £1 0s 0d
Phillippe Smythe h. £2 0s 0d
John Smythe h. £5 6s 8d
Margory Chirche widow £1 0s 0d
Julyan Chirche widow £1 0s 0d
Margett of Acris widow 10s 0d

Figure 5.2: The muster certificate for Shellingford, 1522. Why are the
1522 muster certificates so useful to historians?

Gentlemen

The first of Smith's four social divisions were gentlemen. Smith
had most to say about this class because he was one of them,
which is why he subdivided them into two, upper and lower,
groups. 'The first part of Gentlemen of England' were called
'*nobilitas major*'. These were the members of the House of Lords
and in Smith's opinion, no man was worthy of being called or
created a baron unless he had an annual income of a thousand
pounds. 'The second part of Gentlemen' were called '*nobilitas
minor*'. The title and dignity of knighthood could not be
inherited, 'knights therefore be not born but made'. Esquires 'be
all those which bear arms'. Gentlemen 'be those whom their
blood and race doth make noble and known'.

In further defining the upper class and separating them from
the second group Smith wrote the following:

> For whosoever studieth the laws of the realm, who studieth in the
> Universities … and to be short, who can live idly and without
> manual labour, and will bear the port, charge and countenance of
> a gentleman, he shall be called master.

Key term

Burgesses
The most powerful members of a town's citizens. They were often descended from the town's original founders and they also tended to hold the most important offices in the town's administration.

Urban élite

Second were the urban élite, the citizens and **burgesses** of the large towns and cities. This group included merchants, retailers and craftsmen who had made their wealth by trade. Smith had little to say about this group, perhaps because he understood them the least, having been brought up and educated in a rural world.

Yeomen

Third were the yeomen, who were 'next unto the nobility, knights and squires'; a yeoman was a 'freeman born English' and had the means to enjoy an annual income of 40s (£2). Smith considered them a more significant group than the urban élite, whom he felt did not fit easily into his rural framework.

Labourers

'The fourth sort or class amongst us' were the day labourers, poor husbandmen and all 'artificers' (wage labourers). 'These have no voice nor authority in our commonwealth, and no account is made of them, but only to be ruled.'

As historians Anthony Fletcher and Diarmaid MacCulloch have pointed out, Smith was 'not making a sociological analysis; he was describing power'.

It must be remembered that this was an élite viewpoint, and it is not possible to be sure of the author's motives for writing the book. It may be that he was depicting society as he thought it should be, rather than showing it as it actually was in the middle of the sixteenth century. Again, he might, like the Norfolk rebels, be nostalgically looking back to a society that he thought was vanishing.

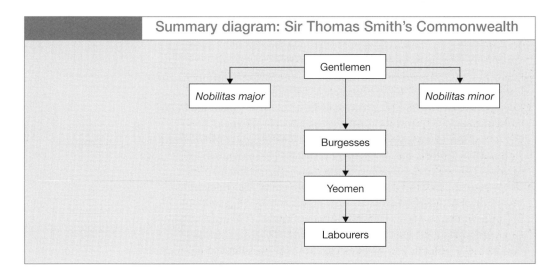

Summary diagram: Sir Thomas Smith's Commonwealth

4 | Mid-Tudor Society and the Theory of Social Crisis

Key question
Is there any evidence to support the theory that mid-Tudor society was in crisis?

It was once thought that the popular rebellions and the élite power struggle in 1549 indicate a social crisis at all levels of society. In view of the apparent stability in all the social hierarchies this conclusion is no longer considered valid. In social terms neither the urban nor the clerical hierarchies displayed any signs of pressure. The clergy and urban élites appear to have supported the Crown and the maintenance of order and stability. Furthermore, no drastic change can be seen in the pattern of social development among the lower orders.

Conflict among the élites?

A number of suggestions have been put forward to support the contention that competition among the élites had reached crisis point by the middle of the sixteenth century. Revisionists have modified or reinterpreted this traditional viewpoint.

Traditional interpretation

1. The numbers of the élites was increasing more rapidly than the rest of the population, particularly after 1500, because the economic conditions favoured them and their diets and health improved. There is certainly evidence to suggest that the size of élite families was increasing by the middle of the century. For example, William Hyde esquire of Denchworth in Berkshire, who died in 1557, had 13 children, and his eldest son had 10 children. Land and office had to be found for the offspring of the upper classes, which led to greater competition.
2. There were signs of increasing competition for land between the rising gentry and the aristocracy. For example, the demand for land among the élites had begun to exceed supply. This competition for land was not caused just by the increased numbers of gentry and yeomen but by the improving commercial opportunities available to landowners. Many of the great estate owners, whose land was still tied up with long leases, wished to obtain additional land so that they could take advantage of the upturn in the economy. In addition, leaseholders were anxious to convert their leases into freehold. This situation is seen as being potentially dangerous for the Crown, as it was causing instability among the élites.
3. The English Reformation and the redistribution of Church lands had a significant impact on élite society. This was the largest redistribution of land since the Norman Conquest and would have a considerable impact on the structure of élite society. It has been estimated that in 1500 the nobility had an average annual income of £1000 compared with £130 for knights, £58 for esquires and £14 for gentlemen. However, the market in Church lands caused wide disparities of wealth within each rank. For example, by 1548 Somerset had an annual income of £7400 from his estates, much of which came

from his success in acquiring ecclesiastical property. Fellow members of the Privy Council – Northumberland, Herbert, Paget, Russell, Rich and Wriothesley – had similarly enriched themselves with Church lands. The unequal acquisition and distribution of Church property led to envy and conflict.

4. The rivalry for power between the rising gentry and the aristocracy had intensified. Henry VII and Henry VIII were accused of deliberately trying to change the social composition of the aristocracy by promoting new families at the expense of the ancient nobility. Former gentry families such as the Seymours and Dudleys, through a combination of military careers, public office, the seizure of Church lands and royal favour, had risen rapidly to the top ranks of the social hierarchy.

Revisionist interpretation

1. Doubts have been expressed about the effects the increasing numbers of élites would have had on society by 1569. It has been estimated that:

   - in 1500 there were 55 nobles, 500 knights, 800 esquires and 5000 gentlemen
   - by 1550 the number of nobles and knights had not changed.

   Although the numbers of esquires and gentlemen had risen, it is thought unlikely that the rate of increase greatly exceeded the general population growth of one per cent per year.

2. The competition between the gentry and the aristocracy is now seen in terms of traditional élite rivalry for land and power. The buoyant land market, fuelled by the availability of Church property between 1536 and 1554, more than met the needs of the land-hungry élite. On the other hand, many gentry did not compete for or acquire Church lands. For example, the ancient family of Pusey in Berkshire demonstrated that in the favourable economic conditions it was possible to prosper even without acquiring additional lands. In 1522 Thomas Pusey's wealth had been estimated at £8. When his grandson Philip died in 1573 he left £238 in his will. This represents an increase of over 2300 per cent in 50 years, whereas the rate of inflation was only 200 per cent over the same period. The increase was due in part to converting long leases (99 years) to shorter ones (20 years) and in taking advantage of greater commercial opportunities.

3. By 1558 the secularisation of Church property had had very little effect on the structure of élite society. With the exception of the immediate vicinity of London, where city merchants were very active in the land market, the land had gone to consolidate the position of the existing aristocracy and gentry. Only a small amount of land appears to have passed into the possession of new owners from the towns or industry. Success or failure was by no means dependent on the ability to buy Church property. For example, the Essex family from north Berkshire was perhaps the most successful in the county in accumulating Church lands. Their annual landed income increased from £160 in 1522 to

£238 by 1553, but further land speculation and changes in land value led to their bankruptcy by 1600.

4. The idea that the early Tudors deliberately tried to change the social composition of the aristocracy by promoting new families at the expense of the ancient nobility is now thought to be unfounded. Old noble families such as the Percys, Nevilles and Poles had fallen through royal disfavour. Others, such as the Howards, survived the displeasure of the monarchy to rise again. The Brandon family, which had risen rapidly through royal marriage, fell back into obscurity because it failed to produce male heirs. Among the lesser élites a gap was starting to develop. Some of the 'greater' gentry began to rival the aristocracy for wealth, while many of the 'parish' gentry became barely distinguishable from yeomen. This is regarded as part of the traditional pattern of success or failure – a 'wheel of fortune' with families rising, falling and stagnating.

Lower order discontent?

If there was social conflict and crisis in mid-Tudor England, the popular uprisings of 1549 suggest that it was caused by problems among the lower orders. The difficulty is to decide whether the problems were caused by social tensions. There is no reason why the comparatively stable, non-élite society of the late fifteenth and early sixteenth centuries should have radically altered by the middle of the century. The problem is considered to lie in the economic conditions, which no longer favoured the lower orders. Rising population and inflation brought prosperity to the élites, but eroded the standards of living for the masses – a situation on which R.H. Tawney, one of the early pioneering social historians, commented in 1912: 'Villeinage [serfdom] ceases but the poor laws begin'.

Key question
What evidence is there to support the theory of lower order discontent?

Population pressure

There is ample evidence to support such an interpretation of the problems in 1549. It is estimated that the population was rising at the rate of one per cent per year, and possibly faster, up to the middle of the century. This would have meant that the population level of 2.3 million in the 1520s may have reached some three million by 1550. This, it is thought, might well have put a strain on food production and created a Malthusian crisis (see page 26), which was made worse by the harvest failure in 1549. The greater number of people enabled landowners to push up the level of rents, while employers were able to keep down wages.

In contrast, inflation, which is estimated to have run at four per cent per year over the whole country during the 1520s and 1530s, was made worse by the debasements of the coinage in the 1540s (see pages 47, 56–8) and may have reached over 200 per cent by 1550. For the growing number of cloth workers the decline of the Antwerp cloth market (see pages 28–9) resulted in heavy job losses in the country's largest industry. Furthermore, the comparative lack of popular unrest in the 1550s can be explained by heavy mortality caused by severe epidemics of plague and 'sweating sickness' in 1551 and 1552, and of influenza between 1556 and 1558 and of smallpox in 1562, which relieved population pressure (see pages 15–16).

Social conflict?

Did the popular rebellions of 1549 (see pages 151–2) offer clear proof of social conflict directed particularly against the gentry? It is true that in the West Country and in Norfolk the rebels were antagonistic towards the local gentry. The Privy Council described both uprisings as social conflict which threatened to undermine the whole fabric of society. However, historians now regard such statements as government propaganda intended to unite the élites behind an increasingly unpopular administration.

Much of the resentment towards the gentry centred on the accusation that they were using the Reformation to enrich themselves and to exploit their tenants. But there is little reason to see why the sale of Church lands should have had any great

Illustration showing a family forced to become vagrants in search of work. Are the poor depicted in a sympathetic way?

effect upon the tenants. Another major cause of resentment was that the rebels, like the government, mistakenly blamed enclosure for the adverse economic situation (see below). It is difficult to see how this could have had an immediate effect in 1549. The great bulk of enclosures had taken place before 1520, and most of these were in the Midlands, where there were no popular uprisings.

Clearly, enclosure did alter the pattern of community life in the villages, but it was part of the changes that had been in progress since the end of the fourteenth century. In any case, much of the enclosure had been carried out by mutual consent among the husbandmen, to improve agricultural production.

Adverse economic conditions

Social conflict was really the reaction of the masses to economic hardship. It is estimated that during the sixteenth century at least 50 per cent of the rural and urban non-élites lived on, or below, subsistence level, even in good years. Discontent, therefore, was always just below the surface, and broke into revolt at times of widespread unemployment and food shortages, such as in 1549. On such occasions the ruling élites were always accused of economic and political exploitation.

Of course, it can be argued that this was a social crisis because the élites were responsible for maintaining a social structure that placed them in a highly privileged position. It is suggested that the rural rebels were largely illiterate and inarticulate, and relied on rumour and hearsay to explain problems that they did not understand. For this reason local issues and grievances became of paramount importance, and they judged the past to have been a vanished 'golden age' of prosperity to which they wished to return. Consequently, many of the grievances of such uprisings belonged more to a 'folk memory' of past events rather than to current issues. Ket's Rebellion in Norfolk (see pages 138–40) is a good example of this interpretation.

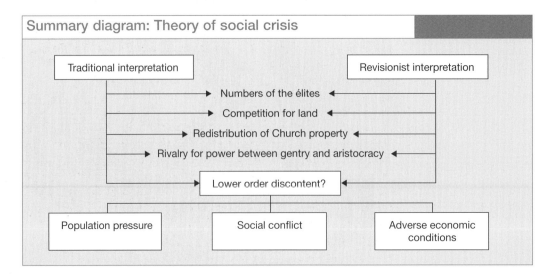

Summary diagram: Theory of social crisis

Traditional interpretation — Revisionist interpretation

Numbers of the élites

Competition for land

Redistribution of Church property

Rivalry for power between gentry and aristocracy

Lower order discontent?

Population pressure — Social conflict — Adverse economic conditions

5 | The Key Debate

Was there a crisis in society?

The process of social change, although controversial, is generally easy to trace. Both the élites and the lower orders had been affected by change.

- Among the élites the emergence of the gentry from the ranks of the feudal aristocracy is still seen as a highly significant development. By the middle of the century the new structure had been strengthened by the sale of monastic and other Church lands.
- Among the lower orders there had been considerable change over the same period. The servile, feudal peasantry had disappeared, to be replaced by a new hierarchy of yeomen, husbandmen, cottagers and labourers.

Although a great gulf existed between the élites and the non-élites, the majority of the lower orders were freer and more prosperous than they had been 200 years before. There were already signs of increasing commercialism and competition at all levels of society. However, in the middle of the sixteenth century there still seems to have been considerable social stability, and little sign of social crisis. It was over the next century, when continued rise in population added to social pressures, that real signs of tension within society began to emerge.

Mid-sixteenth-century England was still an unruly nation, and violence was present at all levels of society. The government and the élites expected and feared outbreaks of popular rioting during the summer months as part of the normal course of events. These might be caused by village sports or quarrels between neighbours. A bad harvest, local enclosure or unpopular taxation might cause more widespread disorder, as in 1549 (see pages 151–2).

Nevertheless, there appears to have been a considerable degree of co-operation between social groups, particularly at local levels. The growing number of county studies and the research into gentry and noble families is revealing the different motives governing social relationships among the élites, and their attitudes towards the lower orders.

The lack of evidence makes it harder to investigate opinions among the non-élites. However, the official keeping of parish registers after 1538, and the growing number of wills and inventories left by people of relatively low social status helps historians to gain an insight into the lives of the ordinary people. Considerable attention continues to be given to the study of popular culture and disorder, and in particular to the family and the role of women in society.

At all levels mid-Tudor society appears to have been more in a process of fairly stable evolution than in a state of crisis and conflict. There was considerable underlying continuity, although significant differences had emerged. Society appears to have reached a point where the changes taking place over the previous two centuries had been consolidated. English society was about to enter the next phase of its development, which was to bring even greater structural change.

6 A Crisis in the Economy?

POINTS TO CONSIDER
This chapter examines the extent to which the English economy had developed by 1569. In pre-industrial societies changes in population levels had a huge impact on the economy, and this chapter examines how agriculture and industry changed and developed during this period. Additionally, it will examine the causes and effects of rising prices, enclosures and trade recession. Finally, it will consider how effectively Tudor governments tackled these economic problems.
  These issues are examined as six themes:

- Population and inflation
- Agriculture
- Industry
- The mid-Tudor trade recession
- Towns, unemployment and urban recession
- Was there a crisis in the economy?

Key dates

1349	Black Death and the beginning of recurrent bubonic plague epidemics
1470s	Beginning of population increase and inflation
1500	Prices started to rise more quickly than wages
1537–48	Series of good harvests
1549	Poor harvest and widespread popular discontent
1552	Plague and sweating sickness checked population rise
1552–3	Trade embargoes marked beginning of decline of Antwerp and beginning of commercial slump
1554–6	Severe harvest failures
1556–8	Influenza epidemics caused fall in population
1558	Loss of Calais

1 | Population and Inflation

The history of the middle years of the sixteenth century was shaped as much by underlying changes in society and the economy as by the actions of the ruling monarchs. The expansion in population and the onset of inflation had a profound effect on the lives of ordinary people. For some, they brought wealth and opportunity, but for others they made the difference between life and death.

Key question
Why is there a debate over the changing rates of population growth and its effects during the sixteenth century?

Population: recovery and growth

There is considerable debate over the changing rates of population growth and its effects during the sixteenth century, particularly in the period between 1500 and 1558.

Population recovery 1470–1522

After the sharp demographic decline following the Black Death and the subsequent plague cycle (see page 15), population levels are considered to have ceased to fall by about 1470. This was followed by a slow recovery from about 1.5 million in 1470 to some 2.3 million by the 1520s.

Black Death and the beginning of recurrent bubonic plague epidemics: 1349

Beginning of population increase and inflation: 1470s

Key dates

There is broad agreement about this pattern of demographic decline and recovery, but not about the causes for the revival. There is little dispute that the bubonic plague, carried by the fleas of the black rat, was the cause of the initial catastrophic population losses. What is less clear is what caused the recovery after 1470. Bubonic plague was still endemic, along with a number of other diseases such as influenza, cholera, malaria and typhus. This makes it difficult to maintain that a fall in the rate of mortality was a major reason for a regrowth in population.

However, some historians believe that people were beginning to build up immunity to some forms of disease. Others suggest that vulnerability to epidemics varied and changed between age groups. The reason for recovery in population levels could have been that young adults were becoming less susceptible to diseases. If more young women survived, increased numbers of children were likely to be born, which would account for a rise in population. Alternatively it is claimed that there was a drop in **infant mortality**, which would have led to a rise in the demographic levels.

Population growth 1522–60

The situation between 1522 and 1560 is equally uncertain. It is estimated that the population was growing at approximately one per cent per year until 1560, when it possibly just exceeded three million. However, the rate of expansion was not even. It is suggested that there was only a very slow improvement until 1540, followed by rapid growth over the next decade, and that by 1569 population levels were falling back again.

Once again there is no single explanation for this pattern of events. A major factor was the presence of endemic disease. From the end of the fifteenth century a new virus had joined the killer

Infant mortality
Term used to describe the death rate among children, usually under five years of age. In the medieval and early modern periods, infant mortality rates were high owing to complications at birth, poor diet, disease, and poor health and hygiene.

Key term

Figure 6.1:
Population
distribution in the
sixteenth century.
What do these figures
suggest about where
people lived?

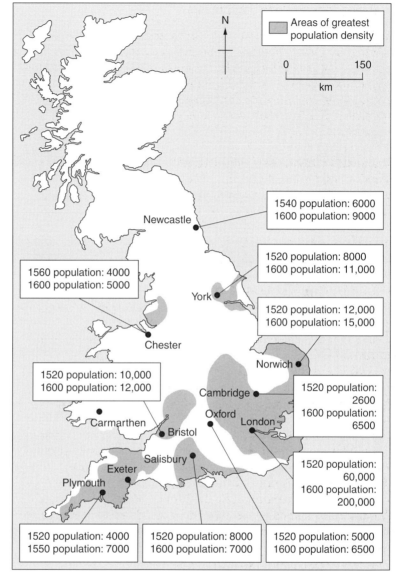

diseases that were already present. The 'English sweat', a fever
that spread more quickly than the plague, was particularly
virulent between 1485 and 1528, and could kill within 24 hours.
It struck particularly at young adults, and it is thought that this,
by reducing the birthrate, slowed the rate of population increase
up to 1540. Moreover, there were four serious outbreaks of plague
between 1500 and 1528, and another in the late 1530s, to which
adolescents were especially vulnerable.

However, it is felt that the comparative absence of epidemics
between 1528 and 1560 might well account for the sharp
demographic increase in the 1540s. A fall in infant mortality
might have been a major cause for more children surviving into
adulthood.

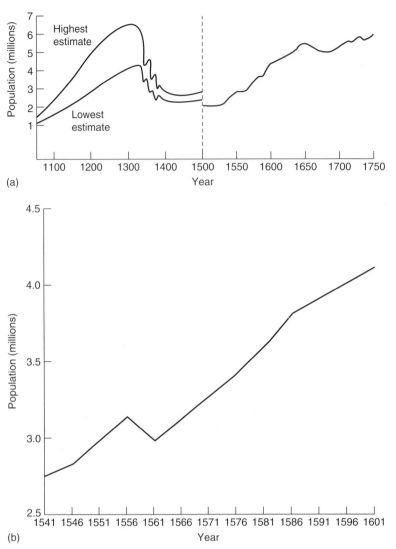

Figure 6.2: English population change and population figures. What do these figures reveal about population change?

Checks to population growth 1551–69

The substantial check to population increase in the 1550s is easier to explain. In 1551 and 1552 there were fresh outbreaks of plague and sweating sickness. Even more serious was the influenza epidemic which ravaged the whole country between 1556 and 1558. It is estimated that it had a mortality rate of at least six per cent, and that the population might have been reduced to under three million. The smallpox outbreak was equally dangerous though not as widespread. The most notable casualty of smallpox in 1562 was Queen Elizabeth but she recovered.

To add to the difficulties of obtaining a clear picture, there were considerable local variations in population densities, the rate of increase or decline, and the incidence of disease. In broad terms the south-eastern section of England was more heavily populated than the north-west because of the different farming regions (see page 185).

Towns, particularly London, which had high concentrations of people, were especially susceptible to epidemics, but the rate of recovery was normally rapid. East Anglia was the most highly populated area, while the north of England had the least number of people per square mile. In sparsely settled areas epidemics were less likely, but the rate of recovery from any population losses was slower.

Variations in recovery and growth

There is ample evidence from abandoned properties and plots of land in both towns and villages that the population during the first half of the sixteenth century had not recovered from earlier losses.

- In north Berkshire the village of Hinton, even by 1573, had not recovered the level of population that it had in 1381.
- In contrast, a survey of the nearby market town of Wantage in the 1550s estimated that the town's population was 1000; a figure confirmed by calculations from the parish registers. This compares with a population of 600 in 1522 – a rise of 66 per cent over 30 years, and twice the estimated national average. The level of increase in the neighbouring villages was lower, and in some cases there was an actual decrease.

It is very difficult to pinpoint the causes of such discrepancies in the countryside, and between villages within a few miles of each other. Much of the similarly varied demographic fortunes of towns in early Tudor England can be attributed to the random outbreak of disease. The three largest towns after London – Norwich, Bristol and York – all suffered severe epidemics in the middle of the century. Indeed, it is calculated that the population of Norwich remained stationary between 1522 and 1565, which is in marked contrast to the growth of London and some other towns.

A Malthusian crisis?

Key question
Was there a Malthusian crisis by 1549?

Evidence in favour of a Malthusian crisis by 1549

Although the evidence for rising population levels is complicated, and often contradictory, it has been suggested that there may have been overpopulation by 1549, leading to a Malthusian crisis (see page 26). The effect of the 'mini-ice age' was to introduce cooler and wetter weather, which is considered to have shortened the growing season. These conditions persisted throughout the sixteenth century, with alternating spells of good and bad weather. The result was that there were sequences of good, poor and very poor harvests.

There were bad harvests from:	There were good harvests from:
• 1527 to 1529	• 1537 to 1542
• 1549 to 1551	• 1546 to 1548
• 1554 to 1556	

Only the exceptionally bad harvests of 1555 and 1556 were poor enough to produce an actual famine, on a wide scale. However, there were problems at a local level, such as the chronic food shortages in Coventry during the 1520s and in Norwich in 1532.

The poor harvests in the 1520s and 1550s coincided with epidemics and increased the mortality rate, while the plague epidemic of the late 1530s occurred during a run of good harvests and had less effect. Epidemics and runs of good or bad harvests affected the underlying demographic trend. The almost unbroken run of good harvests during the 1540s lowered grain prices, and so raised living standards for the mass of the population. In turn, this encouraged earlier marriage, and so intensified the upward spiral in population levels. Consequently, the poor harvest of 1549 created a subsistence crisis, which was an underlying cause of the widespread popular unrest in that year.

Evidence against there being a Malthusian crisis by 1549

On the weight of the existing evidence it is no longer considered likely that there was a Malthusian crisis in 1549. Population growth was not checked in 1549 and continued to rise until the influenza epidemics of the 1550s. Even at its height in 1550, the population level was only about half that of the early fourteenth century. Consequently, even with enclosure and increased regional specialisation (see pages 25–7), there was ample farmland to support the population. Moreover, as there had previously been a long run of good harvests, an adequate supply of stored grain remained, even in the towns.

Lower order hostility towards enclosure in Norfolk and elsewhere was not because it created local grain shortages, but because husbandmen felt that gentry competition was undermining their own agricultural specialisation (see page 27). In any case, the mid-century harvest failures appear to have been caused by abnormally wet summers rather than over-cropping. The harvest failures in the mid-1550s were much more severe, but by then population levels had fallen back because of high mortality rates during the epidemics.

Causes other than food shortages must be found to explain the widespread lower order discontent in 1549. Even so, the sharp increase in population during the 1540s helps to explain the government's anxieties over enclosures, vagrancy and the need to maintain the acreage of arable land.

Inflation

Inflation, which is estimated to have been 400 per cent over the whole of the century, is seen as another major contributor to the economic pressures that existed by the middle of the century. By 1550 the rate of inflation reached 200 per cent over the first half of the century, and the very high levels of inflation reached by 1549 contributed to the widespread popular discontent.

Key question
Was inflation a major contributor to the economic pressures that existed by the middle of the century?

Causes

1. *Rising population.* A rising population, which increased demand, was the underlying cause of inflation. However, this alone does not explain the pattern of inflation during the first half of the century.

2. *Rising prices and rents.* The '**price scissors**' occurred soon after 1500. Prices and rents continued to rise until after 1550. By the 1530s grain and meat prices were increasing quite rapidly in town markets, and doubled between 1510 and 1530. Historians attribute this trend in part to the poor harvests of the 1520s, but prices showed no sign of falling even by the late 1520s after a run of good harvests. The reason for this was that commercial farmers were still concentrating on pasture for wool production rather than crops for food. This, and enclosure, are seen to be the underlying causes for the upward spiral of rents. By the 1540s population pressure added to the upward movement of inflation.

3. *Debasements of the coinage.* Other forces were at work to create high inflation by 1550. Debasements of the coinage (see pages 47, 56–8), which began in 1526, became very frequent in the 1540s, when the government was desperately trying to raise money to finance the wars against France and Scotland (see page 47). By increasing the amount of money in circulation while devaluing the coinage, debasement caused very rapid inflation of prices.

4. *The Reformation.* At the same time the Reformation contributed to this process. Gold and silver ornaments, seized from the monasteries, chantries and churches, were melted down and turned into coins, so adding to the volume of debased coinage in circulation.

5. *Disease.* By 1553 the deaths caused by epidemics had eased population pressure and so slowed the rate of inflation. At the same time, government reforms of the currency reduced the amount of coinage in circulation. The effect was to reduce the rate of inflation still further, which might help to explain the lack of popular unrest during the bad harvests of the mid-1550s.

Key term

Price scissors
Economic term used to describe the point when prices and rents overtook wages.

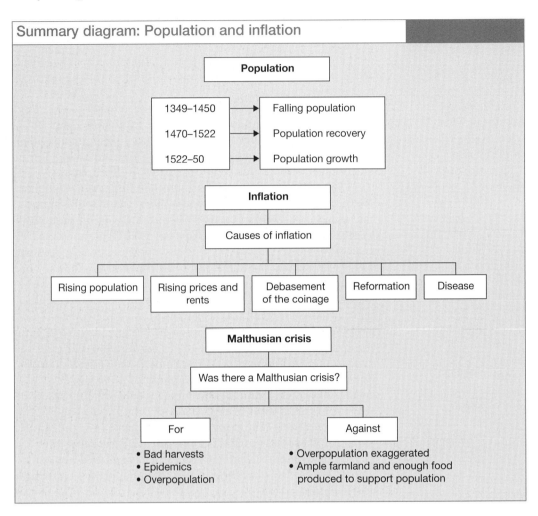

Summary diagram: Population and inflation

2 | Agriculture

Key question
Why did agriculture influence the economy?

As the largest sector in the mid-sixteenth-century English economy, and the employer of the bulk of the population, agriculture had a considerable influence on the economy. However, as agricultural development is now seen as a very slow evolutionary process, it is difficult to pinpoint precisely what stage it had reached by the mid-century.

Changes in land usage

Apart from importing food from abroad, pre-industrial farmers had two basic ways in which to increase output to feed rising populations:

- The easiest method was simply to clear and cultivate more land.
- The more difficult option was to produce a greater quantity of food from the same amount of land.

During the medieval population expansion, the problem had been met by clearing more land. However, this had eventually meant cultivating increasingly marginal land unsuited to arable

Figure 6.3: The distribution of different types of farming practices in sixteenth-century England and Wales. What does this map tell us about farming practices in the Tudor period?

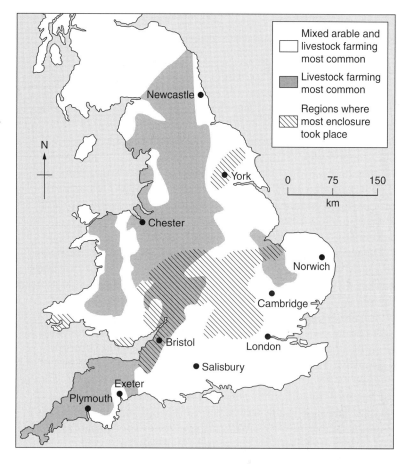

farming. In the end, this had resulted in poorer yields and harvest failures. The result was a subsistence crisis – there was not enough food for the families of the poor to survive – and the breakdown of the late medieval economy.

By the fifteenth century there was no problem in feeding the drastically reduced population. This enabled farmers to abandon the poorer land, which had been made even more marginal by the change to cooler and wetter weather conditions. Whole areas, such as the Brecklands in Norfolk and Dartmoor in the West Country, were virtually abandoned. In every county many villages on the poorer or wetter soils were deserted, and were never reoccupied. This meant that large tracts of previously cultivated land reverted to grassland and pasture, which enabled more cattle and sheep to be kept.

The remaining areas of arable were on the richer soils or, at least, those soils that would support cultivation with the extra quantity of manure available. This means that English agriculture should have been able to move on to the more advanced stage of producing sufficient food from a smaller acreage of arable land. The evidence suggests that without the constant pressure to produce cereals, farming began to become more specialised. This raises the question as to why England in 1550, with a population of only just over three million, appears to have been barely able to feed this comparatively small number of people.

Changing methods

Land usage

Key question
When and why did farming methods change?

Part of the answer lies in the changes in agriculture taking place after the collapse of the late-medieval economy. One of the problems with medieval farming was that it had been largely dominated by 'peasant production methods'. A peasant smallholder had had to produce a range of foodstuffs from the land in order to meet all the needs of his family. This form of production took no account of the wide variety of soil types or their suitability for general farming. Therefore, peasant cultivation was often inefficient and wasteful.

However, even during the Middle Ages, peasants had had to adapt their farming techniques to meet the differing conditions imposed by moorlands, fens or forest. After 1350 the reduction in the number of smallholdings meant that gentry, yeomen and husbandmen could begin to specialise within the broader agricultural zones. The two major zones are divided by a line running from Newcastle in the north-east to Exmouth in the south-west. The upland area west and north of this line has thinner soils with a cooler, wetter climate, making it more suitable for pastoral farming. The lowland area to the south and east of the line has richer soils with a warmer and drier climate better suited to arable farming. Within these zones specialisations began to develop, such as dairy farming in Wiltshire or cereal production in East Anglia.

New crops and techniques

This growing agricultural variety makes it difficult to decide how far farming had progressed by the middle of the sixteenth century. During the sixteenth century new techniques, crops and methods of **field rotation** were introduced. A number of new crops, such as clover and lucerne, were being grown to improve fodder for animal feed. Industrial crops such as saffron, woad and rapeseed were being grown to produce dyes and oils for textile manufacture. At the same time it is suggested that improvements were being made to the techniques of breeding cattle and sheep.

Enclosure

A vital part of this process of improvement was considered to be the spread of enclosure from about 1450 onwards. This, it is thought, enabled the growth of more efficient medium-sized farms, which had **flexible field systems**. These new layouts began to replace the old three-field system, where an individual farmer's land was scattered in small plots across the open fields. At the same time much of the common land was enclosed and brought under more intensive cultivation. It was these developments that are considered to have enabled the introduction of greater specialisation and new techniques.

Key terms

Field rotation
System where different crops are rotated between fields.

Flexible field systems
Farmers could grow what crops they wanted where they wanted, either in large open fields or in enclosed fields.

Key term

Up and down husbandry
A system under which land was used alternatingly over a number of years as arable and then for pasture.

The technique of '**up and down husbandry**' is seen to have prevented soil exhaustion, and to have maintained a better balance between arable and grazing land. Further improvements were made to grazing land by the use of floating water meadows – riverside pastures that were flooded every year with the aid of sluices so that the river silt would enhance the quality of the grass.

Assessing mid-Tudor agriculture

The reason why enclosure and commercialisation were blamed by the government for the economic problems is that, although changes were taking place in agriculture, there had been little improvement in the level of cereal production by the mid-sixteenth century. Indeed, it is believed that enclosure was the cause of this problem.

Enclosure

In the first half of the sixteenth century, the gentry and yeomen, who were mainly responsible for enclosure, were clearly looking for the most profitable crops to gain a good return on their investment. During periods of high population grain prices rose, and so enclosed fields, which were ideal for growing cereals, were used for this purpose.

Rising population

It is thought that in response to a rising population, increasing numbers of commercial farmers converted to cereals. By the seventeenth century production was so efficient that grain prices actually fell in spite of a continued rise in population. However, population increase was almost imperceptible until after 1540. For this reason farmers were slow to shift to cereals, preferring to use enclosed land as sheep-runs, so as to profit from high wool prices.

Specialisation

Whatever type of specialism was adopted, new agricultural regions created problems for grain supplies during the first part of the sixteenth century. Not only did these new agricultural regions lower the overall national cereal output, they became increasingly dependent upon surrounding areas for grain and other farm products.

   Many such areas were created by yeomen and husbandmen responding to local demands and adapting to the types of soil on which they farmed. A good example of this is Wiltshire, where the heavy soils were particularly suited to cattle-raising, and dairy farming became a speciality. Small dairy herds were attractive to husbandmen because they could be managed with family labour, and brought in a regular income from milk, butter and cheese. Larger scale cattle-rearing and fattening was usually outside the scope of the husbandmen because it required more money. For a regional farming structure to work efficiently a good infrastructure of roads and navigable rivers was needed so that produce could be moved rapidly from one part of the country to another.

The government and local authorities were aware of the problem. Attempts were made to improve river navigation, particularly on the Thames, and local landowners worked with the town authorities to improve roads. However, it is considered that little real progress was made until after the 1560s.

A contemporary view of the situation

Such a view is supported by Sir Thomas Smith in another of his books, *A Discourse on the Commonwealth of this Realm of England* (1560s). This takes the form of a dialogue or debate by a doctor, representing the academic view, discussing the state of the economy with various members of society such as a knight, a

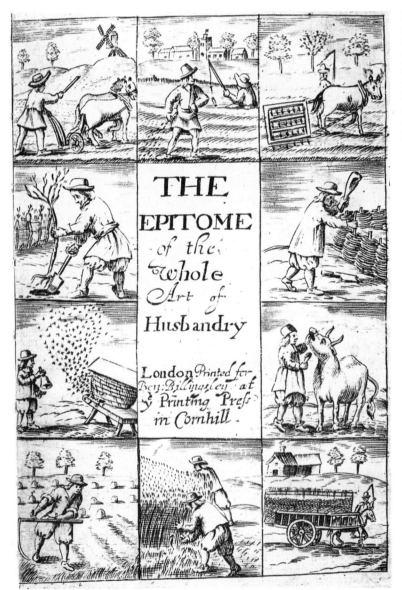

Everyday rural scenes depicted in a contemporary publication *The Art of Husbandry*. How reliable are the illustrations in depicting the everyday life of the lower orders?

merchant and a husbandman. After suggesting that the debasing
of the coinage had doubled prices in his lifetime, the doctor goes
on to discuss the cost and shortage of grain. He suggests that the
best way to get more grain was either to make it as expensive as
wool, or to reduce the price of wool.

This view of the economy confirms that it was not just the
gentry and yeomen who were failing to grow enough grain, but
that husbandmen were equally to blame for any shortfalls. The
reason for this was the low price of grain in comparison with wool
and other animal products over the previous decades, which had
led to the conversion of arable to pasture. It is interesting to note
that husbandmen were just as keen to enclose their land as the
larger commercial farmers, and regarded enclosed holdings as
more efficient than the old open fields. Husbandmen clearly were
being adversely affected by increased rents and other agricultural
overheads.

At the same time they were just as ready to react as the larger
commercial farmers to market forces. This, along with rising
rents, was a major cause of popular hostility towards the gentry.
Wool was seen as the quickest way of making a profit from land,
but sheep-runs were a large-scale undertaking and outside the
scope of most husbandmen. It was such commercially based
rivalry that was an important underlying cause of the disorders in
1549.

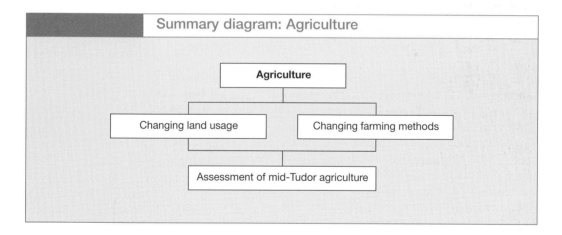

Summary diagram: Agriculture

Key question
What were the effects
of industrial
development during
the sixteenth century?

3 | Industry

Developments in industry show whether or not the mid-Tudor
economy was becoming more advanced. The agricultural sector
was just about able to feed the population, except in bad harvest
years. Less land was under cultivation so that, as the population
began to rise, surplus labour became available to work in industry.
For this to happen more jobs had to be created in both rural and
urban industries.

Heavy industry

Heavy industry used to be considered the most dynamic part of the sector. It was suggested by J.U. Nef in *The Rise of the British Coal Industry* (1932) that there was a Tudor industrial revolution led by rising coal production. This idea was based on the once popular theory that there was a severe timber shortage in Tudor England, and that there was consequently a sharp increase in the use of mineral fuels. The expansion in the industrial use of non-agricultural raw materials, such as coal, was seen as being vitally important in the development of early capitalism. Such operations needed expensive equipment on a centralised site and a small, but highly skilled workforce. Mining and metal-working, along with other specialised and capital-intensive undertakings such as dyeing, brewing, glass and paper-making, are regarded as the real signs of a new, capitalistic economy.

Key question
How significant was the development of heavy industry?

Problems in the coal industry

These ideas are no longer accepted. It is now thought that any shortages of wood or charcoal were purely local. No sudden rise in demand for coal can be seen until the end of the sixteenth century. A major problem for expansion in heavy industry was the difficulty and cost of transport. Unlike raw materials from agriculture, coal and other minerals were only to be found in certain areas. Consequently, industries associated with these products were very localised because of the cost of carrying heavy materials more than a short distance. It is not considered that any great expansion was possible until real improvements to river navigation and sea transport began in the second half of the sixteenth century.

Another difficulty preventing the expansion of heavy industry was that English technology was very backward in comparison with that of the continent. Problems of drainage and ventilation meant that mining operations had to be open cast. Coal was mined in south Wales, the Weald of Kent, the Forest of Dean and parts of the Midlands, but only for local use. The main coal-producing area was Northumberland and Durham, and increasingly large quantities were shipped to London from the end of the fourteenth century. However, this 'sea coal' was used largely for domestic fires and not for industrial purposes.

The metal industries

Before the second half of the sixteenth century only small quantities of coal were used in industry. Another important consideration was that coal was unsuitable for iron smelting. Iron ore, like coal, was mined in various places, but mainly in the Weald of Kent and the Forest of Dean, where there was a plentiful supply of timber for making charcoal to smelt the ore.

At the end of the fifteenth century, gentry and yeomen ironmasters in the Weald began to use a new type of blast furnace, fuelled by charcoal and powered by water, which had been introduced from the continent. By the 1550s, 26 of these new furnaces were in use in the Weald, making it a major producer of cast iron, which was used particularly for making naval guns and shot. However, pig iron was still the major output. This was converted into bar iron in a forge fuelled by charcoal and driven by water. The bars of iron were then distributed on pack animals to blacksmiths in the towns and villages for making into tools and other small objects such as door handles.

Apart from the technological advance in iron production, little real progress was made elsewhere before 1560. Tin was mined in Devon and Cornwall mainly for export. Much the same can be said for lead and zinc mining in Shropshire and the Mendips. Although a new blast furnace for smelting lead, which only used half as much fuel, was introduced, the metal-working industries were on a very small scale. It was only after the 1570s that copper, pewter, brass and silver production began to become important.

Other specialist, centralised industries such as brick, tile and glass-making, bell-founding and gunpowder manufacture, were still very localised. New, sophisticated processes such as paper-making were only just being introduced.

Assessment of heavy industry

By the mid-sixteenth century heavy industry had had little impact on economic growth, and was still at the stage of catching up with continental technology. However, if this sector cannot be said to have made any positive contribution to industrial expansion, neither can it be considered to have added to the economic problems of the mid-century.

Rural industry

<table>
<tr><td>

Key question

How important were the changes in rural industry?

</td></tr>
</table>

In the thirteenth century many urban textile and leather craftsmen had moved to the countryside to avoid the power of the guilds and the high cost of living in towns (see pages 28–9). There they set up new industries to make use of the cheap rural labour force. Crafts such as spinning, weaving, glove-making and basket-making had traditionally been carried out by peasant families in their own homes to supplement their incomes. Craftsmen were able to use this semi-skilled workforce to establish an industry outside the jurisdiction of the town guilds. This was the beginning of the rural textile industry that was to remain dominant until the eighteenth century. Unlike the guilds, which produced small quantities of high-quality, expensive goods, rural industries manufactured large amounts of less well-made, but much cheaper, products.

The rural cloth industry

The largest branch of rural industry was textile manufacturing. The significance of this form of cloth production was that it was large scale and exported increasing quantities of semi-finished textiles to the continent. By the sixteenth century this industry was organised by clothiers. Generally these were merchants from a nearby town, or local yeomen and prosperous husbandmen. Raw materials such as wool or yarn were purchased by the clothier, who distributed them to his workforce for manufacturing in their cottages using their own tools.

There was a significant division of labour because the various stages of manufacture were separated, and only the clothiers sold the completed piece of cloth. It also meant that the clothier had no large outlay to provide buildings or equipment, as was the case in heavy industry. The only high-cost buildings required were the water-driven fulling mills to felt and thicken the woollen cloth by shrinking and rolling it so that the fibres interlocked, and in most cases existing flour mills could be used for this purpose. The capital costs were the purchase of the raw materials and the wages for the workforce.

However, it is thought that many of the rural workforce, particularly the weavers, remained self-employed, and were not entirely dependent on wages. The development of a major exporting industry in England is considered to be a significant economic advance. The main areas of clothmaking were East Anglia, the West Country and parts of Yorkshire.

Competition between rural and urban industries

Although the rural textile industry is seen as the major contributor to England's economic expansion up to 1570, it did create a number of problems. As the putting-out system was free of guild regulations it was not necessary for those taking part in it to have served an **apprenticeship**. This caused resentment among the members of the town guilds who saw it as unfair competition. The situation was made worse by the government's failure to enforce regulations in the countryside. Consequently, by the early sixteenth century, apart from textiles, a variety of allied trades, such as leather crafts, had become firmly established. These also competed with the more expensive products of the urban guilds.

> **Apprenticeship**
> Time served by students learning a trade from master-craftsmen.
>
> **Key term**

Government legislation

From the beginning of the sixteenth century the government repeatedly passed legislation to try to exert greater control over rural industry. In part this was in response to complaints about shoddy workmanship and poor-quality goods levelled at the putting-out industry by the towns. At the same time the State was trying to take greater control over the economy in general. However, attempts by the authorities to remedy the situation were generally crude and heavy-handed.

In 1559 Sir William Cecil suggested restoring the unpopular Vagrancy Act of 1547 (see page 57). Furthermore he recommended that servants and labourers should not be allowed to leave their villages, and no one should be apprenticed unless his father was a gentleman or merchant, and owned land worth at least 10 pounds a year.

Assessing mid-Tudor industry

The poor state of industry suggests that the Tudor economy had not advanced significantly by the 1560s. Consequently, no effective transfer of labour was taking place from the agricultural to the industrial sector. The situation was made worse by the down-turn in exports, which created further unemployment in the textile trades.

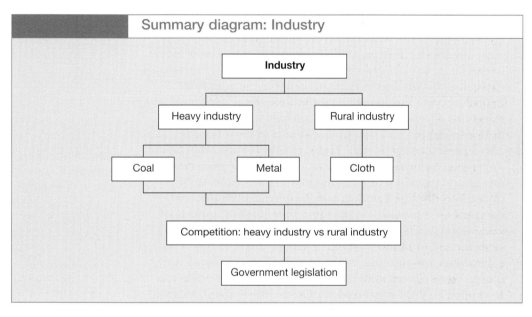

Summary diagram: Industry

4 | The Mid-Tudor Trade Recession

By the 1550s there was widespread destitution in the textile trades and in the towns. The long period of ever-rising cloth exports had ended, so bringing a sustained period of expansion from the 1460s to an abrupt halt. It is agreed that the basic cause of this problem was the decline of the Antwerp cloth market, but there were a number of other contributory factors, which need to be considered to understand the economic difficulties in mid-Tudor England.

Long-term causes

The underlying problem can be traced to developments in the fifteenth century.

Key term

Hanseatic League
Merchants from the mainly German city ports on the Baltic Sea who came together to form a trading union and thus dominate trade in northern Europe.

1. *Exports.* By the 1440s textile exports had risen to some 55,000 cloths a year, while wool exports had fallen to an annual 9000 sacks. In the middle of the century trade was adversely affected by the general western European trade recession.
2. *Diplomatically weak.* England was in a weak diplomatic position after defeat in the war with France and the beginning of the Wars of the Roses. Consequently, English merchants lost control of their markets in central Europe and the Baltic to their main commercial rivals, the German merchants of the **Hanseatic League**. When trade recovered in the 1460s, almost

half the English cloth exports were controlled by the Hanse and other foreign merchants.

3. *Merchant Adventurers.* The English share of the trade had become monopolised by the Merchant Adventurers, who were a powerful group of traders. They owed their dominant position to the large loans that they gave to the Crown, in return for which they were granted privileges denied to other English merchants. Driven out of other continental markets, the Merchant Adventurers established themselves at Antwerp in the Netherlands. This was to have a number of important consequences for English trade up to the 1550s. The Netherlands was a major centre for the dyeing and finishing of cloth, and this made it very convenient for the export of English textiles. Furthermore, at the time of the Merchant Adventurers' removal to Antwerp, the city was becoming the main commercial and financial centre in western Europe.

4. *The Antwerp–London 'funnel'.* This created what is known as the Antwerp–London 'funnel'. The monopoly of the Merchant Adventurers meant that English cloth exports came to be channelled through London, which controlled 90 per cent of the trade by the 1550s. At the same time English imports of wine, spices, manufactured goods and luxury items became concentrated on Antwerp. One beneficial effect of this commercial axis was that by the middle of the sixteenth century some 70 per cent of the country's overseas trade was controlled by English merchants. On the other hand, English ports such as Bristol, York, Hull and Southampton declined, and many merchants outside London complained that they were being excluded from the continental market.

Short-term causes

The link with Antwerp created a variety of problems through its very success.

1. Much of the rise in the volume of exports in the 1540s was the result of the repeated debasement of the English coinage. This, by reducing the value of sterling against continental currencies, artificially stimulated demand for English goods abroad by making them cheaper, and so made the slump after 1550 even deeper.

2. The importance of the trade to both England and the Netherlands made it a pawn in diplomatic exchanges and foreign policy. The early Tudors frequently used the threat of withholding cloth exports to try to force the Habsburg Empire into wars against France. Such a policy finally helped to bring about the decline of Antwerp when England's relationship with Charles V broke down during Northumberland's temporary alliance with France in 1550 (see pages 55–6). Both sides placed restrictions on trade, and this forced English merchants to begin to look for new markets.

3. Although the Antwerp market did not finally collapse until the 1570s, its preceding decline left English trade in a very

exposed position. During the first half of the sixteenth century the volume of exports to Antwerp had made English merchants disinclined to seek out alternative markets. In spite of advice, such as that given by Robert Thorne in his book *Declaration of the Indes* (1530s), very little effort was made to establish new trade outlets within Europe, or elsewhere in the world. It was not until the initial slump in the trade to the Netherlands in the early 1550s that the Privy Council and the London merchants began to promote exploration in the search for new markets. The establishment of the Muscovy Company in 1553 was the first step in this direction.

4. The underlying cause of the decline of the Antwerp market was the change in the pattern of demand. Both European and colonial buyers began to favour lighter types of fabric made of silk, cotton or linen mixed with wool, instead of the heavy English woollen cloth. This meant that during the second half of the sixteenth century English manufacturers not only had to find alternative markets, but also had to restructure to meet the new technical developments.

Assessing mid-Tudor trade

Clearly the concentration on trade with Antwerp eventually proved disastrous for the English economy. In part, the problem was political, arising from England's reliance on Habsburg support in the wars with France. Fear of offending the Spanish Habsburgs meant that only limited attempts were made to break into their monopoly of world trade. The loss of Calais ended any lingering dreams of regaining a continental empire. Deteriorating relations between England and Spain under Elizabeth I opened the way for a more vigorous search for markets outside Europe. This was to be the basis for the expansion of world trade in the seventeenth century.

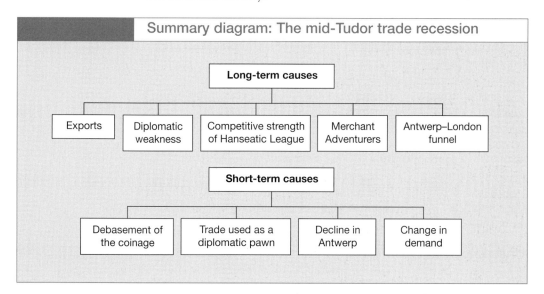

Summary diagram: The mid-Tudor trade recession

Long-term causes

| Exports | Diplomatic weakness | Competitive strength of Hanseatic League | Merchant Adventurers | Antwerp–London funnel |

Short-term causes

| Debasement of the coinage | Trade used as a diplomatic pawn | Decline in Antwerp | Change in demand |

5 | Towns, Unemployment and Urban Recession

Key question
What was the 'urban crisis'?

The commercial backbone of England's economy had long been based on three key activities: foreign trade, regional trade and the local market town trade. The last of these proved the most dynamic during the sixteenth century. The town, with its market and regular fairs, was an essential part of the rural economy because it brought producer and consumer together. Towns stimulated trade and encouraged growth in the economy.

The towns

Mid-Tudor England had many towns but few of them were large. London was six times larger than its nearest rivals, Norwich and Bristol. It has been calculated that only about seven per cent of the country's population lived in towns of over 5000 inhabitants.

The estimated populations of the largest English and Welsh towns in 1550:

London	80,000
Norwich	12,000
Bristol	10,000
York	7000
Newcastle	6000
Exeter	6000
Salisbury	5000
Oxford	5000
Carmarthen	2500

Unemployment in the 1550s was made worse by what used to be called an 'urban crisis'. In some respects this was considered to be a consequence of the development of the rural textile industry. The first stage of urban decline came from the effects of competition from the more cost-effective putting-out system. Then, in the fifteenth century, towns were adversely affected by the population losses caused by the Black Death and the continued influence of the plague cycle. Urban populations declined rapidly, especially because their crowded living conditions produced higher mortality rates.

The situation was made worse by the fall in overall population which drastically reduced the flow of migrants needed to maintain, or increase, the number of town dwellers. When population levels began to recover during the first half of the sixteenth century, the situation was reversed. Towns faced the problem of having to house, feed and employ large numbers of young and generally unskilled migrants from the countryside. At the same time, town guilds had to meet growing competition from the rural industries.

Unemployment and urban recession

Key question
How serious a problem was unemployment and the urban recession?

While some towns went into temporary eclipse, others actually expanded. In any case, the picture is distorted by the abnormal expansion of London, which was a reflection of the city's monopoly of the Antwerp trade. London was becoming recognised as the centre of government and the capital of England. Urban historians tend to see the rapid expansion of London as a positive development. London's emergence as a capital city is regarded as having become an engine for economic growth by the end of the sixteenth century.

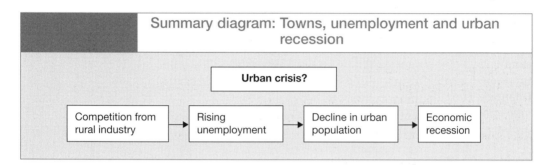

Summary diagram: Towns, unemployment and urban recession

Urban crisis?

Competition from rural industry → Rising unemployment → Decline in urban population → Economic recession

6 | The Key Debate

Was there a crisis in the economy?

Although the mid-Tudor economy appeared to be in a weak state there is no clear evidence that it was in crisis.

Agriculture
Agriculture had become more efficient through enclosures, specialisation and commercial farming. However, because of over-concentration on wool and other animal products, it was barely able to feed the increased population by 1550, a problem that was not to be fully overcome until the next century.

Industry
There was a similar amount of change in industry. Heavy industry was still in the process of catching up with continental technology. The rural textile industry suffered temporary collapse in the 1550s after a century of expansion, but was already adapting to new demands by the second half of the century. The slump in the Antwerp cloth market in the 1550s had forced English merchants to begin to seek new markets in Europe, and to take an interest in world trade. The main difficulty was that the economy was unable to find employment for the surplus labour released from agriculture and created by a rising population.

Debasements of the coinage
Debasements of the coinage helped to increase inflation and made goods and borrowing more expensive. Rising rents, prices and unemployment, along with static wages, curtailed demand among the bulk of the population. In turn, this acted as a disincentive for people to invest in either agriculture or industry.

Taxation

The ruinously high levels of taxation from the 1520s were a further deterrent to investment. The cumulative effect of high taxation had, by the mid-century, seriously limited the cash reserves of all but the wealthiest landowners and merchants.

Political problems

It can be argued that where there were problems they were more political than economic. The two mid-century decades were characterised by almost continuous warfare, which was the culmination of the wars started by Henry VIII in the 1520s. This protracted conflict disrupted the economies on both sides of the Channel. The situation was made worse by diplomatic manoeuvrings which artificially created slumps by stopping overseas trade.

Unemployment

By the 1550s unemployment was becoming a problem in many towns. As population levels rose there were no extra jobs in agriculture, and younger people had to find employment elsewhere. They travelled to the towns to seek work, which was often not available because of the lack of urban investment. There is no real sign that rising unemployment was a key factor in the popular discontent in 1549. This is not to say that there was not widespread hardship in many areas.

Lack of investment

There was an underlying problem of a lack of investment and demand in the English economy. The rural élites favoured building country mansions and buying luxury goods to maintain their lifestyle rather than investing money to improve their estates. Similarly, the wealthy urban élites were more interested in improving their social position by purchasing country estates than expanding and improving their business interests. This situation continued until the inflationary spiral ended in the 1650s. Until then landowners and industrialists were content to live off the profits generated by rising prices without making investments.

Despite the disruptions caused by war, high taxation and debasements of the coinage, economic progress was maintained.

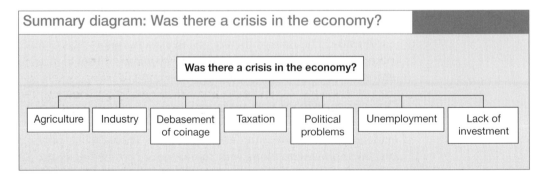

Summary diagram: Was there a crisis in the economy?

Was there a crisis in the economy?

Agriculture | Industry | Debasement of coinage | Taxation | Political problems | Unemployment | Lack of investment

Study Guide: AS Question

In the style of OCR

Study the five sources on social and economic problems 1546–50, and then answer both sub-questions. It is recommended that you spend two-thirds of your time in answering part (b).

(a) **Study Sources A and C.**

Compare these sources as evidence for landlord–tenant relations.

(b) **Study *all* the sources.**

Use your own knowledge to assess how far the sources support the interpretation that enclosures were the *main* reason for social and economic problems between 1546 and 1550.

Social and economic problems 1546–50

Source A

From: A Supplication of the Poore Commons, *1546. A social commentator attacks the rise of oppressive landlords.*

Many landlords oppress the common people. They have increased their rents, so that they charge £40 rather than 40 shillings [£2] for a new lease, and £5 not 5 nobles [almost £2] for its annual rent, so we now pay more to them than we earn. The result is that many thousands of us who once lived honestly upon our labour must now beg, or borrow, or rob and steal, to get food for our poor wives and children. They also compel others to surrender their rights to hold leases for two or three lives and to accept instead leases for just twenty-one years.

Source B

From: Sir Thomas Smith, A Discourse of the Common Weal of this Realm of England, *1549. The economic problems of the time are discussed in an imaginary dialogue between a small farmer, a merchant and a knight.*

Small farmer: These enclosures ruin us all, for they make us pay more for our land so we have no money to put to ploughing.

Merchant: There is a shortage of all things which we grow in this land or which we buy from overseas, and food is more expensive. If enclosures are the cause, then they should be removed.

Knight: Enclosures cannot be the cause of the shortage of cattle, for enclosures encourage and protect cattle. All things are more expensive now, but you can raise the price of the goods you sell, whereas we gentlemen have nothing to sell and yet have to pay higher prices.

Source C

From: Thomas Becon, The Jewel of Joy, *written in about 1550. A religious work blames 'greedy gentlemen' for society's economic problems. The author had been chaplain to Protector Somerset.*

The cause of all this wretchedness and beggary in the commonwealth are the greedy gentlemen, who are sheep-masters and graziers. While they work for their private profit, national prosperity declines. Since they began to be sheep-masters and feeders of cattle, we neither have food nor cloth at a reasonable price. This is no surprise for they fix the market so the poor man has to pay their price, or starve and die of cold: for they have no pity for the poor. As St Paul wrote, 'All seek their own advantage, and not those things which belong to Jesus Christ'.

Source D

From: Robert Crowley, The Waie to Wealth, *1550. Another Protestant clergyman, one of the Commonwealth writers, considers the social and economic causes of the popular rebellions in 1549.*

Rebellion is a dangerous disease and its causes must be rooted out. If I should ask a poor man what is the cause of rebellion, he will blame the great farmers, lawyers, gentlemen, knights and lords. Men of greed; men who take our houses from us, and enclose our commons. If I should ask these greedy men what is the cause of rebellion, they will say that the peasants are too wealthy, they are disobedient, they would destroy gentlemen. They will try again to compel the King to grant their requests, and will be punished for it, as happened last year.

Source E

François van der Delft, letter to Emperor Charles V, 19 July 1549. An ambassador in England writes a brief but accurate account of the risings of 1549.

The revolt of the peasants has increased and spread, so that now they have risen in every part of England, asking for things just and unjust. They demand they may use the land that once used to be public property, and that land leased to them shall be considered to be of the same value now as in the time of Henry VII, who died in 1509. This last request is very difficult to meet. In Kent and Essex the risings ended when foodstuffs were taxed at a reasonable price.

Exam tips

(a) First of all make sure you are comparing the correct two sources: Source A with Source C.

- Focus: here the focus is on *landlord–tenant relations*. This should be kept clearly in mind throughout, as the purpose of the *comparison*.
- Links: similarities and differences should be cross-referenced point by point and *linked* to the question, *landlord–tenant relations*. In planning, highlight aspects of source content that link to these key terms.
- Avoid a formulaic approach. Think about the sources in the light of their historical context, and show your understanding of their significance in answering the question.
- Provenance: it is important to start by focusing on *who, what, when, why* and *to whom* the source was written and its *tone*. Not all of these aspects may be relevant to this particular question, so avoid a formulaic approach. Concentrate on the most significant aspect(s).
- Content: try to balance similarities and differences of content in the light of their provenance, integrating content with provenance.
- Analyse: the detail, sentence by sentence, cross-referencing in the light of the question. Compare the reliability or usefulness of the two sources in answering it.
- Judgement: decide which of the two sources provides the better evidence of landlord–tenant relations and give convincing support for your decision. This may be based on usefulness, reliability, whether the view is typical, more complete, better informed, written at a significant date or some other relevant criterion.

The *provenance* (*nature and purpose*): Source A is a 'supplication of the poore commons' or a list of problems suffered by the poor, written on their behalf by an educated commentator in order to draw the government's attention to them, as they have no political voice of their own in their dealings with their landlords. Source C, on the other hand, is a religious work, drawing attention to disregard for the poor by the gentry class. So, at face value, they have a similar purpose of speaking up for uneducated poor people. However, the authorships and dates are revealing. Source A is written at the end of Henry VIII's reign by an anonymous writer, suggesting that the government, and its gentry allies, would not support the views it expresses. Source C, on the other hand, is written by Somerset's chaplain, at a time when Somerset's government were attempting to help the poor with humanitarian policies.

Context shows that, by that time, ideas such as Hales Commission had a good deal of support among 'commonweal' men at Court. The *context* of Source C's publication is

Somerset's fall from power, so its purpose may be to try to justify Somerset's policies after the 1549 rebellions.

Source content is similar in that both refer to poverty caused by high costs, in Source A, rents and in Source C, food and cloth. The result in both cases is to increase the number of beggars, causing resentment. However, in Source C, landlords are fixing the markets to keep prices of goods artificially high whereas in Source A they are rack-renting and introducing new short-term leases. The moral tone taken in Source C reflects its religious author, and he quotes St Paul to shame the landlords for having no pity for the poor, a view echoed in Source A where earnings have not been raised in line with prices, causing some poor people to resort to stealing. The anonymous author may outrage conservatives who held a good deal of influence with Henry VIII in 1546, and likewise, the author of Source C would have had little support from the faction that replaced Somerset, so both authors are reporting landlord–tenant relations at a time when they will have little support from the current government.

Judgement might view Source A as the better evidence for *landlord–tenant relations*, as it is more genuine in its purpose of trying to draw attention to the problem of increasing landlord–tenant tensions. Source C, on the other hand, may be trying to justify and support a fallen minister.

(b) In order to answer this part of the question:
- The sources should be grouped by their point of view: sometimes a source contains more than one point for cross-reference.
- The significance for the question, of the views in the content of the sources, should be developed using accurate historical context and terminology.
- Relevant aspects of the provenance of the sources should be linked to answering the question. This 'provenance' might be authorship, date, nature, purpose, audience, tone.
- Accurate knowledge and terminology should be integrated into the answer to verify, qualify or evaluate the views in the sources as well as their provenance.
- A judgement should be reached on the 'value' of the sources in linking to the interpretation in the question, where 'value' might be judged by:
  - reliability and/or usefulness of content and provenance
  - completeness of content or aspects deliberately ignored
  - limitations of the sources as a set.

Things to avoid:

- Do not use the sources as illustrations of an essay-style answer.
- Do not merely *describe* or *paraphrase* source content, but always *use* it to argue.

- Do not use the sources as a mine for extracting *references*. Their purpose is to validate or qualify the interpretation in the question, enabling you to use them in effective argument.
- Do not make 'stock' comments about the provenance of sources, especially common with secondary authors, e.g. 'he is an eminent historian so we can trust his view'. Always link comments on provenance to the focus of the question.

Sources C–E suggest that enclosures were the main reason for social and economic problems at this time, whereas Source B seems doubtful that they were the *main* reason. Sources A–C and E also suggest that inflation was a major reason. Sources D and E blame unruly peasants who ask for unjust demands, whereas Source C mentions a decline in religious duty.

Sources C and D refer to 'greedy gentlemen, who are sheep-masters and graziers' and Source D to 'men of greed; men who take our houses from us, and enclose our commons'. Content, provenance and context should be integrated to develop this idea and a judgement reached on how far enclosure played a part in problems such as poverty, unemployment, vagabondage and depopulation of villages. Source B, on the other hand, argues that enclosure cannot be the reason for a shortage of cattle, as land has been enclosed specifically to graze them. Food shortages often resulted, aggravated by bad harvests and epidemics. The provenance of Source B is important. As an economist but also a gentleman himself, Sir Thomas Smith blamed government debasement of the coinage for inflation and the resultant social and economic problems of inflation and poverty. A judgement should be reached evaluating the significance of enclosure in the light of contextual knowledge, source content and provenance.

A–C and E also suggest that inflation was a major reason. Source A suggests that rack rents and new short leases were the main cause of poverty and vagabondage, giving useful statistics to emphasise just how much prices had risen. This might be cross-referenced with Source E, which mentions requests for prices to return to the 1509 level. Source E also mentions increased government tax as a reason for inflation. Whereas Somerset's chaplain, perhaps justifying him, in Source C suggests that greedy landlords fix the market, causing inflation, Sir Thomas Smith argues the case that producers of goods cause inflation by raising their prices, whereas gentlemen have nothing to sell so are not to blame for social and economic problems. Knowledge might be used to qualify this view in cross-reference with Source A, as the sale of monastic land had allowed gentry to gain land for enclosure but also to rent out on short leases at inflated prices. A judgement should be reached evaluating the significance of enclosure in the light of contextual knowledge, source content and provenance.

A judgement should be reached evaluating how far the sources support the interpretation overall. This is likely to reflect the reliability and use of the sources as well as changing historical context and the relative importance of a range of reasons.

Final tips:

- The limitations of the set of sources should be supplied from relevant own knowledge, not merely suggested less appropriately, e.g. 'the sources would be more useful if they told us the unemployment figures'. This comment adds little to the evaluation.
- The grouped sources should drive the answer, and an evaluative argument should be created by integrating context with source content and provenance.

Marks are awarded for synthesis, bringing together all the elements of the answer. Therefore the final paragraph of conclusion is *very important* and will play an important part in gaining marks. It should bring together all the threads of the argument and judge how far the sources, as a set, support the interpretation in the question. If the sources are limited or unreliable, they will not support the interpretation effectively.

Further Reading

G.W. Bernard, 'Politics and Government in Tudor England', *Historical Journal*, 31 (1988), 159–82.

Philip Caraman, *The Western Rebellion* (Tiverton, 1994).

D.C. Coleman, *The Economy of England, 1450–1750* (OUP, 1977).

E. Duffy, *The Stripping of the Altars* (OUP, 1992).

G.R. Elton, *England under the Tudors* (Methuen, 1955).

N. Fellows, *Disorder and Rebellion in Tudor England* (Hodder & Stoughton, 2001).

A. Fletcher and J. Stevenson, *Order and Disorder in Early Modern England* (CUP, 1985).

C. Haigh, *English Reformations: Religion, Politics and Society Under the Tudors* (OUP, 1993).

N. Heard, *Tudor Economy and Society* (Hodder & Stoughton, 1992).

Christopher Hill, 'Marxism and History', *The Modern Quarterly NS 3* (1948), 52–64.

Eric Hobsbawm & T. Ranger (eds.), *The Invention of Tradition* (CUP, 1992).

W.K. Jordan, *Edward VI: The Threshold of Power – The Dominance of the Duke of Northumberland* (George Allen & Unwin, 1970).

J. Loach & R. Tittler (eds.), *The Mid-Tudor Polity, c. 1540–1560* (Macmillan, 1980).

J. Loach, *Parliament under the Tudors* (OUP, 1991).

J. Loach, *A Mid-Tudor Crisis?* (Historical Association pamphlet, 1992).

D.M. Loades, *The Mid-Tudor Crisis, 1545–65* (Macmillan, 1992).

D. MacCulloch, *Tudor Church Militant: Edward VI and the Protestant Reformation* (Penguin, 1999).

D.M. Pallister, *The Age of Elizabeth: England under the Later Tudors 1547–1603* (2nd edn, Longman, 1992).

Paul Slack, *Poverty and Policy in Tudor and Stuart England* (Longman, 1988).

Alan G.R. Smith, *The Emergence of a Nation State 1529–1660* (Longman, 1984).

Paul Thomas, *Authority and Disorder in Tudor Times 1485–1603* (CUP, 1999).

R. Tittler, *Mary I* (Longman, 1983).

P. Williams, *The Later Tudors: England, 1547–1603* (OUP, 1995).

John Warren, *The Past and its Presenters* (Hodder & Stoughton, 1998).

Glossary

Absolution   Forgiven for committing a sin.

Absolutist   Similar to dictatorship where the ruler has absolute power, i.e. unchallenged rule.

Act of Six Articles   Passed in 1539, the Acts were intended to protect and promote Catholic religious ideas and prevent the further spread of Protestantism in England and Wales.

Act of the Ten Articles   Passed in 1536, the Act was intended to promote Protestant religious ideas in England and Wales by stripping away many of the traditional festivals, relic-cults, shrines and parts of the Church service.

Anglo-Catholicism   Term used to describe the English Catholic Church set up in 1534 with the king as its head rather than the Pope.

Anti-clericalism   Hostility to, and unpopularity of, the Church and its priests.

Apprenticeship   Time served by students learning a trade from master-craftsmen.

Arable   Farming land set aside for the growing of crops.

Armada   The Spanish invasion fleet of 1588.

Atlantic trade   The triangular trade route between Europe, America and Africa.

Bondmen   Peasant farmers who had no freedom to choose where they lived and worked. They were tied to the manor on which they were born and brought up.

Book of Homilies   A book containing a list of sermons and other religious tracts for use in daily worship.

Bourgeoisie   Term used by Marxist historians to describe the middle class of lawyers, landowners and merchants.

Bureaucracy   The means by which a State is governed by officials responsible for routine administration.

Burgesses   The most powerful members of a town's citizens. They were often descended from the town's original founders and they also tended to hold the most important offices in the town's administration.

Calvinism   A term used to describe the influence and religious ideas and teachings of John Calvin of Geneva, a radical Protestant religious reformer who attacked the Catholic Church's wealth and privileges.

Catholic élites   The most powerful and influential Catholic politicians and landowners in the kingdom.

Chancellor   Senior minister in the royal government who had control of the Great Seal used to authenticate and give legal force to laws.

Chantries   Small religious houses endowed with lands to support one or more priests whose duty it was to sing masses for the souls of the deceased founder or members of the founding organisation.

Christian humanism   The teaching of the original classical texts in their original Latin and Greek, and the study of the humanities as the basis of civilised life.

Class war   Used by some historians to help explain the causes of the disorder and rebellions that occurred during the reign of Edward VI. The resentment of the poor and economically vulnerable was directed towards the wealthy and powerful élites.

Commercial market economy Landlords leased out their land in larger units to commercial farmers for greater profit which resulted in smaller tenant farmers being forced off the land to work for wages in agriculture.

Commercially oriented A system whereby landowners and merchants became more businesslike in order to make a profit.

Commonwealth A community of shared interests where everyone, in theory, worked for the common good.

Constitution The rules and regulations that determine how a country is governed.

Constitutional monarchy A system whereby a monarch governs the kingdom within the limits of an agreed framework of rules that includes institutions such as the Privy Council and parliament.

Consubstantiation The belief that the sacramental bread and wine given by the priest to parishioners in church were a symbolic representation of the body and blood of Christ and therefore remained unchanged at communion.

Convocation An assembly of clergy that discussed Church matters, passed Church laws and regulated the way the Church was run.

Cottagers Poorer peasant farmers who were obliged to work on the landowner's land either for free or for a fixed sum of money.

Counter-Reformation Catholic reaction against the spread of Protestantism. Led by the Pope, the Catholic Church attempted to reconvert Protestants and bring them back to the Catholic faith.

Country party Made up of those among the élites who did not hold office or enjoy royal favour, and generally lived on their estates in the countryside.

County militia Non-professional military force raised from among the able-bodied local population that lived within the bounds of a county.

Coup d'état French term to describe a rebellion that removes the head of State and the government from power.

Court party Seen as consisting of the members of the Privy Council, government officers and courtiers, all of whom held office and enjoyed royal patronage.

Craft guilds Similar to trade unions, formed to protect and promote the particular trade of their members.

Custom and excise Taxation imposed on the import of goods.

Debasement of the coinage A process whereby the government tried to preserve its gold and silver reserves by reducing the amount of precious metal that went into making coins.

Deflation The reduction of the amount of money in circulation in order to increase its value.

Diocese A district under the pastoral care of a bishop.

Dissolution of the monasteries The closure of the monasteries of England and Wales by Henry VIII between 1536 and 1540.

Divine right Belief that monarchs were chosen by God to rule the kingdom and that their word was law. To challenge their right to rule was the same as challenging God.

Doctrinal orthodoxy The traditional or long-held beliefs of, in this instance, the Catholic Church and religion.

Elizabethan Church Settlement Term use to describe the organisation, ritual and teaching of the Church of England as enforced by Acts of Parliament.

Enclosure The enclosing of land by fences or hedges in order to divide large, open fields into smaller more manageable units.

Entry fines   A custom by which a fixed sum of money was paid on taking up a tenancy by inheritance or by sale.

Eucharist   The Christian Sacrament commemorating the Last Supper, in which bread and wine are consecrated and consumed.

Evangelicals   People who recruit followers to their particular brand of religion.

Exchequer   The centre of the Crown's financial administration since the twelfth century. It had two functions: to receive, store and pay out money, and to audit the Crown's accounts.

Excommunicate   To cast a sinner out of the Roman Catholic Church. When dead, an excommunicate could not be buried on consecrated ground and the soul would go to hell.

Extreme unction   The act of being anointed with oils as part of a religious rite or ceremony.

Factions   Rival or opposing political groups led by powerful noblemen or noble families. Factions fought for control of the monarch.

Feudal crisis   The breakdown in the relationship between lord (master) and vassal (servant). The relationship changed from one based on rewards of land for service to one based on money payments.

Feudalism   The political and social system of medieval England. The system was based on the relationship between lord (master) and vassal (servant): in a ceremony known as homage the vassal promised to serve his lord in war and peace in return for land.

Field rotation   System where different crops are rotated between fields.

Flexible field systems   Farmers could grow what crops they wanted where they wanted, either in large open fields or in enclosed fields.

Forty-Two Articles   A list of essential doctrines drawn up by Cranmer and intended to form the basis of the new Protestant Church of England.

Habsburgs   Family name of the ruling family of Spain and Austria. The head of the family from 1519 until his retirement in 1555 was Charles V who, as Holy Roman Emperor, also ruled Germany, the Netherlands and parts of Italy.

Hanseatic League   Merchants from the mainly German city ports on the Baltic Sea who came together to form a trading union and thus dominate trade in northern Europe.

Heresy laws   Laws to punish those people who reject the State religion and the teachings of the Church.

Higher clergy   The bishops and two archbishops of England and Wales.

Holy Roman Empire   Collection of states of varying sizes that covered central Europe (Germany and Austria) and northern Italy that was governed by an elected ruler, the Emperor.

Hundred Years' War   Fought between England and France for control of France between 1338 and 1453.

Husbandmen   Tenant-farmers who rented their land from the local landowners.

Iconoclasm   The act of breaking, destroying or defacing religious images such as wall paintings or stained glass, and statues like those depicting Christ and the Virgin Mary.

Impotent poor   Those who were too old, too young or too sick to work.

Infant mortality   Term used to describe the death rate among children, usually under five years of age. In the medieval and early modern periods, infant mortality rates were high owing to complications at birth, poor diet, disease and poor health, and hygiene.

Inflation   Price rises in goods, materials and foodstuffs.

Injunction   A law or decree issued by the Crown to compel the clergy in the Church of England to follow a particular order or practice.

Inns of Court   Located in London, the Inns of Court provided a university-type education for those wishing to study and practise law.

Jesuits   Set up in 1540 by the Spaniard Ingatius Loyola, the specially trained order, known as the society of Jesus, spearheaded the Catholic Counter-Reformation in Europe.

John Hales and the commonwealth men Hales was an MP and government minister who is thought to have been part of a group concerned with the economic and social welfare of the citizens of the State, especially its poor.

Justices of the Peace   Magistrates, largely landowners, who enforce the State's rules and regulations in local courts of law.

King's peace   The idea that as the king was appointed by God his law was the highest authority which brought order and protection to the people.

Laity   Term used to describe the non-clerical general population, the parishioners as opposed to the priests.

Legislative programme   The key points of a government's plan to govern the country by passing laws, deciding levels of taxation and controls on trade.

Litany   Recital of religious teachings contained in the Book of Common Prayer.

Lord Lieutenant   Local military officer with the power to call musters and assemble an armed militia.

Lutheranism   A term used to describe the influence and religious ideas and teachings of Martin Luther of Wittenberg in Germany. His protest against the corruption and wealth of the Catholic Church and criticism of the Pope led to him being thrown out of the Church (1520s), after which he set up his own Protestant Church.

Malthusian crisis   Socio-economic theory of T.R. Malthus (d. 1834), an English clergyman and economist who argued that when a country's population outstrips food production the result is famine.

Marian government   Term used to describe the government of Mary I.

Marxist   Historians who see historical change as a series of events caused mainly by social and economic tension leading to conflict between the poorer and richer classes.

Mercenary army   Professional troops who serve for pay.

Millenarianists   Radical thinkers who believed in social reform whereby a kingdom's wealth would be distributed equally to all citizens.

Minority government   Government by councillors when the ruler is a child or minor.

Monopoly   Total control of trade by one country to the exclusion of others.

Muster   The method by which the Crown mobilised the people for war by calling out the militia. Each county was obliged to raise, train and maintain a militia of able-bodied men for active service.

Nationalistic   People who are particularly proud of their country and who might distrust or even hate foreigners.

New World   Term used to describe the continent of America.

Office of Crown Lands   Department set up to manage the estates (most of which had been inherited from previous monarchs) that belonged to the reigning monarch.

Ordination   Ceremony in which holy orders were conferred on priests enabling them to serve in parishes.

Paraphrases   A book containing a list of religious phrases, meanings and explanations for use in daily worship.

Pasture   Farming land set aside for the rearing of animals.

Paternalistic   The idea that a monarch would govern his kingdom and rule his subjects as a father would his house and family.

Patron   A wealthy and powerful individual who uses his influence to promote the career of a supporter.

Pilgrimage of Grace   Popular rebellion in northern England (1536–7) caused by distrust of Cromwell and discontent over religious changes, particularly the closure of the monasteries.

Plague cycle   Term used to describe the regular occurrences of plague. For example, the Black Death of 1348–51 was followed by plague outbreaks in 1361–2, 1369, 1393.

Poor Law of 1536   This required the better off members of each parish to collect money to support the impotent poor.

Poor laws   Laws passed to deal with the poor and vagrant in society. Because they did not understand the causes of poverty and vagrancy and they feared rebellion, many of the early poor laws had been designed to punish and control the poor. However, by mid-century some attempt was made to assist the poor by promoting charity and providing work.

Predestination   Belief that a person's life has been mapped out by God before birth and cannot be changed.

Price scissors   Economic term used to describe the point when prices and rents overtook wages.

Privy Council   Élite body of councillors drawn from the nobility and more powerful gentry who met with the monarch on a regular basis to offer their advice, frame laws and govern the country

Proclamations   The Crown's official or public announcements that included the right to make new laws, especially when parliament was not in session.

Protestant   Term used to describe those who had protested against and separated from the Roman Catholic Church.

Purgatory   A place between heaven and hell.

Puritans   Protestants who wished to purify the Anglican Church and purge the State religion of any Catholic practices.

Putting-out system   Manufacturing system whereby the raw material is put out for others to finish off.

Recession   A fall in the demand for goods which leads to a drop in prices and unemployment.

Recusants   Catholics who refused to conform to the State religion and refused to attend church services.

Reformation   The religious changes of the sixteenth century in England and continental Europe.

Regency Council   A select group of noble councillors who govern the kingdom on behalf of a ruler who is a child. Between 1547 and 1549 the Council was headed by Somerset to rule on behalf of Edward VI.

Renaissance   Rebirth of learning and the arts, which encouraged writers and artists to become part of what was called the spirit of new learning.

Repeal   The procedure in parliament whereby laws are cancelled and removed from the book listing current laws known as the Statute Book.

Revisionists   Historians who believe that older or more traditional interpretations and ideas in history should be regularly reviewed and changed if necessary.

Royal Household Term used to describe the living arrangements of the monarch. It consisted of servants who looked after the monarch's person and his financial and political affairs.

Royal prerogative Certain rights held by the monarchy enabling it to make proclamations, enforce the royal will, and suspend or repeal acts of parliament.

Royal progresses Royal visits served to overawe those who witnessed them and to remind the people of the might and majesty of the monarch.

Royal Supremacy Act of Parliament restoring the Crown as Head of the Church of England. Elizabeth was proclaimed Supreme Governor of the Church.

Ruling élites The landowning class of nobles and gentry who attended parliament and the Court, and who controlled the forces of law and order, government and administration both locally and, in the case of the more powerful, centrally.

Salic Law A law originating in France and dating from the eleventh century, which excluded females from succeeding to the throne.

Sedition Action or speech that incites rebellion.

Self-sufficient rural economy Growing enough food to feed the nation without having to rely on foreign imports.

Seminaries Religious institutions of learning designed to educate and train priests.

Seminary priests Priests who were trained in the seminary college of Douai and sent across Europe to educate people in the Roman Catholic faith.

'Slavery' Act of 1547 Described as 'the most savage of all Tudor poor laws', the statute stated that sturdy or able-bodied vagrants should be branded with the letters V and S and subjected to forced labour or slavery for repeat offenders.

Sovereign State A country in which the monarch has supreme power over the State: government, law, the economy; and the Church: doctrine, appointments and property.

State papers Documents drawn up by ministers that record the decisions made and show the decision-making process undertaken by central government.

Statute law Laws passed in and by parliament.

Succession Acts Acts of Parliament passed to clarify and enforce the right of succession to the Crown of England.

Temporal wealth Church wealth that is calculated in land, property and goods.

Thirty-Nine Articles Articles that set out Protestant beliefs and the method of worship in church services.

Tithes Tax amounting to 10 per cent of a parishioner's income (usually paid in goods) levied by the Church.

Transubstantiation The belief that, at the moment of consecration the bread and wine change in substance, though not in appearance, into the actual body and blood of Christ.

Treason Act Law passed in parliament to punish those who betray the State and its monarch. Political and religious disloyalty was punishable by death if convicted under the Treason Act.

Tree of Reformation Term used to describe the location of Ket's council of justice which sat under an old oak tree.

Tudor revolution in government Theory first put forward in the 1950s by G.R. Elton to explain the changes that took place in government under the guiding hand of Cromwell.

Twelve Decrees Term used to describe the key 12 points drawn up by Pole at the Westminster Synod. They included the need for every parish priest to be properly trained, educated and permanently resident. To help the hard-pressed clergy, Pole commissioned a newly edited Catholic New Testament and a new Book of Homilies to replace Cranmer's Protestant edition. However, they were never used.

Up and down husbandry   A system under which land was used alternately over a number of years as arable and then for pasture.

Vagrancy   Term used to describe the wandering poor who have no permanent work or home.

Valois   Name of the ruling royal family of France between 1328 and 1589.

Wars of the Roses   The sequence of plots, rebellions and battles that took place in England between 1455 and 1485. The idea of the warring roses of Lancaster (red) and York (white) was invented by Henry VII after he seized the throne in 1485.

Westminster synod   Also known as the London Synod, this was a meeting of the important clergy under Cardinal Pole who wished to consolidate and promote Roman Catholicism in the kingdom and to plan the future of the Church.

Whig interpretation of history   Belief that historical events are shaped by great men or women, so that the study of history should be seen in terms of personalities rather than events.

Yeomen   A social class of richer peasants that may have been as wealthy as some of the gentry but were below them in social class.

Zwinglian   Huldrych Zwingli was a Swiss Protestant religious reformer who believed that local religious communities should have the right to control their own affairs without interference from either the Church authorities or State officials.

Index